ETHNICITY AND THE WORK FORCE

* * * * *

VOLUME IV

**ETHNICITY AND
PUBLIC POLICY**
SERIES

ETHNICITY AND PUBLIC POLICY
SERIES

*   *   *   *   *

VOLUME I

ETHNICITY AND PUBLIC POLICY (1982)

VOLUME II

ETHNICITY, LAW AND THE SOCIAL GOOD (1983)

VOLUME IIII

ETHNICITY AND WAR (1984)

VOLUME IV

ETHNICITY AND THE WORK FORCE (1985)

ETHNICITY AND THE WORK FORCE

WINSTON A. VAN HORNE
EDITOR

THOMAS V. TONNESEN
MANAGING EDITOR

UNIVERSITY OF WISCONSIN SYSTEM
AMERICAN ETHNIC STUDIES COORDINATING
COMMITTEE/ URBAN CORRIDOR CONSORTIUM

University of Wisconsin System American Ethnic Studies
Coordinating Committee/Urban Corridor Consortium
P. O. Box 413, Milwaukee, WI 53201

International Standard Book Number ISBN 0-942672-06-2 (cloth)
International Standard Book Number ISBN 0-942672-07-0 (paper)
Library of Congress Catalog Card Number: 85-50235

UNIVERSITY OF WISCONSIN SYSTEM AMERICAN ETHNIC STUDIES COORDINATING COMMITTEE

DR. WINSTON A. VAN HORNE
University of Wisconsin–Milwaukee
Chairperson, AESCC

DR. PETER J. KELLOGG
University of Wisconsin–Green Bay

DR. LIONEL A. MALDONADO
University of Wisconsin–Parkside

DR. WILLIAM J. MURIN
Director, Urban Corridor Consortium

DR. MELVIN C. TERRELL
University of Wisconsin–Oshkosh

MR. THOMAS V. TONNESEN
Program Coordinator, AESCC (ex officio)

The University of Wisconsin System American Ethnic Studies Coordinating Committee (AESCC) wishes to acknowledge the contributions of its former members, as well as those of the Urban Corridor Consortium Steering Committee and the University of Wisconsin System American Ethnic Studies Advisory Committee.

PREFACE

Whenever one meets someone new at a social occasion, a question which almost inevitably is asked within a very short time is "What do you do for a living?" For reasons that are both easy and difficult to understand, learning of one's occupation during such an encounter becomes almost, if you will, a preoccupation. At least in American society, and perhaps in all of Western society and certain other parts of the globe, the answer to this query goes far in aiding us, at least we believe, in getting a fix on a person. Admittedly, there is a socioeconomic class variable in the frequency of this question, nevertheless it is a prevalent one indeed.

Why is it so? What an individual "does for a living" (his/her *work*) serves an important definitional function. To a large extent we define and make judgments about a person by his/her occupation, perhaps because our own self-identification and esteem are so strongly tied to our work. Our work goes far in providing each of us with our role and function in society, and we need to look no further than the connection between unemployment and suicide to realize the powerful hold that work has on our psyches.

Similar arguments hold true for racial and ethnic groups. By studying the occupational level of an ethnic or racial group's members, judgments can be made about their status in society. Just as, during the individual encounter, we tend to judge our own position and occupation by what the other individual's line of work is, so too do members of ethnic and racial groups perceive their own position, and are perceived by others, by how well or poorly they compare to other groups. In that we live in a society where individuals (and, by inference, groups) must compete, rightly or wrongly, to secure employment, the scorecard-like results of this competition reveal some inequalities and injustices that an egalitarian society must address. Our society and the members of its various ethnic and racial groups could not improve if there were not more innings yet to be played. The essays in *Ethnicity and the Work Force*, the fourth volume to be released in the *Ethnicity and Public Policy* series, use an interdisciplinary approach to give a good indication of how a number of ethnic and racial groups currently see the score.

As always, there is a cast of characters to which gratitude is owed. To continue the metaphor, our team has had a stable roster for some time now, and this has made the publication of subsequent volumes in the series so much easier. Works with collected essays from various authors demand considerable copy editing, and Joanne Brown has again done a superb job. The phrase "the patience of a saint" might have first been coined for Linda Jallings, who has again guided us through the production and publishing maze. Noteworthy are the roles that Sharon Gutowski plays in colloquium organization and Jeanne Decker in marketing and sales. To these and others associated with the *Ethnicity and Public Policy* series, we hope they have found value in their contributions because we know their work has added value to the series.

Thomas V. Tonnesen

CONTENTS

INTRODUCTION

Winston A. Van Horne

University of Wisconsin-Milwaukee

In their work individuals imprint themselves upon timeless time, and by their work they make themselves known to the generations and ages. The concept of work force in a political society is at once a philosophic idea and a sociologic category. Philosophically, work force is an open-texture concept covering the totality of the units of energy that constitute a people's labor power, which creates tangible and/or intangible objects of differential value. A society's work force is coterminus with the labor power of its people. Put differently, every unit of energy that actually creates objects or has the potential to do so is factored into the calculation of a society's labor power and, correspondingly, the actual or potential work of its people. Conceptualized thusly, the work force of a given society is inclusive of the labor power of each of its members. The open texture of the concept of work force is grounded axiomatically in the metaphysics of the participation of each and every part in the whole, and the extension of the whole into each and all of its parts.

The ontological grounding of the concept of work force gives it its open texture philosophically. There is not, however, a one-to-one correspondence between ontological reality and social reality, and so the ontology of work force is constrained by the sociology of labor power. Socially discrete units of energy drive the labor power that produces the work of a society. Work is a social category, and it is differentiated by the social value of the energy of its labor power. The work force of a society is thus a concrete expression of social value. It expands or contracts, is dynamic or static, and either egalitarian, meritocratic, egalitarian-meritocratic, ascriptive or ascriptive-meritocratic contingent on the dominant societal values of a particular historical epoch.

An egalitarian work force values each unit of energy in labor power equally arithmetically; a meritocratic work force values the energy of its labor power in the context of geometric equality; an egalitarian-meritocratic work force mixes arithmetic equality and geometric equality in differentiating the value of the energy of its labor power; a work force that is ascriptive values the energy of its labor power on the basis of ascribed traits; and an ascriptive-meritocratic work force mixes ascribed traits with geometric equality in recognizing the value of the energy of its labor power. Social category thus determines social value, and the social value of the energy of labor power determines its position within the work force of a given society.

As one reads the chapters of this volume, one observes radically different as well as complementary conceptions of the opportunity structure of the American work force, and the life chances of different ethnic/racial groups within it in specified/specifiable historical epochs. The opportunity structure of a society is grounded in its traditions and institutions. As one reflects on the opportunity structure of American society after the Civil War and through the mid-twentieth century, one observes the force of traditions and institutions that constrained severely the behaviors of ethnic/racial groups striving to maximize their life chances. Herbert Hill's discussion of African Americans and Ronald Takaki's presentation on Japanese Americans, for example, portray vividly the impact of the opportunity structure of an ascriptive-meritocratic/egalitarian-meritocratic society on the life chances of these groups.

American labor unions, until quite recently, have been fundamentally ascriptive by race and ethnicity. Hill observes that "[t]otal exclusion or segregation was enforced as national policy by most labor unions in the early decades of the twentieth century. The aim of white labor organizations to restrict black workers to the lowest rungs of the job ladder was increasingly successful." If one did not possess the requisite ethnic/racial attribute or set of attributes, one was systematically excluded from membership. Hill discusses brilliantly—with a rare confluence of conceptual perceptivity, analytical rigor and moral outrage—the societal costs of ascriptive union membership for African Americans and Asian Americans. African Americans were perceived to be "hordes of ignorant blacks, . . . huge strapping fellows, ignorant and vicious, . . . [possessing] but few of those attributes that [whites] have learned to revere and love, . . . [and] whose predominating trait was animalism." Notice was served to Asian Americans that the "maintenance of the nation depended upon the maintenance of racial purity," and "Caucasian civilization['s] . . . uplifting process is not to be interfered with in any way" by Oriental civilization. This is the sort of sophistry, jingoism, arrogance, chauvinism, idiocy, perversity and vainglory that tended to corrode the moral vision and skew the moral arithmetic of whites, who either perceived and understood, perceived but did not understand, or failed to both perceive and understand the social significance of being the beneficiaries and heirs of ascriptive group membership.

Within the framework of ascriptive group membership grounded in race and ethnicity, the opportunity structure of American society permitted some individuals to ascend the ladder of social recompense through tangible and intangible returns for demonstrated performance. Meritorious work could be, and was, demonstrated and recognized within the ethnic/racial exclusivity of white-dominated social groupings. But this very opportunity structure which so advantaged whites constrained severely the chances of nonwhites to demonstrate through their work that they deserved to climb the ladder of social recompense. Indeed, so foul was the force of ascriptive group membership that nonwhites were usually denied the recognition and returns for demonstrated performance in their work. How poignant is Takaki's observation that

> Japanese workers were very aware of the plantation hierarchy and the limits on the possibility of occupational advancement for them. "Lunas [foremen] were all Portuguese," observed Minoru Hayashida of the Puunene Plantation on Maui. "Above that was the Caucasian field boss called 'o luna,' the big foreman." Another Japanese worker, knowing he would never be able to get ahead on the plantation, expresses his frustration. Told by an interviewer that he would be promoted and become a "big shot" if he had "the stuff," the laborer retorted: "Don't kid me. You know yourself that I haven't got a chance. You can't go very high up and get big money unless your skin is white. You can work here all your life and yet a haole [white man] who doesn't know a thing about the work can be ahead of you in no time. [Indeed], even where Japanese workers were employed in the same occupational categories as whites, they found themselves paid different and lower wage rates.

The critical point here is that ascriptive group membership grounded in race and ethnicity constrained severely and brutally the life chances of Japanese in the work force of Hawaii's sugar plantations, just as it expanded liberally but often unduly the possibilities of whites' ascent on the ladder of social recompense. What was true of the Japanese on the Hawaiian islands was also true of blacks, as well as of Indians and Hispanics, on the American mainland.

The odiousness of the impact of ascriptive group membership grounded in race and ethnicity on nonwhites is all too obvious from a reading of the chapters by Hill, Takaki, Steve Talbot and Lionel Maldonado. Yet one cannot but be struck by the plight of the Jews, Poles, Irish and Italians, even though they were all covered by the socially protective umbrella of abstract white in American society.[1] Each of

these groups experienced the hurt, anguish and trauma of ethnic stig-
matization, which excluded them from a range of societal benefits that
ascriptive group membership had for generations locked away as the
special preserve of those of British Isles and Western/Northern European ancestry. Barry Chiswick informs us that "'Gentlemen's agreements' in employment and 'restrictive covenants' in housing were
mechanisms for excluding Jews" from full participation in the society.
Helena Lopata notes that Theodore Abel "found native farmers highly
prejudiced against . . . Polish immigrants, whom they found working
so hard as to sacrifice many of the 'niceties of life' in an effort to obtain
land." Lawrence McCaffrey observes that Anglo-American Protestants, "[c]onvinced that Irish poverty, filth, alcoholism, crime, violence, improvidence and mental and physical disorders polluted the nation, . . . resented their presence." And Humbert Nelli tells us that
"[d]uring the first years of immigration before Italians learned American labor practices, they were often used as strikebreakers. . . .
Through such activities, [they] gained an unsavory but not fully deserved reputation as scabs." The crucial underlying point here is that
each of these white ethnic groups felt the hurt of ascriptive exclusion
that was experienced by their nonwhite counterparts. But there is a
difference—a profound difference rooted in the vile racism of the color
line—which W.E.B. Du Bois correctly diagnosed as *the* problem of the
twentieth century, even though he later changed his mind.

White ethnics are white. This is an obvious tautology, and in strict
deductive logic it gives one no new information about the world. Yet,
in the context of the ideology that grounds the social-psychology of
white racism, it tells us much about the world. Nelli's observation that
"before Italians learned American labor practices, they were often used
as strikebreakers" offers an invaluable, though perhaps unintended, insight into the socialization of white ethnics into the dominant Anglo-
American culture. Virulent and truculent racism has been ingrained
into Anglo-American culture for centuries. (Former U.S. Ambassador
to the United Nations Andrew Young was excoriated for stating on
British television that the English played an instrumental role in the
spread of racism through their colonial activities and policies, even
though his observation withstands a close and rigorous scrutiny of
British history.) Anglo-Americans were socialized into their racism by
their British kith and kin, and it was transmitted intergenerationally
by the culture of the society.

White ethnics who immigrated to America soon learned that it was
profitable materially and/or psychologically to incorporate into the be-
lief-attitudinal complex that guided their behaviors the racist sentiments which suffused the dominant culture. And so the Irish, Italians,

Poles, Jews, *et cetera*, quickly learned one of the key practices of organized labor in America, namely, *keep the nonwhites out*. It is little wonder that Booker T. Washington sought to keep the white ethnics who were flooding the shores of America at the end of the nineteenth century out of the country, when he appealed to white Southerners in his "Atlanta Exposition Address," saying:

> To those of the white race who look to the incoming of those of foreign birth and strange tongue and habits for the prosperity of the South, were I permitted I would . . . say . . . "Cast down your bucket where you are." Cast it down among the eight millions of Negroes whose habits you know, we shall contribute one third to the business and industrial prosperity of the South. . . . Cast down your bucket among . . . people who have, without strikes and labor wars, tilled your fields, cleared your forests, built your railroads and cities, and brought forth treasures from the bowels of the earth, and helped make possible this magnificent representation of the progress of the South. Casting down your bucket among my people, helping and encouraging them as you are doing on these grounds, and to education of head, hand and heart, you will find that they will buy your surplus land, make blossom the waste places in your fields, and run your factories. . . . As we have proved our loyalty to you in the past, . . . so in the future . . . we shall stand by you with a devotion that no *foreigner* can approach. . . .[2]

But racism, most foul and odious, impelled his white listeners to hear in his address only what they wanted to hear, that is, Washington's willingness to keep the races separate socially when he proclaimed: "In all things that are purely social we can be as separate as the fingers, yet one as the hand in all things essential to mutual progress."[3] Racism, most cruel and perfidious, opened widely the ears of his white audience to the first clause of the preceding sentence, but deafened them to its second clause. Washington perceived a necessary connection between the stemming of the tide of white ethnic immigration and the mutual progress of black and white Southerners, and so he linked the two inextricably both explicitly and inferentially. The racism of white Southerners and their Northern kith and kin was such, however, that although they often loathed the new white immigrants, they nonetheless found them preferable to blacks and other nonwhites in the context of the ascriptive norms that permeated the opportunity structure of the society.

The white ethnics, who were themselves subjected to the degradation of vile and vulgar discriminatory practices, quickly absorbed the social-psychology of racism, carried by the culture of their new society, as they strived to protect their interests and enhance their life chances under the socially protective umbrella of abstract white. So well did they absorb the social-psychology of racism that Samuel Gompers, a Jewish immigrant and the president of the American Federation of Labor from 1886 to 1924 (with the exception of 1895), was disposed to posit that the "maintenance of the nation depended upon the maintenance of *racial purity*," as we learn from Hill's chapter. (My italics.) The chilling irony of this postulate is too obvious for comment at the end of the twentieth century. The puzzlement of McCaffrey is well founded when he observes that "[o]ne of the frustrating mysteries of human nature is that seldom do those who experience the pain of persecution develop much empathy for other victims of discrimination." Could it be that after nearly two centuries of disputation about his ideas, the utilitarian philosopher Jeremy Bentham is indeed correct, to wit, human beings are stimulated by self-interest to maximize behaviors that bring them pleasure and minimize those which cause them pain? If this is really so, will not the ones who themselves suffer "the pain of persecution" fail to "develop much empathy for other victims of discrimination" if, for whatever reason(s), rational or irrational, decent or vulgar, sound or unsound, they perceive such empathy to occasion greater pain than pleasure? When he was asked why it was that the slave driver often whipped those in his charge more severely than either the slave master or the overseer, Frederick Douglass replied, "Everybody, in the South, wants the privilege of whipping somebody else."[4] Racism provided white ethnics, as well as other whites, with those whom they could readily whip, even as it facilitated access to the work force of a largely ascriptive-meritocratic society under the protective umbrella of abstract white.

The force of racism in constraining unduly the life chances of non-whites in American society echoes resonantly in the chapters by Hill, Takaki, Talbot and Maldonado. Racism was the efficient cause of the opportunity structure that evolved in a largely ascriptive-meritocratic society to assure the persistence of the social marginality of most non-whites in relation to the instrumentalities of power and authority. Even though the ascriptive-meritocratic society of the late nineteenth century and early twentieth century has evolved into a largely egalitarian-meritocratic society at the end of the twentieth century, it is nonetheless the case that the advantages secured by whites from the earlier opportunity structure have persisted intergenerationally. It is a recognition of this fact that impels Hill to conclude his chapter by saying:

> The current conflict over affirmative action is not simply an argument about abstract rights or ethnic bigotry. In the final analysis it is an argument between those who insist upon the substance of a long-postponed break with the traditions of American racism,

and those groups that insist upon maintaining the valuable privileges and benefits they now enjoy as a consequence of that dismal
history.

What one observes here are two competing perspectives of American
history and visions of American society.

In one perspective and vision the society was fundamentally ascriptive-meritocratic though marked by noticeable traces of an egalitarian-
meritocratic social order. Over time the egalitarian-meritocratic attributes of the society have superseded its ascriptive-meritocratic ones,
and this holds out substantial promise to nonwhites in the context of
the persistent evolution of the society's opportunity structure. But
there is a catch. The advantages that whites enjoyed when the society
was largely ascriptive-meritocratic have been frozen in place, and form
the plateau from which new social formations begin. One quickly
grasps the significance of this point when one considers, for example,
the freezing into the economy of the housing and automobile industries' inflated prices of the 1970s, even though in the 1980s the inflation
of prices in these industries has been a fraction of what it was a decade
earlier. The prices of cars and houses are substantially higher today
than what they would have been were it not for the stagflationary seventies. In like manner, the advantages of whites today are substantially greater than they would have been were it not for the opportunity structure of a largely ascriptive-meritocratic society of another
historical epoch.

The plateau of advantage and privilege from which whites strike out
today in order to maximize their life chances troubles Hill, Takaki,
Talbot and Maldonado. They believe that a reconstruction of this plateau is vital if whites and nonwhites alike are to truly enjoy the benefits, as well as bear their proper share of the burdens, of our egalitarian-
meritocratic society. Hill's discussion of affirmative action, for example, is clearly set in the context of reconstructing the plateau of white
advantage and privilege, if we may so speak. This sets him apart from
those who share the perspective and vision that since the late nineteenth century American society has been fundamentally egalitarian-
meritocratic, though marked by distinctive traces of an ascriptive-
meritocratic social order.

As the decades and generations of the twentieth century have succeeded one another, those who perceive the society to be largely egalitarian-meritocratic at the end of the nineteenth century believe that
there has been an inverse relation between the expansion of its egalita-
tian attributes and the contraction of its ascriptive traits. An expan-
sive, open and accessible opportunity structure has become even more
so, as those who were heretofore constrained by undue barriers as they

strived to maximize their life chances have observed the erosion of those constraints. Indeed, even at the outset of the century, the egalitarian-meritocratic possibilities of the society were such that they could be exploited to improve markedly the lots of those who had the determination of will, strength of character and agility of mind to do so. This perspective and vision of American society is observed clearly and distinctly in Nelli's chapter, and with varying degrees of perspicuity in the chapters by McCaffrey, Lopata and Chiswick. What accounts for this difference of perspective and vision between the authors scrutinizing the lots of four nonwhite groups in the work force and those who discuss how four white ethnic groups have fared?

Is one set of authors more attuned to the vulgarity and sordidness of undue discrimination in American society through succeeding cross sections of historical time? I think not. One can readily share with Chiswick and McCaffrey the pain of discrimination suffered by the Jews and the Irish respectively. Is one set of authors more sensitive to the possibilities and limits of the work force over historical time than the other? Again, I think not. Takaki and Talbot are no more sensitive to the constraints of the work force in relation to Japanese Americans and American Indians than are Lopata and McCaffrey vis-à-vis Polish Americans and Irish Americans. Indeed, one cannot read this volume without being struck by the conspicuous similarities in the experiences of both white and nonwhite ethnic/racial groups in the work force—in spite of differences most profound. Could it be, then, that one set of authors is impelled by the historical context of the social logic of the groups they scrutinize to emphasize a particular form of discrimination—racial discrimination—much more than the other? I believe so. Racial discrimination is perhaps the most vulgar, sordid, vile, corrupt, perverse, reprehensible and repugnant of all forms of discrimination. It is known and understood in a special way by those who suffer/have suffered it. This special way of knowing and understanding racism is transfused into the ones who steep themselves in the experiences of those who are/have been the objects of racist behaviors, and this impels them in their analysis of American society to focus on what Takaki has termed the "hard dark line" of race in another book.[5] The life histories and prospects of the nonwhite and white ethnic groups discussed in this volume have thus been instrumental in shaping the perspectives of American history and visions of American society that have emerged in relation to participation in the work force.

The fact that no single perspective, vision, paradigm or model has emerged might be disappointing to one in search of universal laws, deductive nomological explanations and a general theory of ethnicity. Still, one should be encouraged by the isolation of what I shall term categories of demarcation and partial explanations of the phenomena of ethnicity in the context of the work force, as work towards a general theory of ethnicity continues.

First, there is a critical, nay, fundamental distinction between voluntary and involuntary incorporation into American society. Voluntary incorporation entails volition by which one freely and without coercion strives to belong to a given social order, and a decision by the society through its institutions that one should be included in its membership. Involuntary incorporation entails the subjection of one to the rules and institutions of a particular body politic regardless of one's will and preferences. The long-term severity of involuntary incorporation is made worse by the "principle of cumulation," that is, the successive accumulation of discrimination in the work force that spills over into other spheres of social life. This is true regardless of the particular form that involuntary incorporation may have taken—slavery in the case of blacks, military conquest for Mexican Americans and frontier expansion for American Indians. The net result is that a group's place in the work force is best understood in terms of cumulative effects. This helps to clarify the mosaic of many groups' relative social position and work force experiences in America. Put differently, the structured disadvantages of some have a compounding negative effect on them, while serving simultaneously as structured advantages for others with their own interaction and compounding positive effects.

Second, the dynamic nature of industrialization in America and the changing opportunities this has presented to successive arrivals of ethnic/racial groups in different cross sections of historical time are of vital importance in any serious discussion of ethnicity and the work force. The chapters of this volume document the empirical fact that initial work force participation varied significantly for the groups discussed. Moreover, their fortunes depended substantially on the labor power needs at the time of their arrival. Subsequent work force niches, rates and degrees of dispersion from initial slots varied with the fluctuations of the society's political economy. The importance of the political economy as it has evolved through preindustrial, industrial and postindustrial capitalist social formations within a culture that transmits racism intergenerationally, in conjunction with the time of arrival in structuring the possibilities of a particular group within the work force, constitutes one of the major contributions of this volume. American society has never been homogeneous racially, ethnically or culturally. Thus the sensitivity of the authors to regional variations, since all the groups were/are not scattered uniformly throughout the nation, contributes to one's knowledge and understanding of differences within, as well as between, the groups.

Third, the adaptability, as well as the sameness or distinctiveness, of new arrivals in relation to the dominant values of the civic culture and the institutions of power and authority that structure the political economy have been/continue to be the most critical general determinants of group *qua* group success in the society. The ones whose physical and cultural attributes approximate most closely those of the dominant Anglo-American social norms, mores and ethos appear to have fared best. This observation is substantiated when one takes an in-depth, long-term view of a range of group experiences in America. Groups with unique attributes, particularly physiognomic ones, as well as ones representing persistent "cultural markers," tend to penetrate the society's opportunity structure with enormous difficulty, and often orbit on the margins of the political economy. During times of social unrest or a steep downturn in the business cycle, which incidentally have occurred at predictable intervals throughout the twentieth century, such groups are often blamed for society's ills and become ready scapegoats for the travails and woes of the land. This slice of social reality is discussed by some of the authors, who draw a line of demarcation between class concerns and status concerns.

Class solidarity, in whatever measure it has ever existed between nonwhites and white ethnics, has usually given way to racial and ethnic divisiveness during times of downsweep in the business cycle, and intense, even vicious, competition for scarce resources. The erosion of class solidarity has resulted in marked status differences within the work force. Having been established, these status differences have developed a life of their own; they have become deeply entrenched, differentiating criteria in the social order. In a very real sense, they have become another means of group stratification within the work force. Moreover, they tend to spill over into other areas of social life, given the primacy of work in the allocation of rewards in the society, and create innumerable suspicions, frictions and tensions between nonwhites and white ethnic groups.

Fourth, the political philosophy that grounds the political economy of American capitalism precludes conceptually, theoretically and empirically a one-to-one correspondence between the labor power of the working age population and its utilization in the work force. The logic of capitalist production necessitates that some able-bodied individuals are always out of work; their labor power either goes unutilized or underutilized by the work force throughout their lifetime. These persons form what Maldonado has termed "a reserve labor pool," which may be exploited or discarded as the business cycle dictates. This pool is peopled by whites and nonwhites alike, but even here race makes a difference.

Organized labor's role in the exclusion of nonwhites from the work force is documented meticulously in this volume. Lacking the protective shield of unions, and naked before the cultural animus towards nonwhite skin, nonwhites were most susceptible to the vicissitudes of the business cycle. They were, and by and large still are, the last hired and first fired. Behaviors induced by business cycles were underpinned by social norms and reinforced by cultural attributes. A cultural ethos of racism made/make socially acceptable the ready displacement of the least powerful and most vulnerable members of the work force whenever this was/is necessitated by the business cycle. A social norm and business practice over many generations, the displacement of the powerless and vulnerable from the work force received the imprimatur of the nation's highest tribunal in 1977 when the Supreme Court declared that bona fide seniority systems were not constitutionally infirm. (See *Teamsters* v. *United States*, 431 U.S. (1977).) Indeed, citing this decision, as well as that of the *American Tobacco Co.* v. *Patterson*, 456 U.S. (1982) in her concurring opinion in *Memphis Fire Department, et al.* v. *Carl W. Stotts, etc., et al.*, Justice Sandra Day O'Connor observed that "Title VII [of the Civil Rights Act of 1964] affirmatively protects bona fide seniority systems, *including those with discriminatory effects on minorities.*" (My italics.) In short, social norms, cultural ethos, business practices, constitutional law and statute law cohere to protect advantages secured in the ascriptive-meritocratic epoch of American society. What is the significance of this?

Given the Protestant work ethic that inheres in the spirit of capitalism, a job and money are the universal measures of worth and success in the society. "Where do you work?" and "How much do you make?" (a rather vulgar question in polite circles) are, perhaps, the most commonplace questions in the society. Money is the measure of a job's worth in the market economy of capitalism, and an individual's job is the measure of the individual. In a very real sense, then, money is the measure of an individual's worth in the market economy of capitalism, and one's worth increases exponentially with its accumulation. Money means valuableness; penury means worthlessness. This state of affairs is not the most desirable one ethically and morally; it *is* the one that obtains in the real world of the political economy of capitalism. Participation in the work force is thus absolutely critical in terms of one's value in the society. The social category of work force determines one's economic value in the marketplace, and by extension one's social value in the society at large. If I am correct in what has been said thus far, it is obviously *not* in one's self-interest to have one's labor power consigned to the reserve labor pool. Indeed, just as death consigns the lifeless body to the destruction of the grave, termination from the work force consigns the living body to the rot of worthlessness.

The struggle of individuals and groups to keep from descending into the reserve labor pool, and to ascend from it if misfortune places them there, is often self-centered, vicious and brutal. The wage is the primary source of money for most workers in a capitalist political economy. A wage is paid for a job, and it is *generally perceived and believed* that whatever threatens a job also threatens its accompanying wage, even though this is not logically necessarily so. What is important here is not logical reality but social reality. People are usually stimulated to action by the perceived simplicities of their social universe, not the recondite complexities of a logical universe. In an earlier epoch white ethnics used the racially ascriptive security of organized labor as one means of escaping the reserve labor pool, and they struggled with whites and nonwhites alike outside the framework of labor organizations to free themselves from the social debasement of joblessness. They learned quickly the relation between self-worth, self-esteem, self-respect and personal dignity, and work, economic worth and social value. The admixture of egalitarian-meritocratic elements and ascriptive-meritocratic elements of a social order embedded in a racist culture facilitated their activities designed to escape the psychic trauma and social marginality of membership in the reserve labor pool. Today, white ethnics have been in the forefront of the struggle against affirmative action, not because they are uniformly racist—many are not—but because they perceive it to threaten the intergenerational gains that they have made in the work force and society at large.

It matters not that many of these gains were made in an ascriptive-meritocratic and egalitarian-meritocratic context predicated on the exclusion of nonwhites. What is important is that the gains have been made, and self-interest necessitates their protection. The terrors of the cauldron of the reserve labor pool are much to be feared and greatly to be avoided. It matters not that there is no statistically significant correlation between affirmative action and descent into the reserve labor pool. What is important is the perception and belief that there is.

Nonwhites by and large perceive affirmative action as a means of penetrating the work force and rising within it through the framework of established meritocratic principles. As such, *affirmative action is an awfully conservative idea.* It abjures neither the constitutive norms nor generative principles of the society.[6] It constitutes no philosophic declaration of war upon the established values of the political community by which excellence is judged, and it poses no threat to the structure of the political society. It recognizes and subscribes to the primacy of orderly legal change. All it does is broaden participation in the political community in general, and the work force in particular, by providing mechanisms whereby those who have been excluded from a range of societal benefits may have the opportunity to partake of them legally. Grounded in legality, affirmative action is the antithesis of radicality. Still, affirmative action is perceived by many, perhaps most, whites to be a radical idea that rewards the unmeritorious. It is perceived and believed to be a crutch for the undeserving, a formula for dampening, even stifling, initiative and punishing success, and an instrument that produces a deadly unintended consequence—namely, the exacerbation of racial animosities and tensions. And so the struggle continues, within the philosophic and juridic framework that grounds the established social order, as some struggle to leap generations of disadvantage and others strive to protect and defend the gains of intergenerational advantage.

Finally, mention must be made of Chiswick's "hypothesis regarding the trade-off of quantity and quality of children [as] a compelling framework for analyzing group differences in labor market status." Chiswick argues that over the centuries the Jews have been the victims of both discrimination and persecution. They were discriminated against and persecuted in Europe, and they have experienced the trauma of anti-Semitism and the pain of discrimination in America. He observes that "[i]n the century prior to World War II, overt anti-Semitism limited the opportunities of Jews. Discrimination against Jews in access to higher education was widespread, and discrimination in employment varied by the sector of the economy. Heavy industry, banking, insurance and finance appeared to have the greatest difficulty accepting Jews." Given their intergenerational experiences with anti-Semitism and discrimination in America, how is one to account for their place atop the work force in terms of both income and status today? Indeed, Chiswick would reject vigorously any claim that the position of Jews in American society is the product of intergenerational gains made at the expense of nonwhites.

After reviewing and rejecting a number of partial explanations and explanation sketches pertaining to the success of Jews in the labor market, Chiswick hypothesizes that "Jews are more productive in converting education into earnings" than their competitors in the marketplace. He speculates that

[t]his may arise because Jews acquire a higher quality [or more units] of human capital in a year of schooling or because they are more effective in using their human capital in the labor market. The higher rate of return would encourage greater investments in human capital and result in a higher schooling level and higher occupational status. These differences may be the result of *invest-*

*ments made by parents in their children's human capital prior to and
concurrent with schooling.* (My italics.)

Chiswick believes that "[p]arents may be viewed as making rational
decisions regarding the 'number' and 'quality per child' of their children." He notes that "[w]hile 'number' is relatively easy to measure,
investments in 'child quality,' the value of the time and other resources
parents devote to their children, are not easily measured." He further
speculates that "[r]acial and ethnic groups may differ in their optimal
combination of the number and quality of children because they face
different opportunities or 'relative prices.'" He observes that "[f]er-
tility is higher where contraception is more expensive because of cultural or religious proscriptions, it is higher in rural areas where space is
cheaper and children can do productive work at an earlier age, and it is
higher among women who have less schooling or who for other reasons
have poorer labor market opportunities." From this he infers that
"[h]igher levels of fertility imply lower investments of parental time
and other resources per child, and hence lower child quality."

Noting that "American Jews are a predominantly urban population
that, in general, does not have religious prohibitions on contraception," and that "American Jewish women have a high level of education," Chiswick posits and supports with data that Jewish women have
a lower fertility rate than their racial, ethnic and religious counterparts
in the society.[7] Put differently, Jewish parents make rational choices to
decrease the number of their children, but increase the investment of
both tangible and intangible resources in them.

This is a most intriguing hypothesis on a number of counts. First, it
offers a partial explanation for the size of the Jewish population in
America. As rational decision makers concerning the number of their
offspring, Jews have opted to increase their clout in the society through
the quality of their presence rather than the quantity of their numbers.
Second, it suggests that there is a correlation between culture, religion
and quality of child. Cultures and religions that support, or are at least
not hostile to, the rational choice of parents to decrease the total quantity of their children in favor of the total quality of each child maximize
the chances of work force success for its members. Third, cultures and
religions that ground the rational choice of parents to increase the total
quantity of their children at the expense of the total quality of each
child tend to decrease the chances of work force success for its members. Fourth, as schooling, a necessary but not sufficient condition of
child quality, increases, so too does the quality of a child in the context
of probable work force success. Parents who make rational choices
about child quality also make rational decisions about investment in
schooling. Fifth, the rational choice of parents to invest in quality of

child in preference to quantity of children appears to be an intergenerational phenomenon. This is to be expected insofar as the progeny embrace the culture and religion of the parents. Sixth, investment in schooling tends to be replicated intergenerationally insofar as the progeny embrace the culture and religion of their parents, who make rational choices in favor of quality of child rather than quantity of children. Finally, groups marked by parents who make rational choices in favor of quantity of children rather than quality of child would do well to contemplate long and hard on the relation between quantity of children, quality of child and work force success.

Chiswick envisions that as more research is done on his hypothesis, it will be so corroborated that it will become a sound empirical generalization intersecting ethnic/racial boundaries, if not even a universal social law.

I have tarried on Chiswick's hypothesis because it tantalizes one. But will it stand up under tough, hard-nosed, rigorous and dispassionate empirical scrutiny? Chiswick is a rational choice theorist, and his hypothesis is grounded in rational choice theory. As such, it benefits from the logical rigor and conceptual richness of axiomatic rationality, but it also suffers the empirical infirmities of rational choice theory. I cannot scrutinize here the empirical problems and difficulties of rational choice theory that have been discussed by social scientists and philosophers; suffice it to say that if Chiswick's hypothesis is to become either an empirical generalization or a universal social law, its explanatory and predictive powers must be applicable to white and nonwhite groups alike. But Maldonado, after a careful scrutiny of the state of Mexican Americans in the political economy of the work force, informs us that "[a]nalyses of recent data . . . suggest that the experiences of Mexican Americans continue to be *significantly unlike* those of white ethnic groups, and that to apply theoretical models developed on others' experiences is a risky effort at best." (My italics.) Maldonado and Chiswick have different perspectives of American history and visions of American society. These differences shape their axiomatic assumptions, formulation of hypotheses and the grounding of these empirically. Thus we end where we began, with no general theory of ethnicity and the work force, but with an increased knowledge about the possibilities and limits of creating such a theory. Although we have no general theory, what are the public policy implications of what we have learned as the society stands on the threshold of a new century and a new millennium?

The problem and issue of ethnic/racial cleavage will no doubt persist into the foreseeable future inasmuch as they have endured intergenerationally to date. Some groups, taking full advantage of ascribed attributes, have been successful in carving out rewarding and satisfying niches for themselves in the society. Others, however, have found their origins and/or physiognomy to be a persistent source of disadvantage. Enlightened public policy is thus necessary to the creation of a social milieu in which each is truly judged and rewarded on the basis of demonstrated performance that is not the product of ascribed advantages which have been/are foreclosed to some.

Accordingly, those who are authorized to formulate and implement public policy should: (1) Resist overt and covert pressure to have the institutions of government used to resegregate and further segregate the society racially; (2) Replace current affirmative action prescriptions, sanctions, admonitions and exhortations with a *generational leap venture* in which both the public sector and the private sector are required to produce by the end of the first decade of the twenty-first century a new generation of work force participants from among those who have not been the intergenerational beneficiaries of ascriptive advantages. This new generation, of a size approximating the ethnic/racial distribution of its members in the population at large, should be able to compete in the marketplace without the baggage of intergenerational ascriptive disadvantages. How is this to be done? Were a commitment to this end to become national policy and a priority of the first order, the means to do so would be found—just as they were found to accomplish successfully the task of landing a man on the moon in the decade of the nineteen-sixties once President John F. Kennedy and the Congress committed the honor, prestige and resources of the nation to that end. True, social phenomena are much more complex than natural phenomena, as Nobel Laureate F. A. von Hayek is fond of reminding us, and so the task of creating a new generation of work force participants is much more complex than that of landing a man on the moon. Yet it can be done. The agility of mind to overcome the complexities abounds in the society; the only real question is whether the determination of will and strength of character, both collective and individual, can be found in the national soul for the task; (3) Enforce strictly the laws prescribing and proscribing certain forms of behavior that affect the well-being of nonwhites; (4) Take action designed to make good use of the labor power of those who are unable to find niches in the work force. For the ones who are able but unwilling to expend their labor power in the work force, John Locke, the father of liberal political philosophy, said long ago that he who does not work shall not eat, though none should be permitted to starve to death. And Karl Marx, the father of communist political philosophy, instructed us that from each according to his ability, to each according to his work/need. The critical point here is the policymakers should take whatever measures are necessary to assure that the labor power of no one goes to waste; (5) Recognize the social-psychological significance of the transformation of a political economy organized to produce goods into one designed to offer services. As the demands of the work force and the forms of social mobility change in the evolution of a postindustrial society into a technologic society, policymakers should induce the necessary changes in the opportunity structure in order to assure the maximum feasible correspondence between the labor power of the society and the demands of its work force.

By the mid-1880s the promise of the mid-1860s had been dashed to pieces for blacks. The civil rights legislation and constitutional amendments of the mid-1860s through the mid-1870s had been laid waste by the assault of the Supreme Court, the desertion of the blacks' allies, the growing indifference of the nation to black concerns, an increasing emphasis on legal justice over social justice, a noteworthy vulgarization of self-interest, the ascendancy of the old antagonists of blacks and the rise of Jim Crow. While all of this was occurring, new immigrants from Europe who shared the physiognomy of the white population flooded the shores of the land in search of a better life. And a better life they did find, if not for themselves, then for their progeny. In the meantime blacks and other nonwhites were consigned systematically to the backwaters of the society. This is precisely what Booker T. Washington feared and this is exactly what happened. At the turn of the twentieth century, the possibilities symbolized by the Statue of Liberty fired hope in the breasts of the new white immigrants, but for blacks and other nonwhites, for whom this was the land of their birth, liberty was but a dream and justice a dreaded nightmare.

Over the course of the century there has been an undeniable improvement in the lots of nonwhites as an ascriptive-meritocratic society has evolved into a more egalitarian-meritocratic one. But substantial, troublesome and even dangerous inequalities remain in the society's opportunity structure in relation to the life chances of whites and nonwhites. Today, as the society stands on the verge of the twenty-first century, a wave of new immigrants, largely nonwhite, floods the shores of the land in search of a better life. This presents a challenge of even greater proportions than the one presented by the new immigrants at the dawn of the twentieth century. The possibilities of a seemingly boundless frontier and the limitless capacity of an industrial society have given way to the known bounds of the frontier and the limits of the capacity of a technologic society. Indeed, as technologic society matures, there appears to be an inverse relation between the labor power of the society and the need for it in the work force.

As machines prove to be more cost effective than men in the work force, and cost effectiveness enhances profits, the labor power of men becomes increasingly redundant. This redundancy is consistent with profit, a key axiomatic element of the political philosophy that grounds the political economy of the society. Thus, at the end of the twentieth century the society confronts one, if not the greatest, of its challenges in its history. How shall it escape the fate of Rome, as that shining city on the hill absorbed the peoples of the whole world? How shall it make use, and satisfy the needs, of its increased labor power when the evolution of the formations of production, distribution, exchange and reproduction in its political economy makes labor power increasingly redundant? Absent a nuclear holocaust and its accompanying nuclear winter, I shall dare be so bold as to say that the fate of the Republic in history will be determined by how well or poorly it meets this challenge.

NOTES

[1] For a discussion of the idea of abstract white, see Winston A. Van Horne's Introduction to *Ethnicity and Public Policy*, Vol. I (Milwaukee: University of Wisconsin System AESCC/UCC, 1982).

[2] Booker T. Washington, "Atlanta Exposition Address," in Philip S. Foner, ed., *The Voice of Black America* (New York: Simon and Schuster, 1972), pp. 580-581. My Italic.

[3] Ibid., p. 581.

[4] Cited in Kenneth M. Stamp, *The Peculiar Institution* (New York: Vintage Books, 1956), p. 335.

[5] Van Horne, op cit., p. viii.

[6] For a brilliant and insightful discussion of "constitutive norms" and "generative principles," see Paul Schrecker, "Revolution as Problem in the Philosophy of History," in Carl J. Friedrich, ed., *Revolution* (New York: Atherton Press, 1967), pp. 34-52.

[7] The data are somewhat dated.

RACE AND ETHNICITY IN ORGANIZED LABOR: THE HISTORICAL SOURCES OF RESISTANCE TO AFFIRMATIVE ACTION*

Herbert Hill

University of Wisconsin-Madison

Race and Class

Divisions and internal conflicts have shaped the unique development of the American working class. Hostility characterized relations between immigrant and native born, Catholic and Protestant, skilled and unskilled, among ethnic communities and, most importantly, between racial groups. History reveals that workers defined themselves basically in terms of their race and ethnicity. Manifestations of class consciousness that transcended such loyalties were rare and episodic.

Racist ideas and practices in a multitude of forms became a basic characteristic of the most important institution of the working class—labor unions. From the 1860s to the contemporary period, as workers became more union conscious they also became more race conscious, and as labor organizations became more successful they also intensified their racist practices. After the 1930s with the rise of the Congress of Industrial Organizations (CIO), the forms of discrimination sometimes changed, but the substance did not.° The failure of labor historians to confront the extraordinary record of working-class racism has resulted

*The author wishes to express his appreciation to Professors Murray Edelman and Stanley Kutler of the University of Wisconsin, Professor Nell Irvin Painter of the University of North Carolina and Professor Ronald Takaki of the University of California, Berkeley, for their critical reading of the manuscript, and to Stanford M. Lyman, Professor of Sociology, Graduate Faculty of the New School for Social Research, for valuable discussions of race and ethnicity over a period of many years.

°In the late 1930s and early 1940s, during the period of the CIO organizing campaigns in the mass production sectors of the economy, thousands of black workers employed in the steel, auto, packing house and rubber industries, among others, were for the first time enrolled as union members. This, of course, is the historic significance of the CIO in black labor history. In retrospect, however, it is clear that the great promise of the CIO, the

in the failure to develop an adequate theory regarding the nexus between race and class in American labor history and much else that is important and unique in our past.*

The historical record reveals that the embrace of white supremacy as ideology and as practice was a strategy for assimilation by European working-class immigrants, the white ethnics who were to constitute a major part of the membership and leadership of organized labor in the United States. While white ethnics experienced severe hardship due to unjust discrimination, they also benefited from the far more pervasive and brutal discrimination against Afro-Americans. The occupational patterns of discrimination suffered by generations of nonwhites were in fact different in kind from those known to European immigrant workers, and these factors are crucial to an understanding of the development of American labor unions. One consequence of these historical

---

promise of an interracial labor movement, was never realized. All too often black workers were the victims of discrimination after they had been admitted into CIO membership. Some CIO unions permitted segregated units and negotiated discriminatory seniority provisions in union contracts. In both northern and southern states, CIO affiliates often conformed to prevailing racial practices at the work place and in the community. Whatever its limitations—and there were many—the CIO policy was at least an expression of formal equality in contrast to the pattern of exclusion and segregation within the AFL. However, by the time of the merger between the CIO and the AFL in 1955, the CIO policy on race had become an empty formality. The dynamic period of industrial organizing had faded into history, and the CIO leadership now had much in common with the conservative AFL bureaucracy. In retrospect, it is evident that the CIO had little, if any, long-term effect in altering the social conservatism of American labor unions. See Herbert Hill, "The AFL-CIO and the Black Worker: Twenty-Five Years After the Merger," *The Journal of Intergroup Relations*, X:1(Spring 1982): 5-78.

*From John R. Commons in the early years of the twentieth century, to the work of Philip Taft in the 1960s, what usually passed for labor history was really union history. With few exceptions, traditional labor history consisted of institutional studies of labor organizations based largely upon an examination of union records. This literature either ignored racial and ethnic issues, or treated them as footnotes in otherwise extensive works. If traditional labor historians and economists such as John R. Commons, Selig Perlman and Philip Taft mention black and other nonwhite workers at all, it is as a problem for white labor organizations and solely within the context of the institution of the labor union. In reaction to this traditional school, a group of younger labor historians began to emerge in the 1960s. Aware of the limitations of the older group and critical of their methods, this group, whose foremost representatives are Herbert Gutman and David Montgomery, developed what is essentially a neo-Marxian social history. In their revolt against the "old labor history" they proposed "to study the people," in short, to do for American labor history what E. P. Thompson did in his magisterial *The Making of the English Working Class* (New York: Vintage Books, 1963). Much more sophisticated in their view of social processes than their predecessors, the contributions of this group were a significant advance over the work of the traditional labor historians. But this interesting body of work, which introduced important correctives to the Commons-Taft school, is pervaded by an a priori commitment to the concept of working-class consciousness as the decisive force in American labor history, and while acknowledging some relative significance to race consciousness, it implicitly rejects the centrality of race in that history.

realities is that current opposition to affirmative action is based on perceived group interest, rather than on mere philosophical differences about "quotas," "reverse discrimination," and other issues commonly raised in debates. In fact, affirmative action represents a direct assault on the extensive efforts of white ethnics to perpetuate the preferential position and benefits they and their immigrant grandparents and parents enjoyed as Caucasians, at the expense of blacks and other nonwhite groups in American society.

European workers came to the United States with old and complex traditions, from communities of shared religion, nationality, language and history, indeed with all of those elements that constitute a cultural heritage. While there were great differences among these many groups, they shared two characteristics; first, they were white, and second, whatever their past history, they were confronted by one overwhelming problem: Could they become Americans? Furthermore, each successive wave of immigrants was confronted by that same question.

For white labor this issue was not just a theoretical abstraction. It involved fundamental matters of work and status. As successive generations of white immigrants effectively used labor unions to assimilate and become Americans, they acted through the same labor organizations to exclude nonwhites from unionized occupations and from desirable jobs in many industries. Thus, organized labor has played an important role in the inclusion-exclusion process of Americanization.

Immigrant workers were initially isolated from the social and economic mainstream, and they rapidly came to understand that Americanization was the key to success for themselves and for their sons and daughters. In discussing the Americanization process, one has to ask what it is, what does it mean, and perhaps most important, what did the immigrants think it meant? For the purposes of this discussion, the important point is that for immigrant workers the Americanization process was directly linked to the work place. The occupational frame of reference is crucial. Wages and the status that come from steady work could only be obtained by entering the permanent labor force and having access to the job market, and labor unions were a crucial factor in providing precisely such access to large groups of immigrant workers. A major factor over generations of the black working-class experience was that in contrast to the white ethnics, they were systematically barred from employment in the primary sectors of the labor market, thus denied the economic base and stability that made possible the much celebrated achievement and social mobility of white immigrant communities.

Many individual unions, as well as the American Federation of Labor itself, early in their respective histories adopted a policy based on the assumption that because non-Caucasian workers allegedly could not be Americanized, they therefore on a racial basis should be denied union membership and systematically denied employment in unionized occupations. This assumption was of course a self-fulfilling prophecy. Since nonwhites could not be Americanized, they were disqualified from employment and status and assigned to a permanent position as marginal laborers, to be hired only in unskilled and menial classifications at the lowest wages. If nonwhites found it difficult to improve their condition, it was because institutions like organized labor made it so.

For Samuel Gompers, president of the American Federation of Labor from its founding in 1886 until his death in 1924 (with the exception of 1895, when John McBride of the United Mine Workers was president), membership in organized labor turned on the question of a people's assimilability.* The Chinese and Japanese and Afro-Americans were "unassimilable," hence proscribed. Under Gompers, the immigrant Jewish labor leader who came to the presidency of the AFL from the leadership of the Cigar Makers International Union, the federation and most of its affiliated unions organized European immigrant workers, but excluded Asians and later black workers from the ranks of organized labor.

---

*In his autobiography, Gompers writes:

I felt identified with the people of my new home and it was without a question that I accepted American customs and the American life. To my mind the foreigner was the one who did not identify himself with American life and purposes. . . . The first step in Americanizing them [Bohemian workers] was to bring them to conform to American standards of work, which was a stepping stone to American standards of life. . . . By the beginning of the nineties, the racial problem in the labor movement was beginning to assume serious proportions. Our problem was part of the larger national problem, for the majority of immigrants no longer came from Western Europe where language, customs, and industrial organization were similiar to those of the United States but from the countries of Eastern Europe where lower standards of life and work prevailed. As these immigrants flooded basic industries they threatened to destroy our standards . . . . [A]s the number of immigrants rapidly increased and the admixture of various races was too rapid for assimilation, I could not escape the conclusion that some way must be found to safeguard America. . . . I have always opposed Chinese immigration not only because of the effect of Chinese standards of life and work but because of the racial problem created when Chinese and white workers were brought into the close contact of living and working side by side. . . . There was a sort of complacent confidence that America was a melting pot in which all manner of diverse nationalities could be gathered and inevitably, without planning or consideration on our part, Americans would finally emerge. In the absence of constructive efforts on the part of the community, the trade union movement had undertaken to teach foreign workers the economic bases of American standards of life, work, and ideals.

Samuel Gompers, *Seventy Years of Life and Labor: An Autobiography*, Vol. II (New York: E. P. Dutton, 1925), pp. 51-152, 161, 378.

Whatever difficulties white immigrants experienced, they could eventually become naturalized and be granted the rights of citizenship and full participation in the society. (The Naturalization Law of 1790 explicitly limited citizenship to "white" persons.) Success, however, necessitated a response to industrialization and to an ascendant bourgeois social order. For most white immigrants, the response was to seek acculturation and assimilation, a process that required the establishment of identity groups based on ethnicity as a means of progressing into the larger social order.

Joel Kovel contends that racism was functional for this society in that it was a "stabilizing" element of culture. He writes that racism "defined a social universe, absorbed aggression, and facilitated a sense of virtue in white America—a trait which contributed to America's material success. Racism was an integral part of a stable and productive cultural order."[1] The acculturation of white ethnics is in large measure the internalization of this process.*

For the most part the immigrant working class did not develop as a class-conscious proletariat. Instead, the ethnic and racial divisions within the working class reinforced labor market segmentation and led inevitably to the development of a dual racial labor system. Contemporary racial patterns of employment represent the consequences and continuity of a process that has become part of the historical experience of the white working class, an experience that was transformed into the organizational policy and practice of many labor unions. This phenomenon also explains why change in racial employment patterns is so bitterly resisted and why job inequality is so deep-rooted and routinely perpetuated. In the course of becoming "good Americans," the white working class reinforced its own divisions in the context of an emergent industrial division of labor.

The Black Response to Labor Unions and Immigration

White immigrants did not, in fact, always have an easy initial passage into labor organizations. Some unions required citizenship or a declaration of intent as a condition of membership. Others imposed high initiation fees, or required approval for admission by officers of the national organization or the presentation of a membership card from a foreign union.[2] Nevertheless, whatever the initial difficulties for the immi-

---

*For a discussion of the historical antecedents of such beliefs, i.e., membership in the white race as the basis for virtue and citizenship, see Ronald T. Takaki, *Iron Cages: Race and Culture In 19th Century America* (New York: Alfred A. Knopf, 1979), pp. 11-15.

grant, the prospect of eventual acceptance did exist and increasingly so in the last years of the nineteenth century.

In some cases the preferential treatment of immigrants was dramatic. For example, in 1865 the Cigar Makers International Union specifically barred blacks from membership; all the white immigrant needed was the possession of a union card from a labor organization in a foreign country.[3] Not surprisingly, in the 1860s and 1870s this union was composed largely of German-speaking members.[4] The 1870 convention of the Bricklayers Union postponed any decision on the issue of admitting black workers, while at the same time revoking the initiation fee which the white immigrant had been required to pay.[5]

Before the early years of the twentieth century, hostility towards the foreign born characterized some craft unions, especially in the building trades. But after the newcomers organized into ethnic groups such as the United Hebrew Trades* or the Italian Socialist Federation, they established a unified power base and craft unions soon admitted them. In time these immigrant groups achieved control of certain trades and established an "ethnic lock"° on jobs and union jurisdictions within their respective crafts, as in New York City where there was a Greek Furriers local, an Italian Dressmakers Union, and where locals of the Bricklayers Union were either Irish or Italian, while the Painters Union was largely Jewish.[+] A similiar pattern developed in

---

*The United Hebrew Trades, founded in 1888 in New York City, organized immigrant Jewish workers into local unions which later affiliated with national labor organizations, but retained their Jewish leadership and membership base. According to Philip Taft, "The United Hebrew Trades organized locals of Jewish building tradesmen, bakery workers, shoemakers and other trades". Philip Taft, *Organized Labor in American History* (New York: Harper and Row, 1964), p. 679.

°For an interesting description of this development in the industrial context, see Gerd Korman, *Industrialization, Immigrants and Americanizers: The View From Milwaukee, 1866-1921* (Madison, Wis.: State Historical Society of Wisconsin, 1967), pp. 86-88.

+Nationality-based local unions have been illegal since 1945 in New York under the State Anti-Discrimination Law. Title VII, the employment section of the Civil Rights Act of 1964, further requires the elimination of such locals, and some unions moved to disband them. On May 18, 1966, at a tempestuous meeting of the New York Furriers Union Joint Council (then affiliated with the Amalgamated Meat Cutters and Butcher Workmen [AFL-CIO]), the forty-year-old Greek Fur Workers' local was dissolved. The fifteen-hundred-member local union went out of existence and its members transferred to other locals affiliated with the Furriers Joint Council as a result of action by the international union to comply with federal law. (*The New York Times*, [May 19, 1966], p. 22.) Although the Furriers Union and other labor organizations moved to disband nationality locals because of the requirements of the Civil Rights Act, the International Ladies Garment Workers Union (AFL-CIO) continued to maintain two Italian locals in New York City: Local 89 designated as the Italian Dressmakers Union and Local 48 designed as the Italian Cloak Makers Union. According to the report of the general executive board of the ILGWU dated May 12, 1965, Local 89, the largest local in the international union, had a membership of 20,898, and Local 48 had a membership of 8,047. In 1946 a com-

other trades in many cities along the Atlantic seaboard and in mid-western communities with large ethnic concentrations.

Overcoming early hostility, white immigrant groups came to dominate many important unions and to control access to employment in a variety of occupations. This process was in significant contrast to the permanent exclusion and powerlessness of black workers. Clearly the racial factor was decisive.

The widespread resentment at the preferential treatment given to white immigrants by labor unions led many blacks to hold the belief that unions were instruments for the oppression of nonwhite workers by the foreign born. "The greatest enemy of the Negro," said one black leader from Indiana in 1899, "is the trade Unionism of the North."[6] Not surprisingly, the black press over a period of many years was filled with complaints against labor unions and immigrants.

Henry C. Dotry, writing in the *Age* in 1891, reminded his black readers that "usually one of the first things foreigners learn after entering upon these shores is prejudice against the Afro-American, and they strive to bar him from various branches of labor." His predictions were grim indeed: "Experience of riots and distress, strikes and starvation . . . will soon begin to fall on America tenfold. . . . America has become the goal for the criminals and beggars" of Europe.[7]

The Colored American in 1898 and 1899 reported that labor unions were forcing black workers out of their customary occupations—as barbers, coachmen, house painters, teamsters and waiters.[8] Black workers increasingly came to perceive discriminatory labor unions as a conspiracy by foreigners against them. This was expressed in an editorial in *The Colored American* in 1903: "The first thing they do after

---

plaint was filed with the New York State Commission Against Discrimination by a black worker who was barred from jobs controlled by Local 89. (*Hunter v. Sullivan Dress Shop,* C-1439-46). After the commission notified the ILGWU that the existence of nationality-based locals was a violation of state law, the union on January 27, 1947, entered into an agreement with the commission that it would not bar blacks, Spanish-speaking or other persons from membership in the Italian locals. Despite the agreement, and in defiance of state and federal laws, the ILGWU maintained the two Italian locals for another three decades without a single black or Hispanic worker gaining membership in the two locals, which controlled access to some of the highest-paying jobs in the industry. In 1977, because of a declining Italian membership, the union finally eliminated the practice and restructured locals in the New York area. (See *Report of the General Executive Board,* Thirty-Sixth Convention, International Ladies Garment Workers Union, [AFL-CIO], 1977, page 112). For a detailed history of race and ethnicity in the ILGWU, see Robert Laurentz, "Racial/Ethnic Conflict in the New York City Garment Industry, 1933-1980" (Ph.D. Dissertation, State University of New York at Binghamton, 1980); see also Herbert Hill, "The ILGWU Today: The Decay of a Labor Union," and Herbert Hill, "The ILGWU: Fact and Fiction," in Burton H. Hall, ed., *Autocracy and Insurgency in Organized Labor* (New Brunswick, N.J.: Transaction Press, 1972), pp. 147-160, 173-200.

landing and getting rid of their sea legs is to organize to keep the colored man out of the mines, out of the factories, out of the trade unions and out of all kinds of industries of the country."[9]

J. E. Bruce, who lived in Yonkers, New York, was a regular contributor to *The Colored American* under the pseudonym of "Bruce Grit" during the early 1900s. He wrote on these themes again and again. Commenting on a strike against the United Traction Company in Albany, Bruce said that "the leaders of the labor trust in America are largely men of foreign names and antecedents. . . . Who gave them the right to discriminate against the Negro in the labor market? To make him an industrial pariah when he is ready and willing to work? . . . It is a sad commentary on this free land . . . that the barriers in the domain of labor are raised by men of foreign birth."[10]

Bruce continued his attack on the unions a year later, when in 1902 he wrote that labor unions constituted "a gigantic closed corporation— a greedy, grasping, ruthless, intolerant, overbearing, dictatorial combination of half-educated white men." Finally, he declared flatly: "I am against them because they are against the Negro."[11]

World War I and the corresponding increase in industrial production, together with the drastic curtailment of European immigration, offered a new opportunity to black workers. Some Afro-American leaders later ascribed the relatively small black migration to the North during the preceding fifty years to the large foreign immigration.[12] Indeed, the first wave of southern black migrants moved directly into industries and cities which had traditionally been filled by European immigrant labor: railroads, packinghouses, foundries, automobile plants and steel mills, among others. Black workers were now moving into Cleveland, Chicago, Gary, Detroit, Milwaukee, Buffalo and other manufacturing centers.[13] W.E.B. Du Bois, describing the movement northward as tentative and dependent on the war, added: "If for a generation after the present war European migration is restricted, the Negro will have an economic opportunity which no bourbonism can wholly close."[14]

White Supremacy and Organized Labor

In the historical development of white working-class racism, the campaign against Asian immigrant labor was most significant and illustrates the process by which racism was institutionalized within labor unions. From 1850 to 1875 the main thrust of the anti-Asian movement was confined to the western states, but soon thereafter became a national issue. By focusing on a racially distinct people and by obtaining the support of the state in excluding them from entry and from citizenship, organized labor was thus able to lay the ideological groundwork for attacking other nonwhite races. The idea that race was a relevant factor for organized labor was then definitely established, and once having been established it was no longer necessary to adopt or differentiate all the other nice arguments that were needed in the first instance. Thus blacks could be excluded by employing the racial arguments that had been used against the Chinese, simply omitting the cultural ones. Later on the Japanese could be excluded from labor unions by claiming that they possessed the racial traits of the Chinese and, in addition, that they were intrinsically dangerous. The historical evidence suggests that for the black worker, fresh from emancipation and new civil rights laws conferring an abstract citizenship and a dubious equality, the anti-Asian agitation supplied the model for organized labor's discriminatory practices.

The institutionalization of racism within organized labor did not emerge full-blown. It gestated over a long period of time, advancing from stage to stage. Their success in excluding what they called "Mongolians" from the labor force suggested to the leadership of the American labor movement how they would deal with the black worker. In each instance, the objective was the same: to drive workers of the offending "non-Caucasian" race out of the labor force.*

From the start, the organized cigar makers marched in the forefront of the assault on the Chinese. It was the white cigar makers in California who developed a most ingenious method for forcing Chinese workers out of the trade. In 1874 they adopted a white label to indicate that the cigars were made by white union men.[15] On the cigar box was a reproduction of the union label with the following message:

> Buy no cigars except
> from the box marked
> with the trade-union label,
> thus you help maintain the
> white as against the Coolie
> standard of life and work.[16]

The facsimile of the label showed a dragon on one side, the union mark on the other, and the words "White Labor, White Labor." The practice of issuing labels quickly caught on. In 1875 the St. Louis cigar makers followed suit with a bright red one. Finally, at their general

---

*For a discussion of organized labor's role in fragmenting the working class, see Edna Bonacich, "A Theory of Ethnic Antagonism: The Split Labor Market," *American Sociological Review*, 37:5(October 1972): 547-558; see also Edna Bonacich, "Advanced Capitalism and Black-White Relations in the United States: A Split Labor Market Interpretation," *American Sociological Review*, 41:1(February 1976): 34-50.

convention three years later, the Cigar Makers International Union decided on a blue one.[17] Thus, the tradition of the union label was born in the bond of racism.

The Cigar Makers together with other craft unions at that time developed an approach that was to have long-term consequences for the future of labor unions in the United States. The Cigar Makers International Union concentrated solely on organizing skilled workers, leaving the unskilled and disadvantaged to fend for themselves. In this way an "aristocracy of labor" emerged. Members of the Cigar Makers International Union and other craft unions such as those on the railroads, in the printing trades, and among brewery workers, iron molders and other skilled occupations, obtained increasing benefits while the rest of the work force, having no leverage in the open market, stagnated.[18]

In 1884 the Cigars Makers International Union established Local 228 in San Francisco, "the first step," writes Alexander Saxton, "of a long-range plan for driving Orientals out of the trade."[19] The campaign was successful. By the end of November 1885, the large producers capitulated to the demands of organized labor. The Chinese were to be forced out of the industry and replaced by white workers. The target date was January 1, 1886. This target date was not met, but the Chinese were in time eliminated completely from the industry.[20] Similiar campaigns were conducted in the boot and shoe trade and other industries. The process of racial occupational displacement was well underway.

Two men, above all others, were responsible for organized labor's crusade against Asian workers—Adolph Strasser and Samuel Gompers, both immigrants, and both leaders of the Cigar Makers International Union. Although there was no Chinese issue for cigar makers in other parts of the country, they gave unstinting support to their brethren on the West Coast. The predecessor of the American Federation of Labor, the Federation of Organized Trades and Labor Unions, at its first convention in 1881, condemned the Chinese cigar makers of California and recommended that only union label cigars made by white men be purchased.

There is a rather standard interpretation of the attitude of organized labor towards Asian workers stemming from the tradition of the Wisconsin labor economists such as John R. Commons, Selig Perlman and, more recently, Philip Taft. That interpretation argues that American workers, in manifesting a large degree of racism toward Asians, were in fact only responding to the great economic threat Chinese labor posed for whites.* In effect, the traditional labor economists justify labor's racism and attempt to excuse not only the systematic exclusion of Asians from unions, but even the more virulent attacks upon non-whites that often occurred in American labor history. Much of this analysis is derived from contemporary nineteenth-century labor sources, i.e., from the words and writings of union leaders and members, who assumed a priori that the Chinese posed a definite economic threat to their interests, and moreover that the existence of "cheap coolie labor" was largely responsible for the depressed conditions of the American economy after 1873.°

All available evidence indicates that Asian labor was not a direct economic threat to white workers, since the Chinese numbered only 368 outside of the West in 1870.[21] Even the most extreme labor politician could not argue that the depressed conditions of white workers were due to Chinese labor. Three major factors after 1873 kept the Chinese question alive as a national issue. First, the Workingman's Party under the leadership of Dennis Kearney (an Irish immigrant) in San Francisco continued to pressure western representatives in Congress to take action against Chinese labor. Second, the national Democratic Party, attempting to revive itself after the Civil War, pushed its appeal to workingmen through the promulgation of an anti-Chinese position, among others.[22] And finally, the anti-Chinese position became part of the litany of labor after 1870, as indicated by the support given by the Knights of Labor to Chinese exclusion.[23]

These three sources of anti-Chinese agitation were not really sufficient to bring a national, bipartisan campaign to fruition, however. Heretofore the missing link had been the Republican Party. By 1876, though, two key political developments had prepared the Republicans to support Chinese exclusion. The first was the failure of the Radical Republican policy which used blacks as a bulwark against the resur-

---

*According to Selig Perlman, "The anti-Chinese agitation in California, culminating as it did in the Exclusion Law passed by Congress in 1882, was doubtless the most important single factor in the history of American labor, for without it the entire country might have been overrun by Mongolian labor and the labor movement might have become a conflict of races instead of classes." Selig Perlman, *The History of Trade Unionism in the United States* (New York: A. M. Kelley, 1950, originally published in 1922), p. 62. See also John R. Commons, *Races and Immigrants in America* (New York: Macmillan, 1907, pp. 1-7, 141; Philip Taft, *Labor Politics American Style: The California State Federation of Labor* (Cambridge, Mass.: Harvard University Press, 1968), pp. 166-188; and Philip Taft, *Organized Labor in American History* (New York: Harper and Row, 1964), pp. 301-304.

°In California in 1860, the Chinese were 9 percent of the population; in 1870, 8.6 percent, and in 1880, 7.5 percent. In 1882 when the Chinese Exclusion Act was passed, the total Chinese population in the United States was 105,465, with 71 percent living in California. U.S. Bureau of the Census, *Population Reports* (Washington, D.C.: 1860 to 1880).

gence of the southern Democrats, both locally and nationally. The Compromise of 1877 forced blacks out of the political arena and led the Republicans, who had always been a minority party (Lincoln did not receive a majority in 1860), to look elsewhere for political support. This led to the conclusion by Republicans that workingmen were the key to any successful national coalition.

The Chinese Exclusion Act of 1882

Given the activity generated in the ranks of labor, adoption of the Chinese Exclusion Act of 1882 was only a partial victory for labor.* Insofar as national politicians had turned anti-coolieism to their own purposes, the act as it finally stood was more sop than real solution. It of course barred all future Chinese laborers from entering the United States after 1882; but beyond that it did not address itself to the Chinese who were already here. As such, labor had mixed reaction to the bill's passage. Labor leaders vigorously supported the act: Terence V. Powderly had put the entire national Knights of Labor structure to work lobbying for the bill in 1882.[24] But since the Chinese who were in the United States in 1882 were excluded from the act's consideration, the labor movement felt that a Chinese problem still existed. Thus the anti-Chinese position was kept alive after 1882 by the leadership of organized labor. For example, Powderly called for the total elimination of all Chinese in the United States at the end of 1882, even while he and other union leaders celebrated the passage of the Exclusion Act as a labor victory.[25] (The act which forbade the naturalization of Chinese residents was renewed for another ten years in 1892, and in 1902 was extended indefinitely. It was not until 1943, 1946 and 1952 that Chinese, Filipinos and Japanese, respectively, were granted the right to become U.S. citizens.)

After adoption of the Chinese Exclusion Act of 1882, organized labor reasserted its position as the vanguard of the anti-Asian campaign,

---

*See Alexander Saxton, *The Indispensable Enemy: Labor and The Anti-Chinese Movement in California* (Berkeley, Cal.: University of California Press, 1971). Saxton has written a brilliant analysis of the role of anti-coolieism in solidifying the grip of craft unions and their leaders over labor politics and the job market. Prior to 1876 and after 1882, the leadership of the anti-Chinese movement rested with the heads of craft unions of skilled workers—precisely those unions that had the least to fear in terms of economic competition with the Chinese. For the leaders of these unions the anti-Chinese movement became a means by which they could manipulate the political and organizational energy of the entire labor force, skilled and unskilled. Evidently "pure trade unionism" was inadequate in mobilizing workers under the banner of organized labor. What is remarkable about labor's role in the anti-Asian campaign is the all-consuming character of its activity.

much as it had in the 1870s.* This new stage of "anti-coolie" agitation corresponded to a period of national economic decline, and was similar to the activities of the Workingmen's Party movement in 1876. The difference between 1876 and 1882 was not that the Chinese had flooded out of the West into eastern industry as had been feared in 1870 (there were still only 3,663 Chinese living outside of the western states in 1880), but rather that the national political system in the 1870s had given credence to and made acceptable anti-Chinese politics. While 1882 saw the passage of the Exclusion Act, the year also marked the onset of an industrial depression which would serve as the context in which organized labor carried on an extended campaign against Asian workers.

Labor's anti-Asian program, with its clear racist character, was to become a standard policy of the AFL for decades, and in the September 1905 issue of the *American Federationist* Gompers wrote that "Caucasian civilization will serve notice that its uplifting process is not to be interfered with in any way."[26] The president of the AFL later explained that "maintenance of the nation depended upon maintenance of racial purity."[27] At the turn of the century the AFL was actively promoting racist policies against nonwhite workers. The discriminatory pattern was now firmly established and would remain as policy and practice into the modern period.

---

*Gompers and his fellow labor leaders were to continue this activity into the twentieth century. His most comprehensive statement on the subject appeared in a pamphlet of which he was co-author entitled *Some Reasons for Chinese Exclusion: Meat vs. Rice, American Manhood Against Asiatic Coolieism, Which Shall Survive?* This was published by the AFL in 1902 and was brought out again in 1908. Gompers and his co-author, Herman Gutstadt, AFL representative in San Francisco, wrote that "the racial differences between American whites and Asiatics would never be overcome." The superior whites had to exclude the inferior Asiatics by law, or if necessary, "by force of arms." The Chinese were congenitally immoral: "The Yellow Man found it natural to lie, cheat and murder and ninety-nine out of every one hundred Chinese are gamblers." According to Gompers, the Asiatic people were lecherous, loved to live in filthy surroundings and damp cellars, and thus the "instinct of the race remains unchanged." Although the Chinese servant may work faithfully in an "American household," explained Gompers, "he joyfully hastens back to his slum and his burrow to the grateful luxury of his normal surroundings—vice, filth, and an atmosphere of horror." The 1904 AFL convention made a special point of condemning the "Japanese and all . . . Asiatics." (*Proceedings, American Federation of Labor,* 1904, pp. 7-8). The pages of the *American Federationist* were full of alarums and excursions about the "Jap menace." In one notable instance Gompers denounced the famous Japanese socialist, Sen Katayama, who was then visiting the United States. Gompers wrote in the May 1904 issue of the *American Federationist*: "this presumptous Jap . . . from whose leprous mouth . . . came . . . a mongrel's utterances."

Labor's Zeitgeist

It may be objected that the racial views held by Gompers and his colleagues in organized labor should not be singled out for special notice or criticism, for, as some have argued, they merely reflected the *Zeitgeist*. From the end of the Civil War to World War I, white Americans in general attributed their spectacular emergence as an industrial, military and imperial power to their racial superiority. If such were the sentiments of America at large, why should labor in particular be faulted for sharing them?

The fallacy of the *Zeitgeist* argument is that it receives its justification in retrospect from those labor historians who either eliminate or diminish the choices that confronted the individuals and institutions in the period under discussion. The *Zeitgeist* did not command American labor organizations to embrace a policy of racism, and it certainly did not command the AFL, which spoke for the overwhelming majority of organized workers from the 1890s on, to be even more militantly racist than Americans in general.

The responsibility for what the AFL did lay with the organization itself, which is to say that it could have taken an alternative course at the time. It could have practiced what its leaders occasionally preached, namely, that all workers were equal, that no person should be treated as a commodity, that capital was the common enemy of all workers. Instead, the AFL acted on the assumption that non-Caucasians were inferior, that they deserved to be treated as commodities, that race, not differences of class or wealth or power, defined the important issues in society. Organized labor chose the path it walked in the years following the Civil War. In fact, it created its own *Zeitgeist*.

It might be further observed that America's official party of the left at this time, the Socialist Party of the United States, held much the same position on racial issues as the American Federation of Labor. Its executive committee gave the party's seal of approval to racial exclusion laws. Morris Hillquit, one of American socialism's chief theoreticians (an immigrant), supported measures to restrict the influx of "backward races." Victor Berger, also foreign born, the party's leader in Milwaukee and one of its major national figures, and later its first congressman, went much further. On the issue of race he was as extreme as Madison Grant or Lothrop Stoddard, whose book, *The Rising Tide of Color Against White Supremacy*, published in 1920, set forth the most uncompromising white racist position. Berger was vehement about keeping the United States a "white man's" country, and he feared that it might be too late to prevent the United States from degenerating into a "black-and-yellow country within a few generations." For him at least this was a life-and-death struggle, a "fight for my wife and children . . . for all your wives and children."[28] And there was Jack London, whose racism was well known, for it appeared in his novels and short stories as well as in his essays defending socialism. "I am first of all a white man and only then a socialist," he said. These words could have been emblazoned on the party's banner.[29]

Not every American socialist, of course, subscribed to the views of the Bergers and Londons. The radical wing of the party tended to take its universalist principles more seriously. One such radical was Louis Boudin (like Hillquit, a Russian-born Jew). Boudin was among the delegates attending the 1907 congress of the Socialist International at Stuttgart, Germany. There the congress defeated an American proposal favoring the exclusion of undesirable immigrants. Boudin, who argued against the proposal, later explained why nearly all the delegates of twenty-two countries rejected it out of hand. They did so because they were not going to "establish the principle of dividing immigrants along racial lines into 'organizable' and 'unorganizable'" nor to "lay down as a rule of socialist policy, based on such principle of division, the demand for the exclusion of the so-called 'unorganizable' races." The socialist parties of the world were convinced, Boudin went on, that the "principles and demands formulated in our resolution are a snare and delusion, and cannot possibly result in any permanent good to the working class of this country or of the world. These principles and demands are unsocialistic, that is to say, they are repugnant to the permanent and lasting interests of the working class."[30]

Boudin soon received his reply from one Cameron H. King, Jr., who elaborated the views of the Socialist Party's national executive committee. King's article presented the shopworn racist theme in the vestments of Marxian socialism. The logic proceeded as follows: The Socialist Party must be the party of the working class, the party dedicated to Marx's "materialist conception of history," and as an "organization becomes stronger the more accurately it meets the material interests and economic necessities of the people," it also becomes weaker when it falls "into the morass of impractical schemes while pursuing the beautiful but illusory ideals of altruistic utopianism."[31] The workers through their unions have "declared for the exclusion of Asiatic labor."[32] Therefore, the Socialist Party must adopt a similiar position. Only by doing so will it be true to Marx's teachings. Having made his point, King condemned the socialists of other countries for failing to empathize with their American brethren.

King makes it very clear that in the event of a conflict between race consciousness and class consciousness, the socialists must choose the former. They must do so or cut themselves off from the proletariat.

"The time has come," King concluded in language reminiscent of Jack London's,

> for the Socialist Party to decide what its relation shall be to the working class. Are we going to bend the knee in worship of the idealistic phrase, "The Brotherhood of Man," or are we going to affirm our solidarity with American labor and prevent the destruction of its hard won standard of life? In short, are we to remain idealists out of touch with the red-blooded, self assertive life, or are we to take our place in the workingmen's struggle for existence, organizing his forces and always fighting for advances in his means of life.[33]

Racial Exclusion and Job Displacement

Between 1860 and 1914 over twenty-five million immigrants arrived in the United States, and by 1890 the working class was largely composed of new stock immigrants. Herbert Gutman summarizes this development:

> Outside the building trades in nearly all parts of the country, white male workers of old stock were relatively unimportant. Immigrants, their children and Afro-Americans played central roles in the reproduction of the working class and the development of working-class institutions. It could not have been otherwise in places like Leavenworth, Kansas, where Blacks, immigrants and the children of immigrants comprised about 90 percent of the working-class in 1880. And the Leavenworth pattern was typical for the country at large.[34]

In many cities north and south, blacks had once been employed in a great variety of occupations, skilled and unskilled. However, in the last years of the nineteenth century the process of black displacement was well underway, and trade unions frequently were the instrument that forced black workers out of jobs they had traditionally held by replacing them with immigrant white workers after union organization.

George Sinclair Mitchell noted in 1936 that "the Southern trade unionism of the last thirty odd years has been in good measure a protective device for the march of white artisans into places held by Negroes."[35] The white worker and his trade union displaced black labor on street railways, removed Afro-American firemen on railroads, took the jobs of black switchmen and shop workers, replaced blacks in construction work and shipbuilding, and forced them out of tobacco manufacturing and other industries. Mitchell wrote that the "typical city central labor body of Mobile or Savannah or Columbia or New Orleans or Richmond was a delegate meeting of white men drawn from white locals, jealous of every skilled place held by Negroes." The occasional all-black segregated local received little or no help from its international union or the AFL. The result was that black workers who through years of service had acquired the skill needed for craftsmen's work were denied membership in white unions and forced out of skilled and semi-skilled employment. The Machinists, Boilermakers, Carmen and other AFL unions, according to Mitchell, "absolutely forbid Negro membership."[36]

The evidence presented in 1902 by W.E.B. Du Bois in his Atlanta University study entitled *The Negro Artisan* is most relevant. Du Bois investigated the racial practices of many labor organizations and found that forty-three national unions operating in both northern and southern states, including the railroad brotherhoods, had not a single black member. Twenty-seven others had very few black members. Du Bois concluded that the United Mine Workers, an industrial union, was the major exception to the racial pattern. He reported a black membership of twenty thousand out of a total membership in 1901 of 224,000.[37] Du Bois estimated the 1910 black membership as twenty-five thousand,[38] but Spero and Harris believe the figure was probably closer to four thousand since there were about forty thousand blacks in the entire industry.[39] However, the black membership in 1926 was no more than five thousand.[40]

By the turn of the century the process of black job displacement that had begun in the South was also well under way in the North. Here too economic expansion and the quickened pace of industrialization gave rise to new and more attractive jobs, to which blacks were denied entry. At the same time, the emergence of labor unions that excluded blacks on the basis of race also hastened the displacement of northern blacks from skilled jobs.

These trends were accelerated by fluctuations in business cycles. In times of industrial expansion, when labor was scarce, the black "labor reserve" was utilized. But the concomitant losses in periods of recession more than canceled the short-term gains, and blacks were increasingly limited to casual and unskilled jobs in the unorganized sector of the economy.

When employers wished to hire blacks, white workers frequently protested. Between 1882 and 1900 there were at least fifty strikes by whites against the hiring of blacks.[41] Some of these strikes failed, but the success of a number of them meant that blacks were effectively barred from almost all the higher-paid skilled work in many industries.

White labor unions also organized strikes and engaged in other action to force the displacement of black workers from jobs they had long held. In 1890 the Brotherhood of Locomotive Trainmen petitioned the Houston and Texas Central Railroad demanding that all black workers be replaced by whites,[42] and in 1909 white workers struck against the Georgia Railroad to protest the company's practice of hiring black firemen.[43] Ten black railroad workers were killed in 1911 during a strike organized to remove blacks employed by the Cincinnati, New Orleans and Texas Pacific Railroad.[44] Similiar events occurred elsewhere in the railroad industry over a period of many years.[45]

The experience of black workers in both Birmingham, Alabama, and Boston in the early 1900s is indicative of the national pattern. The movement of large numbers of European immigrants into the Birmingham steel mills eliminated the concentration of black workers in many trades.[46] Similarly the data show that in Boston, Irish immigrants displaced and economically surpassed blacks at the turn of the century.[47]

White Unions Against Black Workers

The unions affiliated with the American Federation of Labor and the independent railroad brotherhoods attained their racially restrictive goals by a variety of methods. These included exclusion of blacks and other nonwhites from membership through racial provisions in union constitutions or in the ritual bylaws of local unions; exclusion by tacit agreement in the absence of written provisions; racially segregated units where blacks were admitted; separate racial lines of seniority and promotion in labor contracts; union control of licensing boards; refusal to admit nonwhites into union-controlled apprenticeship and other training programs; negotiating discriminatory labor agreements that adversely affected black workers while excluding them from union membership; and denial of access to hiring halls and other union-controlled job referral systems.

The incorporation of restrictive racial membership clauses in union constitutions antedated the formation of the American Federation of Labor and continued long after its establishment. A typical example of early exclusionary practices is to be found in the 1865 constitution of the Cigar Makers International Union. Article IX stated that "unless said person is a white practical cigar maker," he could not belong to the union.[48] In 1871 the Cigar Makers International Union convention transferred the racial exclusion provision from the national union's constitution to the admission ritual of the local union, where it performed the same function,[49] and the International Typographical Union resorted to the same device, as did other unions later including the Iron Molders Union, the National Association of Machinists, the National Carpenters Union and the Bricklayers and Masons Union. Frank E. Wolfe's study of union membership exclusion, published in

1920, summed up the racial practices of this period: "Indeed, all available evidence supports the conclusion that Negroes were seldom admitted into a union in any part of the country."[50]

Typical of the exclusion clauses in many union constitutions were the following:

The National Association of Machinists (later the International Association of Machinists) specified:

a white, free born male citizen of some civilized country;[51]

The American Wire Weavers Protective Association:

Christian, white, male of the full age of 21 . . . . Foreigners applying for admission must declare citizenship intentions and pay an initiation fee of $1,000;[52]

The Masters, Mates and Pilots:

a white person of good moral character;[53]

The Order of Sleeping Car Conductors:

The applicant for membership shall be a white male;[54]

The Brotherhood of Railway and Steamship Clerks:

A white person, male or female, of good moral character;[55]

The Brotherhood of Railway Carmen:

Any white person between the ages of 16 and 65 years;[56]

Switchmen's Union of North America:

A candidate for admission in a Lodge shall be a white, male person;[57]

Railway Mail Association:

Any regular male employee or certified male substitute of the United States Railway Mail Service, who is of the Caucasian race.[58]

Among the most powerful of the labor organizations at the turn of the century were the railroad unions, which had a membership of over one million by the early 1900s and already possessed the capacity for coordinated national strikes. The railroad labor unions, by virtue of their high degree of organization and militancy, emerged as a vanguard of the organized American working class. They were also among the most militantly racist.

The constitution of the Brotherhood of Locomotive Engineers provided that "no person shall become a member of the Brotherhood of Locomotive Engineers unless he is a white man 21 years of age."[59] Also typical of the railway unions were the Brotherhood of Locomotive Firemen and Enginemen, founded in 1873, and the Brotherhood of Railroad Trainmen, founded in 1883,[60] both of which limited membership to white males by provisions in their respective constitutions. The constitutional provision regarding membership in the Brotherhood of Locomotive Firemen and Enginemen stated the full qualifications as follows: "He shall be white born, of good moral character, sober and industrious, sound in body and limb, his eyesight shall be normal, not less than eighteen years of age, and able to read and write the English language."[61] In 1925 their constitution was amended and the following was added: "Mexicans, Indians, or those of Indian or Spanish-Mexican extraction are not eligible. . . . Natives of Italy are eligible to membership."[62] In 1928 the constitution added a special dispensation for the admission of American Indians to membership, to be granted only by the president of the International Union.[63] The membership qualification of the Brotherhood of Railroad Trainmen also required that an applicant "be a white male, sober and industrious."[64]

Charles H. Houston, general counsel for the Association of Colored Railway Trainmen and Locomotive Firemen, summarized the racial practices of the railroad unions in 1949:

> . . . the Big Four Brotherhoods have been using every means in their power to drive the Negro train and engine service worker out of employment and create a "racially closed shop" among the firemen, brakemen, switchmen, flagmen, and yardmen.[65]

A similiar history of aggression by the railroad labor unions against black firemen and brakemen occurred in northern states as well as in the South. Action was taken by the railway brotherhoods to force black workers out of jobs on the Michigan Central as early as 1863, and on the New York, New Haven and Hartford Railway, the Baltimore and Ohio and other lines during World War I.[66]

During World War II the Brotherhood of Firemen and Enginemen distributed a strike ballot to prevent the hiring of black firemen on the Atlantic Coast Line Railroad. In 1943 President Franklin Roosevelt's Committee on Fair Employment Practices held public hearings on the racial pattern of employment in the railroad industry. The unions remained firm in their policies and practices and successfully defied the committee. Houston, a member of the committee, concluded that the operating railroad brotherhoods had established "the Nordic closed shop" on American railroads.*

Among the many unions that rigidly enforced a policy of nonwhite exclusion into the modern period was the AFL's Seafarers International Union. The leader primarily responsible for its development was

---

*For a detailed analysis of the process of black displacement in the railroad industry, see Herbert Hill, *Black Labor and The American Legal System* (Washington, D.C.: Bureau of National Affairs, 1977), Chap. 13, pp. 334-372.

Andrew Furuseth, a Norwegian immigrant and a major figure in the early organization of seamen, who was also one of the most militant white supremacists of his time. Furuseth frequently invoked racist arguments against non-Caucasian workers, as in his warnings before a congressional hearing in 1915 that whites would be forced from the sea if black and Asian workers were employed on American ships. For a decade Furuseth had lived the brutalized life of a seaman before becoming a union organizer and seeking, by the sheer force of his personality, to persuade Congress to improve working conditions on American merchant ships. Thanks mainly to his efforts, the LaFollette Seamen's Act was passed in 1915.[67]

Historians and biographers have duly acknowledged Furuseth's achievements.[68] But beneath the aura that encircles his life and work lies the specter of racism. Excluding non-Caucasians from American ships was no less important to him than improving the lot of seamen. The most militant Aryan supremacists of the day had nothing to teach him.[69] His racism, moreover, was buttressed by a far-ranging ideology. The power of the white race, he claimed, rested on its mastery of the seas. That control over the world which the white race—or a segment of it—had maintained unimpaired for three thousand years now stood in jeopardy because "Orientals" and other inferior people were replacing whites.[70] Furuseth called for adoption of a law that, in his words, "will mean safety to our part of the human race, national safety, and racial safety as well."[71]

In 1905 Furuseth joined with other officials of the American Federation of Labor in San Francisco, including Patrick H. McCarthy (from Ireland), Olaf Treitmoe (from Sweden) and Walter MacArthur (from Scotland), in establishing the Asiatic Exclusion League. Later in a typical article in the *Seamen's Journal*, the official publication of the union which he headed, Furuseth stated, "Self respecting white men will not serve with Negroes."[72] It should be noted that Furuseth and his associates were responsible for a pattern of racial exclusion in the Seafarers International Union which continued into the contemporary period.[73]

In a study of the racial practices of labor unions published in 1930, Dr. Ira DeA. Reid noted that even though some unions had removed racial exclusion provisions from their constitutions, they continued to exclude nonwhites by tacit consent:

> Tacit agreement, examinations and local determination of eligibility for membership serve as deterrents to Negro inclusion in many unions. The Plumbers have never made an issue of the question of admitting Negroes, though it is generally understood that they are not admitted. Despite persistent efforts of Negro plumbers in Philadelphia, New York, and Chicago to secure

membership, they have not succeeded. . . . . In Philadelphia, the licensing board will not grant licenses to Negro plumbers.[74]

Many construction unions had lobbied successfully in state legislatures and city councils for the enactment of statutes which required that craftsmen such as plumbers, steamfitters and electricians be licensed by state or municipal boards on which union representatives would sit. In a letter written in 1905 by C. H. Perry, secretary of Local Union 110 of the Plumbers Union in Virginia, to the editor of the *Journal*, official organ of the Plumbers Union, the purpose of such lobbying was revealed clearly; namely to "entirely eliminate the black artisan . . . from [the] craft, especially in the southern district, as the Negro is a factor there."[75] By 1925 more than thirty states required licensing boards which included union representatives, thus providing racist labor unions with the legal means to eliminate nonwhites from many trades.

After 1900 when black workers were admitted into some AFL unions, they were usually limited to segregated or auxiliary units. This policy was sanctioned by Article XII, Section VI, of the American Federation of Labor constitution as revised in 1900, which states:

> Separate charters may be issued to central labor unions, local unions or federal labor unions, composed exclusively of colored workers, where in the judgement of the Executive Council it appears advisable.[76]

Union officials soon enforced segregated units as a matter of common practice, and this became the prevailing pattern within the federation. A typical example was the Blacksmiths Union whose constitution stated:

> Where there are a sufficient number of colored helpers they may be organized as an auxiliary local and shall be under the jurisdiction of the white local having jurisdiction over that territory. Colored helpers shall not transfer except to another auxiliary local composed of *colored members, and colored members shall not be promoted to blacksmiths or helper apprentices, and will not be admitted to shops where white helpers are now employed.*[77]

Other labor organizations such as the Sheet Metal Workers Union engaged in similar practices. Article IV, Section I, of the union's 1918 constitution provided that separate charters for black sheet metal workers would

> be granted only with the consent of the white local union established in the locality . . . where there are a sufficient number of Negro sheet metal workers, they may be organized as an Auxiliary Local and shall come under the jurisdiction of the white Local Union having jurisdiction over said locality. Members of Aux-

iliary Locals composed of colored sheet metal workers shall not transfer except to another Auxiliary Local composed of colored members.[78]

Segregated locals often functioned under restrictions and standards imposed by the same international unions that refused to admit black workers. Thus in 1903 the International Brotherhood of Electrical Workers stated in its official publication that "we do not want the Negro in the International Brotherhood of Electrical Workers, but we think they should be organized into locals of their own."[79] One of the major purposes of creating segregated locals and auxiliary units was to prevent blacks from protecting their own interests in the collective bargaining process.

From its inception in 1880, the International Association of Boilermakers had enforced a policy of racial exclusion. When it was admitted to the American Federation of Labor in 1896, the union transferred the "white-only" membership clause from its constitution to the admission ritual of local unions, where it served to effectively exclude blacks.[80] At the 1908 convention of the Boilermakers Union, the delegates debated returning the color bar to the constitution of the international union, but decided that it should remain part of the local union ritual.[81] In 1937 the convention of the Boilermakers Union amended its rules to permit the chartering of all-black auxiliary locals.[82] The leadership of the union requested the change in policy and stated: "The Executive Council, therefore, recommends that this convention authorize the granting of separate charters to colored workers of our trade . . . [and] that the membership of the colored men be confined to such separate locals."[83]

The convention adopted a policy of limiting black workers to segregated auxiliary units, each under the "supervision" of a white local. The bylaws governing such auxiliaries provided that "[a]n applicant for membership must be a colored male citizen of some civilized country, between the ages of sixteen (16) and sixty (60) years."[84] The bylaws for white locals allowed membership until the age of seventy. The auxiliaries were not allowed to have their own business agents but were to use the services of their "supervising" local's agent. Grievances of the auxiliary members would be processed through the grievance committees of the white locals. Black members were denied the right of "universal transfer" among the Boilermakers' locals, retaining only the right to transfer among auxiliary units, with restrictions upon job promotion. The black auxiliaries had no representation on any of the white locals' governing committees or at the union's international conventions. Auxiliary membership provided only half the life insurance coverage received by white members.

Black workers could not seek job promotions without the approval of the white supervising local, since the bylaws provided that

> [a]ny member desiring a change of classification must first receive the approval of his auxiliary lodge, after which it will be necessary for him to receive the approval of the supervising lodge. The application will then be submitted to the International President for final approval.[85]

White locals of the Boilermakers had secured for themselves control of the occupational classification structure and job promotion system. The device of segregated auxiliaries provided a means of controlling and limiting black labor while reserving better-paying classifications for members of the white locals.

Total exclusion or segregation was enforced as national policy by most labor unions in the early decades of the twentieth century. The aim of white labor organizations to restrict black workers to the lowest rungs of the job ladder was increasingly successful. This process was accompanied by a litany of white supremacy within labor organizations. In the September 1905 issue of the *American Federationist*, the president of the AFL wrote that the organization desired no controversy with Negroes, "but if the colored man continued to lend himself to the work of tearing down what the white man has built up, a race hatred far worse than any ever known will result."[86] Also typical is the article in the August 1906 issue of the *American Federationist* which refers to "hordes of ignorant blacks" who possess "but few of those attributes we have learned to revere and love," and who were but "huge strapping fellows, ignorant and vicious, whose predominating trait was animalism."[87]

The Consequences of White Working-Class Racism

Data from cities, north and south, reveal the consequences of organized labor's efforts to remove nonwhite workers from many crafts and industries. In Cleveland, Ohio:

> union policies, both national and local, effectively kept most eligible Negroes out of the trade union movement. The Boilermaker's Union, the International Association of Machinists, and the Plumbers and Steamfitters Union had a national policy of excluding blacks. Other union locals in the city such as the Metal Polishers and the Paperhangers, barred Negroes on their own initiative. . . . In 1870 fully 31.7 percent of all black males in Cleveland had been employed in skilled trades; by 1910 this figure had dropped

sharply to 11 percent. . . . The 1910 Census listed only five black plumbers in the entire city.[88] *

In New Orleans there were 3,460 blacks listed in the city directory for 1870 as carpenters, cigar makers, painters, clerks, shoemakers, coopers, tailors, bakers, blacksmiths and foundry hands. By 1904 the number was below 346, although the black population had increased by more than 50 percent.[89]°

Craft unions in the construction trades were a most important factor in the process of racial job displacement that occurred during the post-Reconstruction period. Prior to emancipation, there had been a concentration of black workers, both slave and free, in the building trades. The construction unions converted these jobs to "white men's work" and forced Afro-Americans out of the skilled trades in the construction industry. This process, which occurred in many cities along the eastern seaboard and throughout the southern states, was described in an 1898 report by John Stephens Durham. He cited Washington, D.C., as an example and wrote that

> at one period, some of the best buildings were constructed by colored workmen. Their employment in large numbers continued some time after the war. The British Legation, the Centre Market, the Freedmen's Bank, and at least four well-built school houses are monuments to the acceptability of their work under

---

*These data are consistent with the pattern for many northern cities and are confirmed by the U.S. Thirteenth Census, 1910, and by several studies. These include W.E.B. Du-Bois, *The Philadelphia Negro* (Philadelphia: University of Pennsylvania, 1899); Mary White Ovington, *Half a Man: The Status of the Negro in New York* (New York: Longman, Greens and Co., 1911); John Daniels, *In Freedom's Birthplace: A Study of the Boston Negroes* (Boston: Houghton Mifflin Co., 1914); and William A. Crossland, *Industrial Conditions Among Negroes in St. Louis* (St. Louis, Missouri: Press of Mendle Printing Co., 1914). Among several valuable studies in the modern period are St. Clair Drake and Horace R. Cayton, *Black Metropolis* (New York: Harcourt, Brace and Co., 1945); Gilbert Osofsky, *Harlem: The Making of a Ghetto* (New York: Harper and Row, 1966); Allen Spear, *Black Chicago: The Making of a Negro Ghetto, 1890-1920* (Chicago: University of Chicago Press, 1967); Stephan Thernstrom, *The Other Bostonians: Poverty and Progress in the American Metropolis, 1880-1970* (Cambridge, Mass.: Harvard University Press, 1973); David M. Katzman, *Before the Ghetto: Black Detroit in the Nineteenth Century* (Urbana, Ill.: University of Illinois Press, 1933); and Kenneth L. Kusmer, *A Ghetto Takes Shape: Black Cleveland, 1870-1930* (Urbana, Ill.: University of Illinois Press, 1976).

°Woodward writes of this period:

Caste sanctioned a division of labor into white men's jobs and black men's jobs. Sometimes aided by employers' policy of hiring, sometimes encouraged by politicians, white labor kept up an unremitting pressure to drive Negroes out of the better paid, more attractive work and further down in the job hierarchy. While at the end of the Civil War Negro artisans are said to have outnumbered white by five to one, they made up only a small proportion of the labor force in most crafts by 1890.

C. Vann Woodward, *Origins of the New South, 1877-1913* (Baton Rouge, Louisiana: Louisiana State University Press, 1951), p. 360.

foremen of their own color. Today, apart from hod-carriers, not a colored workman is to be seen on new buildings, and a handful of jobbers and patchers, with possibly two carpenters who can undertake a large job, are all who remain of the body of colored carpenters and builders and stone cutters who were generally employed a quarter of a century ago.[90]

Durham provides examples of how labor unions prevented blacks from working in many occupations including those of baker, confectioner, printer, cooper, painter and carpenter:

A Negro working in the Government Printing Office can stay on as long as he is in government employment, but once out of public service he cannot secure work as a printer on a union newspaper or in a union office. The Negro, whatever his record, finds all doors closed against him, thus, in our national capital may be observed the effects of the discrimination of labor organizations against the Negro.[91]

In Philadelphia, Durham found the effects of the racial exclusion policy to be even "more manifest." In 1838 the Society of Friends had compiled a directory of occupations in which blacks were employed in Philadelphia. Included were such skilled jobs as cabinet maker, plumber, printer, sail maker, ships carpenter, stonecutter and many others. By the end of the 1890s black workers had been forced out of these and other craft occupations.

The data for New York City reveal that between 1890 and 1910, when the percentage of the total immigrant white population reached 76 percent,[92] the process of black occupational eviction was intensified. This process was described by the social worker and journalist, Mary White Ovington, in a 1906 study, and by other observers during that period.[93]

In the longshore industry, in catering, as wagon drivers, coachmen and stable hands, as house painters, tailors and brickmakers, as hotel and restaurant waiters and in other trades, black workers were steadily forced out of employment. Typical of this development was stevedoring which at the turn of the century provided employment for many blacks. New York was a very active port in the early years of the twentieth century, but as the longshore industry was unionized, specific docks were assigned on an ethnic basis to white immigrant workers, and blacks were increasingly excluded from jobs on the New York waterfront.

In New York and elsewhere, as ethnic groups became occupationally concentrated, the ability of labor unions to provide a measure of job stability and advancement into the larger society for immigrant whites was instrumental in permitting these organizations to function effectively and to expand their influence beyond the work place. By 1890 most labor organizations drew their members and leaders from white immigrant communities, and these communities derived many benefits from the ethnic control of labor unions.

As such unions evolved, they increasingly used their control of jobs—formally or informally—to perpetuate the ethnic character of the work force under their jurisdiction. In practice this meant the systematic displacement and exclusion of nonwhite workers from much of American industry.

Where nonwhites were permitted to work, they were systematically limited to segregated jobs. The inferior status of blacks in the labor force made it possible for whites to receive higher wages and enjoy relatively better working conditions—individually and as a class. Discriminatory hiring practices and segregated seniority and promotional structures in manufacturing industries contributed to the relatively privileged position of white workers and the depressed condition of the black working class.

The greater rate of exploitation of the black worker, locked into an all-black labor classification, subsidized the higher wages of whites. This process was repeated in many industries and codified into collective bargaining agreements. Thus, organized labor and management jointly created a severely exploited class of black labor, rigidly blocked from advancing into many all-white occupations.

The effects of this process on the nonwhite working class were extremely detrimental. The permanent condition of poverty and social disorganization, which was to characterize black life in the urban ghettos of the nation for many generations, was in large measure a direct consequence of the occupational displacement of blacks by white immigrants and the racial practices of organized labor.

Labor and Ethnic Response to Affirmative Action

None of this is to deny the sufferings and humiliation endured by European immigrants to the United States. The Irish, Italians, Poles, Jews and the other groups that immigrated often confronted difficult conditions and much hostility. One indication of public sentiment was expressed in the description of some of the immigrants by Andrew B. White, the first president of Cornell University: ". . . a crowd of illiterate peasants, freshly raked in from the Irish bogs, or Bohemian mines, or Italian robber nests."[94] Furthermore, the virulent anti-Catholic and anti-Semitic outbursts of the period caused much pain and left deep scars in many communities across the nation.

That the white ethnics were frequently victimized is undeniable; also undeniable is the historical evidence that European immigrant groups were quick to embrace ideas of white supremacy, engage in violence against blacks, and resort to racist strategies in the effort to surmount their own disadvantaged position.* For white immigrants, ethnic identification became the decisive factor in determining access to jobs, family stability and advancement. The extensive network of formal and informal ethnic organizations that developed within European immigrant communities was crucial in making possible the eventual

---

*There is a long history of immigrant violence against blacks. In Philadelphia, Irish-led working-class pogroms against the Afro-American community occurred in 1829, 1834, 1838 and 1849. Race riots occurred in Boston, St. Paul, Cincinnati, Toledo and other cities during the Civil War. On March 6, 1863, the Detroit race riot, the major riot in the Midwest, began.

> Exploding racial conflict between immigrants—mostly Irish—and the blacks underlay the midwestern riots, as well as their counterparts in New York, Boston, and the smaller New York cities of Brooklyn, Buffalo and Troy. As recent immigrants, the Irish manifested relatively little interest in the war to preserve the union; the sons of Eire were more concerned about the competition of black laborers for unskilled and service jobs.

David M. Katzman, *Before the Ghetto: Black Detroit in the Nineteenth Century* (Urbana, Ill: University of Illinois Press, 1973), pp. 44-45. In a contemporary account of the race riot in New York in 1863, Joel Tyler Headley, in describing those who attacked blacks, wrote:

> A great proportion of these being Irish, it naturally became an Irish question, and eventually an Irish riot . . . the whole block on Broadway, between Twenty-eighth and Twenty-ninth streets, was burned down. . . . while these fires were under full headway a new idea seemed to strike the mob. . . it now impelled by a strange logic sought to destroy the Colored Orphan Asylum on Fifth Avenue, extending from Forty-third to Forty-fourth street. The slaves were black, ergo, all blacks are responsible for the war. This seemed to be the logic of the mob, and having reached the sage conclusion to which it conducted, did not stop to consider how poor helpless orphans could be held responsible, but proceeded at once to reveal their vengeance on them. . . . soon the massive structure was a sheet of flame.

Joel Tyler Headley, *The Great Riots of New York: 1712-1873* (Originally published in 1873, reissued by the Bobbs-Merrill Company, Inc., Indianapolis, 1970), pp. 149-169, 171. See also Richard Moody, *The Astor Place Riot* (Bloomington, Ind.: Indiana University Press, 1958). Immigrant hostility was also a factor in the widespread violence against blacks in the early twentieth century as in East St. Louis in 1917 and Chicago in 1919. In 1951 the author observed the violence of Poles and other Slavic-Americans against blacks during the Trumbull Park riot, and again in Chicago in 1966 against blacks who were participating in the marches led by the Rev. Martin Luther King, Jr. In Boston, organized groups of whites based in ethnic communities demonstrated against school desegregation and repeatedly engaged in racial violence. Members and leaders of AFL-CIO building trades unions were involved in this activity in South Boston for many years. James Kelley, for example, a former official of the Sheet Metal Workers Union, was head of the South Boston Information Center, the parent organization of a paramilitary racist group known as the South Boston Marshalls. The emergence of such organizations in working-class neighborhoods occurred in several cities involved in school desegregation efforts during the 1960s and 1970s.

success of immigrant groups and the upward mobility of their children. Entry into a specific occupation was often based upon membership in an ethnic group, and many labor unions became the institutional expression of ethnic group interests.*

It must be recognized that whatever the trials experienced by European ethnic groups, they were white in a society acutely conscious of race. They and their descendants substantially contributed to the development of discriminatory patterns, and they were the beneficiaries of practices that victimized nonwhites. The idea that the suffering of white people is more important and worthy of attention than the suffering of black people, and that it is acceptable to obtain advantages at the expense of blacks, permeates much of American society. It is the implicit assumption that is often invoked in the explanations for white racist behavior in the past and present. And whatever the tortured rationalizations, it is this belief that is at the root of the arguments against affirmative action.

Immigrants greatly benefited from the exclusionary racial pattern, as it made possible their entry into many crafts and industrial occupations. As a result of discriminatory practices, immigrant workers obtained a preferential status at the expense of blacks in gaining access to training and jobs reserved for whites only. Over generations this preferential status became an important factor in making possible the economic gains of ethnic communities, in contrast to the declining condition of black workers. The much celebrated success and achievement of white ethnics were in large measure based upon a racist employment structure, one that either limited or excluded nonwhites from participation in the labor force.

That many Irish immigrants in New York City could get jobs as bus drivers with the Fifth Avenue Coach Company was due in large part to the policy of that company not to hire blacks.° The same process operated with Jews in the needle trades, with Italians in construction, and for other immigrant groups in a variety of occupations.

White ethnics advanced themselves by organizing on bloc lines and improved their condition as they enhanced the status of the group. In

---

*In a valuable study, John Bodnar has described "the withdrawal of working class groups into ethnic communities," and of "how ethnicity served as a basis of social organization and adjustment for the newly arrived immigrant worker in an industrial society." John Bodnar, *Immigration and Industrialization, Ethnicity in An American Mill Town, 1870-1940* (Pittsburgh: University of Pittsburgh Press, 1977), pp. xvi-xvii.

°For a history of the discriminatory employment pattern in urban transit systems in several cities and the resistance of white workers to change, see Herbert Hill, *Black Labor and the American Legal System* (Washington, D.C.: Bureau of National Affairs, 1977), Chap. 11 and 12.

many instances labor unions were based on the ethnic communities of their membership, and these immigrants were the beneficiaries of an unstated but effective and widespread preferential hiring system based upon the systematic exclusion of nonwhites.

The elimination of these traditional patterns of discrimination adversely affects the expectations of whites, since it compels competition with black workers and other minority group members where none previously existed. White worker expectations have become the norm and any alteration of the norm is considered "reverse discrimination." When racial practices that have historically disadvantaged blacks are removed to eliminate the present effects of past discrimination, whites believe that preferential treatment is given to blacks. It is, in fact, *the removal of the preferential treatment traditionally enjoyed by white workers at the expense of blacks as a class* that is at issue in the affirmative action controversy.

Excerpts from two federal court decisions involving craft unions, one in Louisiana and the other in New York, reveal how the traditional preferential system for whites was maintained. In *Asbestos Workers, Local 53* v. *Vogler*, in New Orleans, the Court of Appeals for the Fifth Circuit stated:

> In pursuing its exclusionary and nepotistic policies, Local 53 engaged in a pattern and practice of discrimination on the basis of race and national origin both in membership and referrals. It was found to be Local 53's practice to refer white persons of limited experience and white journeymen of other trade unions as mechanic asbestos workers. It was also found to be its practice to refuse to consider Negroes or Mexican-Americans for membership and to refuse to refer Negroes for employment or to accept Negroes for referral for employment. This policy and various acts of discrimination, both prior to and after the effective date of the Civil Rights Act of 1964, were admitted at trial and on this appeal.[95]

In *United States* v. *Lathers, Local 46*, in New York City, the district court found that

> There is a deep-rooted and pervasive practice in this union of handing out jobs on the basis of union membership, kinship, friendship and, generally, "pull." The specific tactics, practices, devices and arrangements just enumerated have amounted in practical fact to varying modes of implementing this central pattern of unlawful criteria. The hirings at the site, the bypassing of the lists, the use of the hiring hall, when it was used at all, as a formality rather than as a place for legitimate and nondiscriminatory distribution of work all reflected the basic evil of preferring Local 46 members, relatives, friends or friends of friends in job referrals. And since the membership of this Local has for so long

been almost exclusively white, the result could have been fore-
cast: the jobs, and especially the more desirable jobs, have gone
disproportionately to whites rather than Blacks.[96]

Commenting on the union's practices in maintaining an all-white
membership and restricting jobs, the court added a sharply worded
statement:

> Because courts may know what all the world knows, practices of
> nepotism and favoritism like those disclosed here could, and
> probably should, be condemned as inevitably discriminatory.
> . . . But there is no need in this case even for so modest a general-
> ization. The whole story is here, in vivid and repetitive detail.
> Giving life and point to an impressive statistical demonstration,
> the Government has shown in case after case the preference of
> whites over Blacks on grounds of nepotism or acquaintanceship.
> The officers of the local did not merely acquiesce in this state of
> affairs; many, if not all, of them have been active participants in
> the pattern of favoritism and its inevitable concomitant, racial
> discrimination.[97]

Predictably, this labor union, that for more than half a century had
systematically excluded blacks and Hispanics, responded to the court-
ordered affirmative action remedy by denouncing "reverse discrimination," but the U.S. Court of Appeals for the Second Circuit rejected the
union's contention and sustained the order of the lower courts.

A different but related pattern has long operated in the industrial
sector, and the case law provides many examples. In 1970, after years
of protest by black steel workers, a federal court found the United
Steelworkers of America (AFL-CIO) and the Bethlehem Steel Corporation in Lackawanna, New York, to be in violation of the law. In
United States v. *Bethlehem Steel Corp.*, the court stated:

> The pervasiveness and longevity of the overt discriminatory hir-
> ing and job assignment practices, admitted by Bethlehem and the
> unions, compel the conclusion that the present seniority and
> transfer provisions were based on past discriminatory classifica-
> tions. . . . Job assignment practices were reprehensible. Over 80
> percent of black workers were placed in eleven departments
> which contained the hotter and dirtier jobs in the plant. Blacks
> were excluded from higher paying and cleaner jobs.[98]

The court observed that discriminatory contract provisions were
embodied in nationwide master agreements negotiated by the interna-
tional union in 1962, 1965 and 1968. The court also noted that "The
Lackawanna plant was a microcosm of classic job discrimination in the
North, making clear why Congress enacted Title VII of the Civil
Rights Act of 1964."[99]

On October 14, 1971, the court issued a decree defining as members of the affected class some sixteen hundred black steelworkers, who were entitled to receive benefits as a result of the court's decision. It is significant to note that in the *Bethlehem Steel* case, the Court of Appeals for the Second Circuit stated:

> Appellees also argue that the morale of employees who did not suffer discrimination will suffer if rate retention and seniority carryover are ordered. But in the context of this case that possibility is not such an overriding business purpose that the relief requested must be denied. Assuming *arguendo* that the expectations of some employees will not be met, their hopes arise from an illegal system.[100]

The court continued with a statement on the expectations of employees who benefited from the seniority provisions of collective bargaining agreements that deprived other employees of their rights:

> Moreover, their seniority advantages are not indefeasibly vested rights but mere expectations derived from a bargaining agreement subject to modification. . . . If relief under Title VII can be denied merely because the majority group of employees, who have not suffered discrimination, will be unhappy about it, there will be little hope of correcting the wrongs to which the Act is directed.[101]

In *Robinson* v. *Lorillard Corporation*, the Fourth Circuit Court of Appeals also dealt with this question:

> We recognize Lorillard's point that changing the minority system may frustrate the expectations of employees who have established departmental seniority in the preferable departments. However, Title VII guarantees that all employees are entitled to the same expectations regardless of "race, color, religion, sex or national origin." *Where some employees now have lower expectations than their co-workers because of the influence of one of these foreladen factors, they are entitled to have their expectations raised even if the expectations of others must be lowered in order to achieve the statutorily mandated equality of opportunity.*[102] (Emphasis added.)

The "expectations-of-white-workers" defense was most convincingly rejected when, in the case of *Franks* v. *Bowman Transportation Company*, the U.S. Supreme Court stated:

> [I]t is apparent that denial of seniority relief to identifiable victims of racial discrimination on the sole ground that such relief diminishes the expectations of other, arguably innocent, employees would if applied generally frustrate the central "make whole" objective of Title VII. . . . If relief under Title VII can be denied merely because the majority group of employees, who have not suffered discrimination, will be unhappy about it, there will be

little hope of correcting the wrongs to which the Act is directed.[103]

In many different occupations, including a variety of jobs in the public sector such as in police and fire departments, white workers were able to begin their climb on the seniority ladder precisely because nonwhites were systematically excluded from the competition for jobs. Various union seniority systems were established at a time when racial minorities were barred from employment and union membership. Obviously blacks as a group, not just as individuals, constituted a class of victims who could not develop seniority status. A seniority system launched under these conditions inevitably becomes the institutionalized mechanism whereby whites as a group are granted racial privilege. But organized labor has repeatedly refused modifications in established seniority systems, and with few exceptions rejects affirmative action approaches as a remedy to eliminate discriminatory patterns. (The Reagan administration has intervened on behalf of white municipal workers and their unions in litigation attacking affirmative action programs in Boston, New Orleans, Memphis and Detroit.)

In this connection it is necessary to note the disingenuous argument of those who state that they are not against affirmative action, but only against "quotas." Affirmative action without numbers, whether in the form of quotas, goals or timetables, is a contradiction; there must be some tangible benchmark, some empirical measure of change. Not to use numbers is to revert to the era of symbolic gesture or, at best, "tokenism."

White ethnic groups and labor unions also frequently argue that affirmative action programs will penalize innocent whites who are not responsible for past discriminatory practices. This argument turns on the notion of individual rights and sounds very moral and highminded. But it ignores social reality. As has been demonstrated in many lawsuits, nonwhites have been denied jobs, training and advancement not as individuals but as a class, no matter what their personal merit and qualification. Wherever discriminatory employment patterns exist, hiring and promotion without affirmative action perpetuate the old injustice.

It is of significance that two historically interrelated groups, white ethnics and organized labor, are in the forefront of the attacks against affirmative action, as both, separately and jointly, participated in the development of discriminatory employment patterns. Since the purpose of affirmative action is finally to eliminate such patterns, it is not surprising that the traditional beneficiaries of job discrimination vigorously oppose the most effective approach to eliminate employment practices that continue to victimize the nonwhite population.*

Before the emergence of affirmative action remedies, the legal prohibitions against job discrimination were for the most part declarations of abstract morality that rarely resulted in any change. Pronouncements of public policy such as state and municipal fair employment practice laws were mainly symbolic, and the patterns of job discrimination remained intact.° Because affirmative action programs go beyond individual relief to attack traditional patterns of discrimination and, if vigorously enforced by government agencies over a sustained period, have the potential of becoming a major instrument for social change, they have come under powerful and repeated attack. It was not until theoretical rights began to be exercised in practice that a well-orchestrated opposition developed on a large scale. As long as Title VII litigation was concerned largely with procedural and conceptual issues, only limited attention was given to the consequences of remedies. However, once affirmative action was widely applied and the focus of litigation shifted to the adoption of affirmative action plans, entrenched interests were threatened.

Among the earliest attacks upon affirmative action were those from organized labor and groups representing ethnic communities. In 1969 after federal courts and government agencies imposed affirmative action requirements in cases involving construction unions (among the

---

*For a comprehensive study that documents the effectiveness of specific affirmative action programs, see Jonathan S. Leonard, *The Impact of Affirmative Action* (Berkeley: Institute of Industrial Relations and School of Business Administration, University of California, Berkeley, July 1983). See also the statement of William T. Coleman, Jr., Chairman, NAACP Legal Defense and Educational Fund, Inc., before the Subcommittee on Constitutional Rights of the Senate Judiciary Committee (Washington, D.C.: June 11, 1981). For other views, see "Report on Affirmative Action and The Federal Enforcement of Equal Employment Opportunity Laws," Subcommittee on Employment Opportunities, Committee on Education and Labor, House of Representatives (Washington, D.C.: February 1982); "Affirmative Action in the 1980's: Dismantling the Process of Discrimination," A Statement of the U.S. Commission On Civil Rights (Washington, D.C.: November 1981); "Statement on Affirmative Action," The U.S. Commission on Civil Rights (Washington, D.C.: October 1977); and "Affirmative Action: The Unrealized Goal," The Potomac Institute (Washington, D.C.: 1973). Among the many studies arguing a variety of views, see especially Marshall Cohen, Thomas Nagel, Thomas Scanlon, eds., *Equality and Preferential Treatment* (Princeton, N.J.: Princeton University Press, 1977) and John C. Livingston, *Fair Game? Inequality and Affirmative Action* (San Francisco: W. H. Freeman, 1979).

°See Herbert Hill, "Twenty Years of State Fair Employment Practice Commissions: A Critical Analysis With Recommendations," *Buffalo Law Review*, 14: 1(Fall 1964): 22-69.

most discriminatory of all labor groups),* the AFL-CIO Building and Construction Trades Department issued a widely publicized resolution which stated:

> Racial quotas, under any guise, are repugnant to all Americans. When a proposal is made to establish racial quotas as public policy, honest men must protest. . . . We prefer the free choice of free men and we are certain that the vast majority of Americans, white and non-white alike, prefer such freedom.[104]

At issue was the Philadelphia Plan[105] which contained affirmative action requirements to remedy generations of overt racial discrimination by the construction unions in Philadelphia, where the federal government was responsible for major construction projects. The order contained a Department of Labor review of its own data, together with information compiled by various government agencies, which showed that nonwhites were excluded from seven crafts: iron workers, plumbers and pipefitters, sheet metal workers, electrical workers, roofers and waterproofers and elevator constructors.[106]

The plan ordered "goals" or "ranges" in the form of minimum percentage requirements of nonwhite employment in specific crafts. The part of the plan initially issued announced that affirmative action commitments would be required of contractors in the pre-award stage of all construction projects involving the expenditure of $500,000 or more of federal funds in the Philadelphia area. No contracts were to be awarded to bidders who did not commit themselves to percentage requirements imposed in the seven affected crafts. This plan provoked the bitter opposition of the building trades unions and the AFL-CIO.

Construction labor unions and the national labor federation lobbied extensively in Congress against affirmative action, and used their political influence to prevent enforcement. George Meany, president of the

---

*There is an extensive literature on the discriminatory practices of the building trades unions and the many judicial decisions involving construction labor organizations. Within the context of this discussion, see Herbert Hill, "The Racial Practices of Organized Labor: The Contemporary Record," in Julius Jacobson, ed., *The Negro and the American Labor Movement* (Garden City, N.Y.: Anchor Books, 1968), pp. 292-320; James E. Jones, Jr., "The Bugaboo of Employment Quotas," *Wisconsin Law Review*, 1970: 2(1970): 341-403; Dennis R. Yeager, "Litigation Under Title VII of the Civil Rights Act of 1964: The Construction Industry and the Problem of the Unqualified Minority Workers," *Georgetown Law Journal*, 59: 6(June 1971): 1265-1296; Herbert Hill, "Labor Union Control of Job Training: A Critical Analysis of Apprenticeship Outreach Programs and the Hometown Plans," Occasional Paper, 2: 1 (Washington, D.C.: Institute for Urban Affairs and Research, Howard University, 1974); William B. Gould, "The Seattle Building Trades Order: The First Comprehensive Relief Against Employment Discrimination in the Construction Industry," *Stanford Law Review*, 26: 4 (April 1974): 773-806; and *The Challenge Ahead—Equal Opportunity in Referral Unions*, a report of the U.S. Commission On Civil Rights (Washington, D.C.: May, 1976).

AFL-CIO, was deeply involved in these actions. Meany's father, an Irish immigrant, had been the president of a New York Plumbers Union local which functioned as a job protective association for Irish workers at the turn of the century, and George Meany became its business agent. While head of the AFL-CIO, he was also the de facto leader of the construction unions which had provided the organizational base of his long career. During a press interview on August 28, 1975, Meany, in response to a reporter's question, stated:

> [T]o say that I've got some responsibility to make up for discrimination that took place 125 years ago is nuts. . . . I don't buy that at all.

> Reporter: Does anybody have a responsibility in contemporary American society? . . .

> Meany: Not that I know of. . . . And to say that we've got to sacrifice our kids and our rights to take care of people who merely say that we've got to be employed because our skin is black, that is discrimination in reverse and we don't buy it.[107]

A major factor in the intransigent resistance of construction craft unions to the requirements of contemporary civil rights laws is that many local organizations continue to be based largely upon ethnic communities. The leaders and members of such unions adamantly believe that the jobs which they control "belong" to their ethnic group. (The larger local unions may consist of several nationality groups, each with their own leadership and a tacit distribution of work.) It is not surprising that the first two contempt citations issued by federal courts under Title VII of the Civil Rights Act of 1964 were against construction labor unions: Local 189, the Plumbers Union in Columbus, Ohio,[108] and Local 46 of the Lathers Union in New York City.[109] Even after decades of litigation, many unions in the building trades have succeeded in evading the legal prohibitions against employment discrimination.*

---

*For thirty-four years Local 28 of the Sheet Metal Workers International Association (AFL-CIO) failed in New York to comply with municipal, state and federal civil rights laws, and has been a defendant before a variety of administration and judicial bodies since 1948. *Lefkowitz* v. *Farrell*, (C-9289-63, New York State Commission for Human Rights) and *EEOC* v. *Sheet Metal Workers, Local 638 . . . and Local 28*, 565 F.2d 31 (2nd Cir. 1977). See also Ronald Smothers, "Union and Employers in Contempt on Job Bias," *The New York Times* (August 26, 1982), p. 1. Among other such cases are those involving Local 3 of the International Brotherhood of Electrical Workers (AFL-CIO) in New York City, *State Division of Human Rights and the City of New York* v. *George Schuck, as President of Local 3, IBEW, AFL-CIO and Thomas Van Arsdale*, Case No. (S)E-NR-58361-78 and Local 542 of the International Union of Operating Engineers (AFL-CIO) in Philadelphia, *Commonwealth of Pennsylvania and Williams* v. *Operating Engineers, Local 542*, 347 F.Supp. 268, (E.D. Pa. 1979). For an analysis of the typical governmental response

In regard to educational institutions, the Anti-Defamation League of B'nai B'rith and the American Jewish Congress both condemned affirmative action requirements, and on June 20, 1972, called on the U.S. Department of Health, Education and Welfare to repudiate "preferential treatment" in federally-funded programs. On August 4, 1972, the American Jewish Committee, in an open letter to President Nixon, urged him to "reject categorically the use of quotas and proportional representation" in civil rights programs, and on January 12, 1973, six national Jewish organizations charging "reverse discrimination" sent a protest to the Department of Health, Education and Welfare urging it to "prevent or eliminate preferential treatment".[110]

The Ukrainian Congress Committee of America, the Polish American Affairs Council and the Italian-American Foundation were among the many other ethnic group organizations that protested against affirmative action programs. In addition to the national ethnic organizations, there were local and regional groups as well as the National Center for Urban Ethnic Affairs and the Ethnic Millions Political Action Committee.* An extensive network based on ethnic communities and

---

to racial discrimination in the building trades, see Herbert Hill, "The New York City Terminal Market Controversy: A Case Study of Race, Labor and Power," *Humanities In Society*, 6:4(Fall 1983): 351-391.

*The organized opponents of affirmative action are responsible for a vast body of material in every conceivable form and much too numerous for inclusive listing here. Nathan Glazer's *Affirmative Discrimination: Ethnic Inequality and Public Policy* (New York: Basic Books, 1975) gathers all the arguments and is representative of the polemic against affirmative action. For a reasoned criticism that places the issue in a historical context, see Alexander Saxton, "Nathan Glazer, Daniel Moynihan and the Cult of Ethnicity," *Amerasia Journal*, 4: 2(1977): 141-150. Typical of the sharp attacks on affirmative action is the statement of Morris B. Abram who was appointed vice-chairman of the U.S. Commission on Civil Rights by President Reagan. See *Consultations on the Affirmative Action Statement of the U.S. Commission on Civil Rights*, Vol. 1 (Washington, D.C.: February 10 and March 10-11, 1981), pp. 25-29; also Miro Todorovich and Howard Glickstein, "Affirmative Action: Two Views," *Civil Rights*, A Staff Report of the Subcommittee on Constitutional Rights of the Committee on the Judiciary, United States Senate (Washington, D.C.: 1976), pp. 69-90. The United Federation of Teachers in New York City and its parent organization, the American Federation of Teachers (AFL-CIO), have been among the most active opponents of affirmative action. Albert Shanker, president of both the New York local and the international union, has since 1972 repeatedly attacked equal opportunity programs requiring hiring goals in his weekly column which appears each Sunday as a paid advertisement of the United Federation of Teachers in Section 4 of the *New York Times*. See for example: "A Quarrel with Quotas" (July 16, 1972); "How Order Number 4 Promotes Employment Quotas" (March 18, 1973); "Preferential Treatment v. Constitutional Rights" (May 13, 1973); "The Quota Principle: Dangerous Arithmetic . . ." (December 9, 1973); "The Quota Mentality v. the 14th Amendment" (October 20, 1974); "Strong Voices Against Ethnic Hiring" (January 12, 1975), and many others later. *Commentary*, published by the American Jewish Committee, has for more than a decade maintained a continuing attack upon affirmative action. The volume for one year, 1972, contains the following: Earl Raab, "Quotas by Any Other Name" (January); Paul Seabury, "HEW & the Universities" (February); "The Pottinger Pa-

labor unions joined together in organized attacks against the principle of affirmative action and against specific programs. Since the late 1960s these groups have conducted a sustained nationwide campaign to discredit affirmative action, have organized political opposition to nullify enforcement, and have repeatedly intervened in the courts.* These actions have also provoked much hostility against the nonwhite population and stimulated racist attitudes and behavior.

---

pers: An Exchange on Affirmative Action" (May); Elliott Abrams, "The Quota Commission" (October); and Paul Seabury, "The Idea of Merit" (December). For a statement of the labor union position, see George Meany, "Labor And The Philadelphia Plan," a pamphlet based on an address by AFL-CIO president George Meany to the National Press Club, January 12, 1970, published by the AFL-CIO (Washington, D.C.: n.d.), unpaged. There is also a multitude of resolutions and statements denouncing "quotas" and "reverse discrimination" in the convention proceedings of many labor organizations and the AFL-CIO, together with frequent material in the trade union press. Among these are *Statement by AFL-CIO Executive Council on Seniority and Layoffs*, (Washington, D.C.: May 6, 1975); *Statement by AFL-CIO Executive Council on Title VII and the Seniority System* (Chicago: July 30-31, 1975). See also "Last Hired, First Fired: Layoffs and Civil Rights," *A Report of the United States Commission on Civil Rights* (Washington, D.C.: February 1977). For an example of the attacks upon affirmative action from influential supporters of Reagan administration policies, see Allen P. Sindler, "Equal Opportunity—On the Policy and Politics of Compensatory Minority Preferences" (Washington, D.C.: American Enterprise Institute, 1983).

*An examination of the *amicus curiae* briefs filed by ethnic and labor groups in the Supreme Court cases involving affirmative action reveals the following: In *De Funis* v. *Odegaard*, 416 U.S. 312 (1974), briefs attacking affirmative action came from the Anti-Defamation League of B'nai B'rith, the American Jewish Committee, the American Jewish Congress and the Jewish Rights Council. The National Organization of Jewish Women filed a brief in support of affirmative action which was endorsed by the Commission on Social Action of the Union of American Hebrew Congregations. The AFL-CIO filed a brief against affirmative action, as did the National Association of Manufacturers. The United Auto Workers, United Farm Workers and the American Federation of State, County, and Municipal Employees filed briefs in support, as did the United Mine Workers, an independent union. In *Regents of the University of California* v. *Bakke*, 438 U.S. 256 (1978), among the groups which filed *amicus* briefs against affirmative action were the American Jewish Committee, American Jewish Congress, Anti-Defamation League of B'nai B'rith, Jewish Labor Committee, National Jewish Commission on Law and Public Affairs, UNICO National (the largest Italian-American organization in the United States), Italian-American Foundation, Chicago Division of UNICO, Hellenic Bar Association of Illinois, Ukrainian Congress Committee of America, Polish American Affairs Council and the Polish American Educators Association. All seven Jewish organizations filed briefs opposing affirmative action; the two Jewish groups that had supported affirmative action in the *De Funis* case did not file in *Bakke*. The American Federation of Teachers, an AFL-CIO affiliate, filed against affirmative action, while some other unions submitted a joint brief in support. In *United Steel Workers of America* v. *Weber*, 443 U.S. 193 (1979), four *amicus* briefs urged the Supreme Court to decide against affirmative action; these were from the Anti-Defamation League of B'nai B'rith, the National Jewish Commission on Law and Public Affairs, the Ukrainian Congress Committee of America and UNICO National. Several unions with large black memberships filed in support. In *Fullilove* v. *Klutznick*, 448 U.S. 448 (1980), the Anti-Defamation League of B'nai B'rith joined with employer groups and the Pacific League Foundation to argue against affirmative action. The Anti-Defamation League filed briefs in opposition to affirmative action in several lower court cases, and has been among the most active of all

An additional element was the emergence of opposition to affirmative action from within academia. The clarion call for an ideological war against affirmative action came from Sidney Hook in a widely quoted article that appeared on November 5, 1971, in the *New York Times*. Hook denounced affirmative action programs in institutions of higher learning and called upon the academic community to resist all such demands from civil rights organizations. Soon thereafter the Committee for a Rational Alternative (later known as the University Center for Rational Alternatives) was formed, followed by the Committee on Academic Nondiscrimination and Integrity, whose national coordinator is Miro Todorovich. These groups, with virtually unlimited access to the media, have conducted a steady drumbeat of attack against affirmative action. It is interesting to note that most of their leaders come from immigrant communities.

Within a historical perspective, the attack against affirmative action is the most recent effort to perpetuate the privileged position of whites in American society. Under the Reagan administration, the power of the national government has been joined with many ethnic and labor groups united in their opposition to affirmative action remedies for the elimination of discriminatory patterns. As the gains of the 1960s are eroded, the nation becomes even more mean-spirited and mendacious.

---

groups in attacking affirmative action in the courts. In 1982 the ADL filed a brief against minority interests in the Boston firefighters case *(Boston Firefighters Union, Local 718, v. Boston Branch, NAACP)* before the Supreme Court, as did the AFL-CIO and the U.S. Department of Justice. On June 12, 1984, the Supreme Court in the Memphis firefighters case *(Firefighters Local Union No. 1784 v. Stotts)* held that layoffs must be made on the basis of applicable union seniority rules, even if advances in minority employment as a result of court-ordered affirmative action are destroyed in the process. Many labor unions and ethnic organizations joined with the Justice Department in urging the Court to rule against affirmative action. In addition to filing *amicus* briefs, the ADL has initiated its own litigation against affirmative action. (See, for example, Press Release, Anti-Defamation League of B'nai B'rith, New York, January 14, 1975.) The American Federation of Teachers has also been actively involved in litigation against affirmative action. In *Chance* v. *Board of Examiners*, 561 F.2d 1079 (2nd Cir. 1976), its New York affiliate, the United Federation of Teachers, intervened against the black and Puerto Rican plaintiffs. Among the other cases in which the AFT or its local union affiliates acted against the interests of racial minorities was the Boston school case decided by the U.S. Court of Appeals for the First Circuit in 1982. Rejecting arguments by the AFT that a district court had ordered an affirmative action plan that amounted to a "forbidden racial preference," the appellate court said that the plan was a "reasonable response" and necessary to "safeguard the progress toward desegregation." *(Morgan* v. *O'Bryant,* 671 F.2d 23 (1st Cir. 1982), cert. den. 103 S.Ct. 62, 103, S. Ct. 178.) Among the many other labor unions which initiated litigation against affirmative action programs were the International Brotherhood of Electrical Workers (AFL-CIO) in *Jersey Central Power and Light* v. *IBEW Local 327,* 542 F.2d 687 (3rd Cir. 1976), and the Communication Workers of America (AFL-CIO) in *Communication Workers of America* v. *American Telephone and Telegraph,* 379 F.Supp. 679 (S.D.N.Y. 1974), rev. 513 F.2d 1024, vac. 97 S.Ct. 724, vac. and rem. 553 F.2d 93(2nd Cir. 1977).

It is necessary to go back to the raging debate over slavery in the 1850s to find circumstances comparable to the controversy on affirmative action. As in the case of slavery, the resolution of this issue will not only determine the future of racial minorities—it will also decide the future direction of the nation.

Racism in the history of the United States has not been an aberration. It has been systematized and structured into the functioning of the society's most important institutions. In the present as in the past, it is widely accepted as a basis for promoting the self-interests of whites. For many generations the assumptions of white supremacy were codified in the law, imposed by custom and often enforced by violence. While the forms have changed, the legacy of white supremacy is expressed in the continuing patterns of racial discrimination, and for the vast majority of black people, race and racism remain the decisive factors in their lives.

The nineteenth-century European migrations to the United States took place during the long age of blatant white supremacy, legal and extralegal, formal and informal, and as the patterns of segregation and discrimination emerged north and south, the doors of opportunity were opened to white immigrants but closed to blacks and other nonwhites. European immigrants and their descendants explain their success as a result of their devotion to the work ethic, and ignore a variety of other factors such as the systematic exclusion of non-Caucasians from competition for employment. As white immigrants moved up in the social order, black workers and those of other nonwhite races could fill only the least desirable places, the only places open to them.

The romanticized and often pietistic histories of the struggles of white immigrants and their labor unions repeatedly ignore the racial aspects of that history, and neglect the fact that white immigrants were labor competitors with blacks, that they used labor organizations to exclude nonwhite workers from the primary labor force in many industries, and that they had the advantage of being white in a social order of racial subordination.

The current conflict over affirmative action is not simply an argument about abstract rights or ethnic bigotry. In the final analysis it is an argument between those who insist upon the substance of a long-postponed break with the traditions of American racism, and those groups that insist upon maintaining the valuable privileges and benefits they now enjoy as a consequence of that dismal history.

NOTES

[1] Joel Kovel, *White Racism* (New York: Pantheon Books, 1970), p. 4.

[2] See French E. Wolfe, *Admission To American Trade Unions* (Baltimore: The Johns Hopkins Press, 1920), pp. 100-112.

[3] Proceedings of the Cigar Makers International Union, 1865, p. 60. Quoted by Wolfe, op. cit., p. 128. See also A. Bergman, "The Rise and Fall of the National Labor Union and Its Relation to the Division Between Negro and White Labor During the Reconstruction Period" (Unpublished Masters Thesis, Columbia University, 1956), pp. 64-65.

[4] Wolfe, op. cit., p. 99.

[5] Bergman, op. cit., p. 65.

[6] Quoted in Kenneth L. Kusmer, *A Ghetto Takes Shape: Black Cleveland, 1870-1930* (Urbana, Ill.: University of Illinois Press, 1976), p. 70.

[7] H. C. Dotry, *New York Age* (May 16, 1891), p. 1.

[8] *The Colored American* (Washington, D.C.: October 29, 1898), p. 1; also July 22, 1899, p. 1.

[9] *The Colored American* (May 23, 1903), p. 1.

[10] Bruce Grit, "The Lessons of the Strike," *The Colored American* (May 25, 1901), p. 1.

[11] Bruce Grit, *The Colored American* (October 18, 1903), p. 3.

[12] See, for example, W.E.B. Du Bois, "The Passing of Jim Crow," *The Independent* (July 14, 1917), p. 54; G. E. Haynes, "Effect of War Conditions on Negro Labor," *Proceedings of the Academy of Political Science* (February 1919), p. 170; C. S. Johnson, "The American Migrant: The Negro," *National Conference of Social Work, Proceedings* (1927), pp. 554-558.

[13] Samuel A. Stouffer and Lionel C. Florant, *Negro Population Movements, 1860-1940, In Relation To Social and Economic Factors*, Preliminary Draft of a Memorandum for the Carnegie Corporation's study of the Negro In America, 1940 (Myrdal Study), Chap. 1, p. 8, Schomburg Library, New York; Lionel C. Florant, *Negro Migration 1860-1940*, Revised Draft of a Memorandum for the Carnegie Corporation, 1942, p. 52, Schomburg Collection, New York Public Library; Carter G. Woodson, *A Century of Negro Migration* (Washington, D.C., 1918).

[14] W.E.B. Du Bois, "The Passing of Jim Crow," op. cit., p. 54.

[15] Lucile Eaves, *A History of California Labor Legislation: With an Introductory Sketch of the San Francisco Labor Movement* (Berkeley, Cal.: The University Press, 1910), p. 386.

[16] Quoted from document in the archives of the California Historical Society (San Francisco, n.d.).

[17] Eaves, op. cit., p. 386; also Lewis Lorwin, *The American Federation of Labor* (Washington, D.C.: Brookings Institution, 1933), p. 367.

[18] John R. Commons, et al., *History of Labor in the United States*, Vol. II (New York: The Macmillan Co., 1918), pp. 301-315.

[19] Alexander Saxton, *The Indispensable Enemy: Labor and The Anti-Chinese Movement in California* (Berkeley, Cal.: University of California Press, 1971), p. 216.

[20] For a detailed account see Saxton, op. cit., pp. 213-218.

[21] U.S. Ninth Census, *Part 1*, Washington, D.C., 1872. For additional data see Mary R. Coolidge, *Chinese Immigration* (New York: H. Holt & Co., 1909, reprinted 1969); Ping Chiu, *Chinese Labor in California, 1850-1880: An Economic Study* (Madison, Wis.: State Historical Society of Wisconsin, 1963); and Stanford M. Lyman, *The Asian in the West* (Reno, Nev.: University of Nevada, 1970).

[22] Saxton, op. cit., pp. 104-112.

[23] See Nicoles Somma, "The Knights of Labor and Chinese Immigration" (Unpublished Masters Thesis, Catholic University, Washington, D.C., 1952).

[24] Ibid., pp. 464-472.

[25] Ibid., pp. 30-39.

[26] Samuel Gompers, *American Federationist* (September 1905), p. 636.

[27] Samuel Gompers, *Seventy Years of Life and Labor: An Autobiography*, Vol. II (New York: E. P. Dutton & Co., 1925), p. 160.

[28] Quoted in Ira Kipnis, *The American Socialist Movements 1897-1912* (New York: Columbia University Press, 1952), pp. 276-286.

[29] Quoted in Phillip Foner, ed., *Jack London* (New York: Citadel Press, 1947), p. 59.

[30] Louis Boudin, "Immigration at Stuttgart," *International Socialist Review*, 8: (February 1908): 491.

[31] Cameron H. King Jr., "Asiatic Exclusion," *International Socialist Review*, 8: (May 1908): 661.

[32] Ibid., p. 662.

[33] Ibid., p. 669.

[34] Herbert Gutman, in Henry Abelove, et al., eds., *Visions of History* (New York: Pantheon Books, 1984), p. 197.

[35] George Sinclair Mitchell, "The Negro in Southern Trade Unionism," *The Southern Economic Journal*, II: 3(January 1936): 27-38.

[36] Ibid.

[37] W.E.B. Du Bois, ed., *The Negro Artisan* (Atlanta: Atlanta University Press, 1902), p. 158.

[38] W.E.B. Du Bois and A. G. Dill, eds., *The Negro American Artisan* (Atlanta: Atlanta University Press, 1912), p. 83.

[39] Sterling D. Spero and Abram L. Harris, *The Black Worker* (New York: Columbia University Press, 1931), p. 80.

[40] Ibid. See also Ira DeA. Reid, *Negro Membership In American Labor Unions* (New York: National Urban League, 1930, reprinted 1969).

[41]*Sixteenth Annual Report of the Commission on Labor, Strikes and Lockouts* (Washington, D.C.: 1901), pp. 413-465.

[42]*Locomotive Firemen's Magazine* (December 1890), p. 1094.

[43]"The Georgia Railroad Strike," *Outlooks* (June 5, 1909), p. 310; cited in Spero and Harris, op. cit., note 39, p. 289.

[44]Spero and Harris, op. cit., p. 291.

[45]See Charles H. Houston, "Foul Employment Practice on the Rails" (based on a report to the Fortieth Annual Convention of the NAACP, Los Angeles, July 1949), *The Crisis* (October 1949), pp. 269-272; "The Elimination of Negro Firemen on American Railroads—A Study of the Evidence Adduced at The Hearing Before the President's Committee on Fair Employment Practices," *Lawyers Guild Review*, IV: 2(March-April 1944): 32; and Herbert Hill, *Black Labor And The American Legal System* (Washington, D.C.: Bureau of National Affairs, 1977), pp. 334-372.

[46]See Paul Worthman, "Working-Class Mobility in Birmingham, Alabama, 1880-1914," in Tamara K. Hareven, ed., *Anonymous Americans* (Englewood Cliffs, N.J.: Prentice-Hall, 1971), p. 185.

[47]See Stephan Thernstrom, *The Other Bostonians* (Cambridge, Mass.: Harvard University Press, 1973), pp. 186-187.

[48]Cigar Makers International Union, *International Proceedings* (1865), p. 60.

[49]The meaning of the elimination in 1871 of Article IX, the exclusion clause in the constitution of the Cigar Makers International Union, is explained in *The Working Man's Advocate* (November 25, 1871), p. 1.

[50]Wolfe, op. cit., p. 114.

[51]"Order of United Machinists and Mechanical Engineers of America," photographic reproduction of original document in Mark Perlman, *The Machinists* (Cambridge, Mass.: Harvard University Press, 1961), frontispiece.

[52]U.S. Bureau of Labor Statistics, "Handbook of American Trade Unions," Bulletin No. 506 (Washington, D.C.: 1929), p. 208.

[53]Ibid., p. 104.

[54]*Constitution and General Rules of the Order of Sleeping Car Conductors*, Article XVI (Effective April 1925), p. 26.

[55]U.S. Bureau of Labor Statistics, op. cit., p. 80. In 1939 the union altered its policy to permit the establishment of segregated all-black local lodges.

[56]*Constitution of Brotherhood of Railway Carmen of America*, Section 6, Clause(a), (adopted 1890, revised August 1921), p. 41.

[57]See *Railway Mail Assn. v. Corsi*, 326 U.S. 88 (1946).

[58]Ibid.

[59]A copy of the union's constitution was introduced into evidence at *A Hearing To Hear Evidence On Complaints Of Racial Discrimination In Employment On Certain Railroads Of The United States*, President's Committee On Fair Employment Practices (Washington, D.C.: September 15-18, 1943), p. 412, Record Group 228, Preliminary Inventory No. 147, Records of the FEPC, National Archives, Washington, D.C.

[60]Brotherhood of Railroad Brakemen of the Western Hemisphere, *Constitution—Revisions and Amendments*, Article 2, Membership Section 1, Constitution of Subordinate Lodges, presented at the First Annual Convention (Oneonta, N.Y.: October 20-25, 1884), p. 9.

[61]*Constitution of the Brotherhood of Locomotive Firemen and Enginemen*, Section 162 (1906), pp. 77-78.

[62]*Constitution of the Brotherhood of Locomotive Firemen and Enginemen*, Article 12, Section 22(b) (1925), pp. 158-159.

[63]*Constitution of the Brotherhood of Locomotive Firemen and Enginemen*, (1906), op. cit.

[64]Brotherhood of Railroad Brakemen of the Western Hemisphere, op. cit.

[65]Charles H. Houston, op. cit., p. 269.

[66]See *Brotherhood of Locomotive Firemen and Enginemen's Magazine* (June 15, 1917), p. 9, and (August 15, 1917), pp. 11-12.

[67]See Jerald S. Auerbach, "Progressives at Sea: The LaFollette Act of 1915," *Labor History*, 2:3(Fall 1961): 346-357.

[68]See, for example, Silas B. Axtell, ed., *A Symposium on Andrew Furuseth* (New Bedford, Mass.: Darwin Press, 1948); Hyman Weintraub, *Andrew Furuseth* (Berkeley, Cal.: University of California Press, 1959); Paul S. Taylor, *The Sailor's Union of the Pacific* (New York: The Ronald Press, 1923); and Joseph Goldberg, *The Maritime Story* (Cambridge, Mass.: Harvard University Press, 1957).

[69]See Jerald S. Auerbach, op. cit., p. 67.

[70]Ibid., p. 347.

[71]Ibid., p. 355.

[72]*Seamen's Journal* (February 1929), p. 35.

[73]See Herbert Hill, op. cit., pp. 218-234.

[74]Ira DeA. Reid, op. cit., p. 38.

[75]Quoted in Spero and Harris, op. cit., note 39, pp. 477-478.

[76]AFL Convention, *Proceedings* (1900), pp. 12-13, 22-23, 117, 129.

[77]U.S. Bureau of Labor Statistics, "Handbook of American Trade Unions," op. cit., p. 55.

[78]*Constitution of the Amalgamated Sheet Metal Workers International Alliance*, Article IV, Section I (1918), p. 8. See also 1926 constitution.

[79]*Electrical World* (April 1903), p. 102.

[80]See Malcom Ross, *All Manner of Men* (New York: Reynal and Hitchcock, 1948), p. 143.

[81]Ibid.

[82]International Brotherhood of Boilermakers, *Report of Proceedings, 1937 Convention* (Kansas City, Missouri: September 1937). See also *Report of the International President and Executive Council to the Sixteenth Consolidated Convention of the International Brotherhood of Boilermakers, Iron Ship Builders, and*

Helpers of America (September 1937), Record Group 228, Preliminary Inventory No. 147, Records of the Committee on Fair Employment Practices, National Archives, Washington, D.C.

⁸³Ibid.

⁸⁴1937 Boilermakers Convention, *Bylaws of the International Brotherhood Governing Auxiliary Lodges*, Article VI (effective January 1, 1938).

⁸⁵Ibid., Article II, Section 15.

⁸⁶Samuel Gompers, *American Federationist* (September 1905), p. 636.

⁸⁷John Roach, "Packingtown Conditions," *American Federationist* (August 1906), p. 534.

⁸⁸Kenneth L. Kusmer, op. cit., p. 68.

⁸⁹See C. Vann Woodward, *Origins of the New South 1877-1913* (Baton Rouge, Louisiana: Louisiana State University Press, 1951), p. 361.

⁹⁰John Stephens Durham, "The Labor Unions and the Negro," *Atlantic Monthly* (February 1898): 222-231.

⁹¹Ibid.

⁹²U.S. Department of Commerce, *Immigrants and Their Children*, Census Monograph No. 7 (Washington, D.C.: 1920), p. 27.

⁹³Mary White Ovington, "The Negro in the Trade Unions of New York," *The Annals of the American Academy of Political and Social Science*, (May 1906). See also J. G. Speed, "The Negro in New York," *Harper's Weekly* (December 22, 1900); H. Tucker, "Negro Craftsmen in New York," *Southern Workmen*, 37 (1908); American Academy of Political and Social Science, *The Negro's Progress in Fifty Years* (Philadelphia: American Academy of Political and Social Science, 1913); and R. S. Baker, "The Negro's Struggle for Survival in the North," *American Magazine*, 65: (1907-1908).

⁹⁴Andrew D. White, *The Forum*, as quoted in Edward C. Banfield and James Q. Wilson, *City Politics* (Cambridge, Mass.: Harvard University Press, 1963), p. 153.

⁹⁵*Asbestos Workers, Local 53* v. *Vogler*, 407 F.2d 1047 (5th Cir. 1969).

⁹⁶*U.S.* v. *Lathers, Local 46*, 328 F.Supp. 429, 3 FEP457 (S.D.N.Y. 1971), aff'd., 471 F.2d 408 (2nd Cir.), cert. den., 412 U.S. 939 (1973).

⁹⁷Ibid.

⁹⁸*U.S.* v. *Bethlehem Steel Corp.*, 446 F.2d 652, 659 (2nd Cir. 1971).

⁹⁹Id., p. 655

¹⁰⁰Id., p. 663

¹⁰¹Ibid.

¹⁰²*Robinson* v. *Lorillard Corp.*, 444 F.2d 791 (4th Cir. 1971) cert. dismissed, 404 U.S. 1006 (1971).

¹⁰³*Franks* v. *Bowman Transportation Co.*, 424 U.S. 747 (1976).

¹⁰⁴*Statement of Policy on Equal Employment Opportunity*, adopted by the 55th Convention of the Building and Construction Trades Department, AFL-

CIO, September 22, 1969, at Atlantic City, New Jersey; also "Excerpts From Building Trades Statement on Hiring Minorities," *The New York Times* (September 23, 1969), p. 12.

[105]Memorandum to Heads of All Agencies from Arthur A. Fletcher, Assistant Secretary, U.S. Department of Labor, *Subject: Revised Philadelphia Plan for Compliance with Equal Employment Opportunity Requirements of Executive Order 11246 for Federally-Involved Construction* (June 27, 1969). Second part issued September 23, 1969.

[106]Ibid.

[107]*News from the AFL-CIO*, Press Release, Department of Public Relations (August 31, 1975), p. 8.

[108]*EEOC* v. *Plumbers Local 189*, 311 F.Supp. 464 (S.D. Ohio 1970).

[109]*United States* v. *Wood, Wire and Metal Lathers, Local 46*, 328 F.Supp. 429 (S.D.N.Y. 1971).

[110]On September 15, 1972, U.S. Secretary of Labor James D. Hodgeson issued a memorandum directing that numerical goals in the hiring of women and racial minorities by federal contractors should no longer be required by contract compliance agencies. The National Organization of Women and the National Association for the Advancement of Colored People denounced this action as a "retreat" and stated that: "For all practical purposes, enforcement of affirmative action plans have come to a halt." Paul Delaney, "Quota Memo Held Job 'Retreat'," *The New York Times* (September 26, 1972), p. 12.

NATIVE AMERICANS AND THE WORKING CLASS

Steve Talbot

Oregon State University

A review of the literature reveals few social scientists giving so much as a nod to the matter of Native Americans in the work force, let alone the more fundamental question of their class position. This may be due in part to the anthropological prerogative: until the 1970s, sociologists, political scientists and economists—those most inclined to look at economic data—seldom trespassed on "turf" traditionally claimed by anthropology. Still, the fact that social scientists (including anthropologists) have generally ignored the subject seems to suggest that they are unaware that Indians work like other Americans. They may have "bought" the common racial stereotype that Native Americans live on government money or continue to subsist by traditional (non-capitalist) economic activities. Neither is true, however, as shall be documented subsequently.

As for the anthropological neglect of the subject, one investigator, Stephen Lagone, searched in vain for economic data by examining twelve drawers of file cards in The Library of Congress under the heading, "Indians of North America."[1] The nation's largest library contains references to approximately eighteen thousand works, but only sixteen cards deal with statistics and eleven with the census; under population and income there are no cards at all.

> The facts speak for themselves; anthropologists upon whom others rely for expert information, have collected data primarily on pre-Columbian life, on the more esoteric and less politically strategic areas of culture, i.e., "primitive" religion, "primitive" art, folklore, material culture and technique, kinship and linguistics.[2]

If this lack of economic research seems odd, take the neglect of the more obvious topics of genocide and racism, areas which, given the history of Indian-white relations, one would suppose deserve some academic attention. Yet there is only one academic work of which I am aware that chronicles the genocide of the Indians—*Who's The Savage?*[3] As for racism, the only substantive work is *Native Americans Today:*

Sociological Perspectives, and this topic is only one of a number of the usual sociological concerns included by the editors.[4]

While our survey of American Indians and labor presented here is hardly definitive, it still may be the first substantive publication by an anthropologist to consider the subject. John Price has authored a very useful book on U.S. and Canadian Indians, written from the refreshing perspective of Native American Studies, but again, like other investigators, he neglects labor and social class.[5] Waddell and Watson[6] edited an important work on urban Indians in 1971, but although it contains an outstanding article by Jorgensen[7] on the cause of Indian underdevelopment, and one by Weppner[8] on the adjustment of Navajo Indians to Denver, the volume as a whole is not relevant to our discussion. Is is therefore fair to say that there is a dearth of published work by the academic community on the economic status of American Indians.

Fortunately, better census data on American Indians and Alaskan Natives have become available starting with the 1970 Census of Population, although these data still leave many important questions unanswered. A breakdown of American Indian data on social and economic characteristics, such as was done in 1970, was not yet available from the 1980 Census at the time of this writing, but an analysis of these new data will also be extremely helpful.

Two other sources are past reports of the U.S. Commission on Civil Rights, which contain information on discrimination in employment, and studies by a handful of non-traditional social scientists, especially the anthropologists Aberle,[9] Clemmer,[10] Jorgensen,[11] Robbins,[12] Pratt[13] and Talbot.[14] The economists Reno,[15] Ruffing[16] and Stillwaggon[17] have also produced important works. These studies have concentrated on the Ute, Navajo, Hopi and Apache populations, and deal mostly with Indian labor only in the context of reservation economic development. The sociologist, Weiss, has undertaken a major investigation of the development of capitalism in the Navajo Nation, providing an excellent historical analysis of factors leading to the formation of a Navajo proletariat.[18] Unfortunately, this doctoral dissertation remains unpublished.

With these acknowledgements and qualifications, it must be said that the chapter presented here is an elaboration of the data and conclusions reached in my book, *Roots of Oppression*.[19] My thesis in that work is that Native American tribes and peoples are locked into underdevelopment by capitalism. Not only do reservations have their natural resources "ripped off"; Indian labor is exploited as well. In fact, the two kinds of exploitation are interrelated and solutions to either problem must take this fact into consideration. I contend that both rural and urban Indians today are found not only mainly in the working class, but at the bottom of the class structure. Their participation in the work force varies, depending upon the "booms" and "busts" in the wider economy at the national level and the fluctuations in federal Indian policy. The exploitation of Indian resources and the discrimination against Indian working women and men foster astronomical rates of unemployment and poverty. Native Americans thus occupy a particularly oppressed niche in the working class of the United States. The material which follows will explore the details and ramifications of these observations.

Population and Demography

The 1970 Census, in which for the first time self-classification for race was used, found a total of 827,091 American Indians and Alaskan Natives, a 46.5 percent increase over the 1960 census enumeration.[20] In 1980, with more efficient census enumeration methods, a total of 1,418,192 were counted.[21]

In 1970 most were living in the West and about half were classified as urban, suggesting a steady migration from the reservation to the city. This inference may be erroneous, however. In the first place, the Census Bureau's urban category includes at least one city of fifty thousand inhabitants and a surrounding "urban fringe." This definition may serve well enough in the East, but in the West a number of rural, small town, and even reservation Indian communities are wrongly lumped into the urban category. I have argued that a more accurate breakdown of the 1970 census data would be 65 percent reservation and rural/non-reservation, and 35 percent urban.[22] (The Census Bureau makes a tripartite distinction: urban, reservation and rural/non-reservation.) In any case, in examining the question of Native Americans in the working class, we are dealing in a sense with both an urban and a rural proletariat.

Although Native Americans constituted only 0.5 percent of the total U.S. population in 1970, it should be noted that their numbers are not uniformly distributed. Reservations, villages and Indian communities are located mainly in several of the western states. In 1970, five states—Oklahoma, Arizona, California, New Mexico and Alaska—accounted for 50 percent of the entire Native American population.

The 1980 Census, with better enumerating methods and what may be an increase in the Native American birthrate, showed a 72 percent increase over the 1970 total. The distribution of the population, however, remained basically the same. Forty-nine percent live in the West, and two-thirds reside in ten states:[23]

California	201,311
Oklahoma	169,464
Arizona	152,857
New Mexico	104,777
North Carolina	64,635
Alaska	64,047
Washington	60,771
South Dakota	45,101
Texas	40,074
Michigan	40,038

Categorization by state does not tell the whole story. The large population in California, for example, is explained not so much by native California Indians as by the great numbers of Indians from other states who have relocated in search of job training and work. The bulk of the population is therefore urban, residing in the Los Angeles-Long Beach and the San Francisco Bay areas. Native Americans in California are mainly an urban proletariat.

Elsewhere, in Alaska and the western United States, the concept "Indian country" is more useful than that of Indian state. The Sioux-Cheyenne-Crow areas of Montana, North Dakota and South Dakota are one such region; the Navajo-Hopi-Apache-Papago/Pima-Pueblo area of Arizona and New Mexico is another; the Inuit and Athabascan Indian village region of Alaska and the Chippewa area of Minnesota are others. In these and smaller Indian regions, the Native American population is often relatively large, if not the majority of the total rural population, and, as we shall see below, forms a significant percentage of the local work force.

Demographic and social characteristics are summarized in Figure 1.[24] In brief, the Indian population is increasing, the median age of Indians is lower than that of the total U.S. population, Indians have larger families (a factor in considering family income and poverty rates), education is slowly improving in grade level but still lags behind the national average, life expectancy is low, infant death rate high, sanitation and health poor, and so on. Overall, Native Americans have the worse social and economic statistics with respect to well-being of any national or racial minority in the nation.

FIGURE 1
STATISTICAL PROFILE OF THE NATIVE AMERICAN POPULATION, 1970

The Indian and Alaskan Native population in the United States is 827,268, or 0.4% of total U.S. population.

Nearly 2/3 (508,000) live in eight states, (in descending order, by number of Indians)	The 10 largest tribes are:
	Navajo
	Cherokee
Oklahoma	Sioux (Dakota)
Arizona	Chippewa
California	Pueblo
New Mexico	Lumbee
Alaska (includes Eskimos & Aleuts)	Choctaw & Houma
North Carolina	Apache
South Dakota	Iroquois
Washington	Creek, Alabama, Coushatta

The Indian population is increasing at a rate four times the national average:

Total U.S. population, 1960-1970   13% increase
Indian population, 1960-1970   51.4% increase

The Indian population is younger than the total U.S. population:

	Male	Female
U.S. median age	26.8 years	29.3 years
Indian median age	19	20
	Under 18 years	Over 65 years
Total U.S. population	34%	9.9%
Indian	45%	5.7%

Indians have larger families than the total U.S. population:

	Total U.S.	Indian	
Families of 5 or more	25%	41%	rural Indian 50%
			urban Indian 32%

Education among Indians is improving—

	1960	1970
High school graduates, 14 and over:		
Rural Indians	13%	23%
Urban Indians	28%	42%

but still lags behind that of the total U.S. population:
Years of schooling completed, 16 years of age and over (median):

Total U.S.   12.1
Indian males   10.4
Indian females   10.5

Indians are moving to the cities:

	1960	1970
Indian population living in urban areas	30%	45%

Indian participation in the U.S. labor force is the lowest of any group:
Population 16 & over in labor force:

	Male		Female	
Total U.S.	77%		41%	
Indian	63%	(rural, 56%)	35%	(rural, 29%)
		(urban, 72%)		(urban, 42%)

Unemployment rate for Indians is 3 times higher than the U.S. total:

	Male		Female	
Total U.S.	3.9%		5.1%	
Indian	11.6%	(rural, 14%)	10.2%	(rural, 10.6%)
		(urban, 9.4%)		(urban, 9.9%)

Indians have the lowest individual and family incomes of any group in our society:

Individual income under $4,000, over $10,000:	Chart A	(see original source)
Family income under $4,000, over $10,000:	Chart B	(see original source)

	Total U.S.	Indian
Families receiving Social Security	20%	47%
Families receiving public assistance	5%	19%

Housing, sanitation and health:

	Urban		Rural	
	U.S.	Indian	U.S.	Indian
Households with severe overcrowding of 1.51 or more persons/room	1.9%	6.4%	3.0%	28.6%
Households without water	0.3%	0.9%	8.7%	67.4%
Households without toilet	0.6%	8.6%	13.6%	48.0%
Families without automobile	19.4%	27.6%	11.7%	31.5%

	Whites	Indians
Life expectancy:	71 years	63-64 years

	U.S. average	Indian average
Infant death rate:	19.2	29.6
(per 1,000 live births)		

The morbidity (illness) rate among Indians is increasing for most reportable diseases and is greater among Indians than any other groups in the population, but the total Indian death rate is decreasing.

	1960	1970
Indian deaths per 100,000 population	910.3	771.7

Source: Department of Health, Education, and Welfare. *A Study of Selected Socio-Economic Characteristics of Ethnic Minorities Based on the 1970 Census.* Volume III: American Indians, July 1974.

Position in the Class System

Although the two are inseparably linked, one can make a conceptual distinction between social class and economic class. Economic class is the primary determinant; the two basic economic classes in capitalist society being capitalists and workers. Capitalists own factories and possess capital; workers "own" only their labor which they sell to the capitalist. Control of the means of production is the key variable. Thus by "economic class" is meant a set of individuals who have the same relationship to the means of production. "Social class," on the other hand, is a "set of freely intermarrying families who share a common lifestyle and a common status or prestige ranking in the society based on a similar economic class position."[25] In this chapter we will use mainly the former concept.

The 1970 Census demonstrated clearly that the Native American population is fully integrated into the capitalist political economy.[26]

The vast majority are workers in terms of economic class. There are no capitalists to speak of, few small business people, relatively few high-income professionals and tribal officials, and a dwindling number of farmers, ranchers and herders. About 60 percent of all Indian men work as operatives, including transport (24 percent), craftsmen, foremen and the like (22 percent), and laborers, excluding farm labor (13 percent). Seventy percent of all Indian women are service workers, including private household workers (26 percent), clerical workers (25 percent) and operatives (19 percent).

Nevertheless, poverty and unemployment characterize the Native American working class. This is indicative of their social class position, reinforced by racism and ethnic discrimination. Unemployment, according to a Bureau of Indian Affairs survey in 1973, is extremely high.[27] The BIA found an overall rate of 37 percent unemployed for the "resident Indian population," about 65 percent of the total Native American population in that year. When underemployment was added, the rate jumped to 55 percent. Unemployment is even higher today, running between 70 and 80 percent on a number of reservations.

The astronomical rate of unemployment naturally contributes to poverty:

> Poverty is extremely severe for those on reservations where incomes are below the poverty line, with rates ranging from 20.3 percent at Laguna Pueblo in New Mexico, to 72.4 percent on the Navajo-Hopi joint use area in Arizona. The average for the 24 largest reservations listed in the 1970 Census . . . is 55.1 percent, and 46.8 percent for "all other identified reservations."[28]

These findings are confirmed by Pratt who has constructed an informative table showing 1970 family income for five major reservations.[29] It is presented here:

TABLE 1
FAMILY INCOME FOR FIVE RESERVATIONS (1970)

	Cheyenne River, S. Dak.	Navajo-Hopi, Arizona	Rosebud, S. Dak.	Cherokee, North Carolina	Ft. Apache, Arizona
Median Income	$3802	$2052	$3423	$4125	$4343
Mean Income	4989	2765	4518	4743	5254
Mean Income Deficit from Poverty Line	2292	2969	1940	1714	2202
Percent of Families Living Below Poverty Line	54.8	77.3	62.9	52.2	53.3
Mean Family Size	5.96	5.74	5.24	4.80	6.09

Source: Raymond P. Pratt, "Tribal Sovereignty and Resource Exploitation," *Southwest Economy and Society,* IV: 3(1978)

In 1983, of the five poorest "counties" in the United States, four were on the Lakota Indian reservations of South Dakota, and the poorest was Pine Ridge, the second largest reservation in the country, where the Wounded Knee uprising took place in 1973.[30]

The urban Indian worker is only relatively better off than his reservation or rural counterpart. This is shown in Table 2, drawn from the 1970 U.S. Census.[31] Median income for urban women was only half of that for Indian men, $2,023 compared to $4,568.

TABLE 2

INCOME AND POVERTY IN 1970: WHITES AND INDIANS

	Family Median Income	Families Living In Poverty (%)
Whites	$10,236	9.9
All Indians	5,832	33.3
Urban	7,323	21.0
Rural, non-farm	4,691	45.1

Source: U.S. Bureau of the Census, *Subject Report, American Indians* (Washington, D.C.: 1973).

Certain Indian populations have been urban workers for decades, while still maintaining their ethnic identity and tribal affiliation. This is true especially of the Mohawk. Blanchard,[32] for example, has given us an anthropological analysis of the Caughnawaga Mohawk in high steel whose occupation, which includes 70 percent of the total work force, dates from the last century. Average yearly earnings for 1978-79 ranged from $14,400 for the younger workers to $21,120 for the older. But such rates of pay, as can be seen from Table 2, are unusually high for the urban Indian worker.

The Indian working class is therefore characterized by massive, chronic unemployment and underemployment, hence, poverty. Indeed, as the 1977 American Indian Policy Review Commission (AIPRC) pointed out:

From the standpoint of personal well-being the Indian of America ranks at the bottom of virtually every social statistical indicator. On the average he has the highest infant mortality rate, the lowest longevity rate, the lowest level of educational attainment, the lowest per capita income and the poorest housing and transportation in the land.[23]

Industries and Occupations

Despite poverty and unemployment, the position of Native American workers in industries and occupations is unique among the minorities. According to 1975 data,[34] they never constitute a significant percentage in any *single* industry. Two of their largest percentages, for example, are 1.8 percent in metal mining and 2.1 percent in sawmills and planing mills. But in Indian country and Alaska, Native American workers often form a significant *portion* of key industries. Alaskan Natives are 10.9 percent of mining workers in that state; Indian workers in Oklahoma perform 5.8 percent of construction and 6.2 and 6.4 percent respectively in durable and non-durable goods manufacturing. In New Mexico they constitute 6.2 percent of those in mining and 4.3 percent of workers in durable goods manufacturing. In Montana they are 6.0 percent of mining and 4.6 percent of durable goods manufacturing workers. And in Idaho, although only 1.3 percent of the work force, they comprise 4.1 percent of the mining industry. In short, for these industries in the Indian states, Native American workers either match or exceed their state work force participation levels.

Table 3 (see p. 74) compares Indian to white and black workers in private industry. It shows that Native Americans have higher percentages in mining and construction than either of the other two groups and, in general, theirs is a very distinctive profile.

Table 4 (see p. 75) makes the comparison for occupations. For those Native Americans fortunate enough to have employment, their pattern is better than that of the other oppressed minorities. In 1975 they exceeded the minority participation rate in private industry in blue-collar and service jobs, and were underrepresented only in the professions.[35] Of particular significance is the fact that they had higher numbers of craft workers proportionately than did black, Hispanic or Asian-American workers. Later, we will see that other data on craft unions confirm this statistic.

Tables 5 and 6 (see pp. 76-77) offer occupational profiles by gender. The occupations of men do not differ significantly from the all-Indian profile. In contrast to black and Hispanic women, who are employed primarily as operatives, laborers and service workers, Indian women have slightly higher numbers proportionately in sales, office and clerical categories. In fact, they fall slightly behind other minority women in blue-collar jobs. This statistic no doubt is explained by Indian women servicing the government agencies—the Bureau of Indian Affairs (BIA) and the Indian Division of the Public Health Service (PHS)—that run the reservations. Their percentage in craft jobs, however, is approximately the same as for white and other minority women, all of which are quite low in comparison to the rates for men.

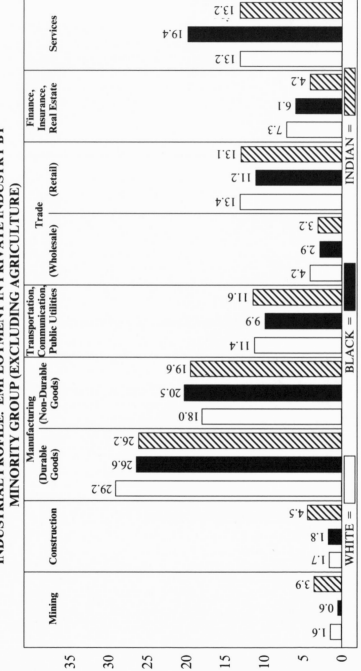

TABLE 3

INDUSTRIAL PROFILE: EMPLOYMENT IN PRIVATE INDUSTRY BY
MINORITY GROUP (EXCLUDING AGRICULTURE)

Source: U.S. Equal Employment Opportunity Commission, "Minorities and Women in Private Industry, 1975," Research Report No. 54
(Washington, D.C.: EEOC, 1977).

TABLE 4

OCCUPATIONAL PROFILE: EMPLOYMENT IN PRIVATE INDUSTRY
BY MINORITY GROUP (EXCLUDING AGRICULTURE)

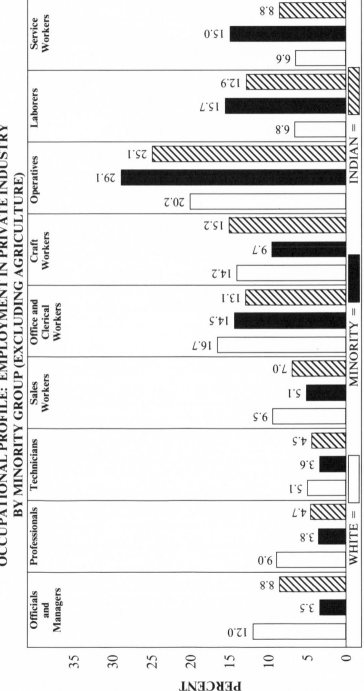

Source: U.S. Equal Employment Opportunity Commission, "Minorities and Women in Private Industry, 1975," Research Report No. 54
(Washington, D.C.: EEOC, 1977), Table 1, p. 1.

TABLE 5
OCCUPATIONAL PROFILE OF INDIAN MEN, COMPARED
TO WHITE AND ALL MINORITY MEN

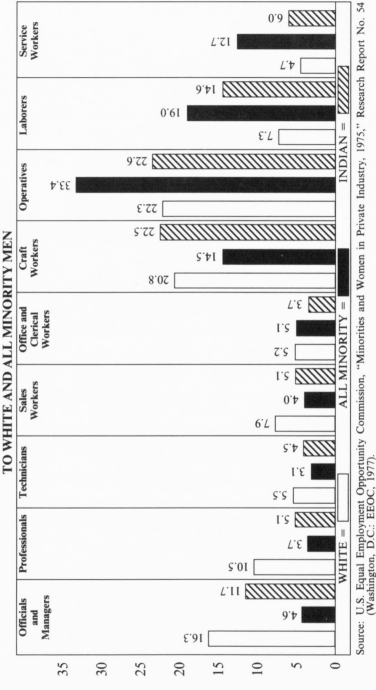

Source: U.S. Equal Employment Opportunity Commission, "Minorities and Women in Private Industry, 1975," Research Report No. 54 (Washington, D.C.: EEOC, 1977).

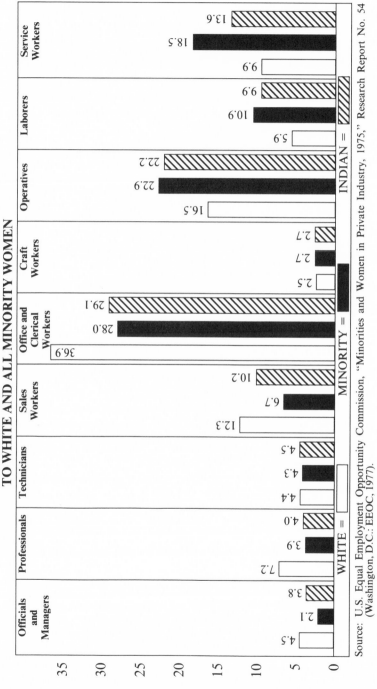

TABLE 6

OCCUPATIONAL PROFILE OF INDIAN WOMEN COMPARED
TO WHITE AND ALL MINORITY WOMEN

Source: U.S. Equal Employment Opportunity Commission, "Minorities and Women in Private Industry, 1975," Research Report No. 54 (Washington, D.C.: EEOC, 1977).

Sorokin[36] reviewed occupational changes of the Indian work force from 1940 to 1960 and found that there had been a rapid decline in employment in agriculture and a rapid expansion in blue-collar occupations; the white-collar jobs category, although increasing for Indians, nevertheless had lagged behind the statistic for non-Indian workers. The percentage of Indian craftsmen tripled, and operatives increased three and one-half times, both higher rates than the case for non-Indians in this twenty-year period. The Indian non-farm labor category doubled in contrast to a decline for non-Indians. There was a definite shift to wage labor during this period and away from agriculture.

In 1939, only 38 percent of reservation income was derived from wages, 26 percent from agriculture, 8 percent from arts and crafts, and 28 percent from various sources of unearned income. In 1964, an estimated 75 percent of total income was derived from wages, with 10 percent from agriculture, 5 percent from arts and crafts, and 20 percent from various sources of unearned income.[37][sic]

We know from other data that this period saw the mechanization of agriculture, which drove Indian farm laborers from the fields. At the same time, independent farmers and stockraisers "went under" economically in the period following the Korean War. The Indian worker apparently turned to non-farm, wage labor.

Participation Rate in the Work Force

The 1970 Census revealed that the Indian labor participation rate is the lowest of the minorities, and that unemployment, a related factor, is three times higher than the U.S. total. Table 7 gives the percentages in relationship to the variables of gender and locality:[38]

TABLE 7

INDIAN PARTICIPATION AND UNEMPLOYMENT, 1970,
BY SEX AND LOCALITY

A. Population (16 & Over) in Labor Force

	Male	Female
U.S.—Total	77%	41%
Indians—Total	63%	23%
Rural	56%	29%
Urban	72%	10%

B. Unemployment Rate

	Male	Female
U.S.—Total	3.9%	5.1%
Indians—Total	11.6%	10.2%
Rural	14.0%	10.6%
Urban	9.4%	9.9%

Source: League of Women Voters Education Fund, *Indian Country* (Washington, D.C.: 1976).

Both Indian men and women lag far behind the U.S. average in their participation rates in the work force, these rates correlating with unemployment. Interestingly, however, although the participation rate for men is lower in the rural than in the urban areas, just the reverse is true for women. Fewer than 10 percent of urban Indian women were in the work force in 1970. This statistic points to the need for additional empirical research.

Only 63 percent of Indian men were in the work force compared to 75 percent for blacks and 80 percent for whites. Tens of thousands of Native Americans are therefore in the ranks of the permanently unemployed. This fact distorts the unemployment rate. The 11.6 percent unemployment rate for Native Americans in 1970 is the official, but not the actual, one.

Native Americans have the lowest individual and family incomes of any group in society: 55 percent in 1970 under $4,000 for men and 80 percent for women, compared to 41 and 68 percent respectively in the total U.S. population. A recent analysis indicates that unemployment lessened somewhat for Indian men between 1970 and 1976, but they were still more than twice as likely to be unemployed as majority males.[39] Despite improvement in median household per capita income, in 1975 they still had only half that available to the majority population.[40]

Cited previously was a BIA 1973 survey which found 37 percent of the "resident Indian population" unemployed. This apparent discrepancy with the official rate is explained by the fact that the federal government's Current Population Survey defines an unemployed person as someone who has no employment, is available for work, and *has engaged in some specific job-seeking activity within the past four weeks*. But on Indian reservations and in isolated Alaskan Native villages, few jobs are available; "to exclude these individuals from the labor force results in a serious under-estimation of Native American unemployment and the available labor pool."[41] It is for this reason that the BIA considers any Native American adult who does not hold a wage job to be unemployed.

Kleinfeld and Kruse[42] have examined both the "discouraged worker" and what they term the "intermittent worker" effect on Native American labor force participation. In their Alaskan research they found that during the North Slope economic boom in 1977, when jobs became available to Alaskan Natives, many Inupiat (Eskimo) worked for only eight weeks or less despite relatively high pay. Investigation identified a number of disincentives from the Inupiat viewpoint: work camps were located far from home; the work entailed a heavy, ten-hour day, seven-day workweek; the Inupiat encountered bigotry from white workers; and the companies made "poor use of Native workers," i.e., there was discrimination in tasks assigned, etc.[43] By contrast, the jobs program of the Native-controlled North Slope Borough, which transformed oil tax revenues into jobs adapted to Inupiat life-styles, was quite successful; the participation rate went up, especially for Inupiat women. For the Inupiat, therefore, participation rates depend not only upon job availability, but also upon working conditions.

The intermittent worker effect relates to the preference for the traditional life-style, particularly by those Native Americans in rural areas. A number of Alaskan Native peoples still actively engage in fishing and hunting, which take place seasonally. Kleinfeld and Kruse found a preference for part-year wage work among Inupiat men so that they could continue to engage in traditional economic activities. They found that, although the annual average labor force participation rate approached national norms, the "male labor force participation at all ages was far below national norms,"[44] hence, the intermittent worker effect.

This intermittent work preference is probably not uncommon for Native Americans generally who seek to carry on traditional pursuits commensurate with ethnic life-styles. Not only subsistence activities like hunting and fishing, but also herding and ranching are favored, even when they are economically unrewarding from the standpoint of income. Stillwaggon found that, although the Northern Ute Indians as a whole are self-supporting, twenty-two still continue to cling to ranching as an occupation even though only three or four of them can make an income from this activity.[45] The others have to find additional income sources to support their ranching activity.

The labor force participation rate for Native American women is only 35.3 percent. This compares with the 40.6 percent for white adult women and 47.5 percent for black women. It is also less than all other ethnic groups, except Puerto Rican women, which is 31.6 percent. Most importantly, one must note that Native American women are at the very bottom of the ethnic list in median income—$1,697 compared to $3,738 for whites, $2,041 for blacks and $1,892 for Mexican Americans.[46]

Discrimination in Employment

This chapter has concentrated on reservation or rural Native American populations because little information exists for urban Indian workers. Traditionally, the studies in anthropology of urban Indians have concentrated on acculturation and adjustment to urban conditions.[47] In the various hearings of the U.S. Commission on Civil Rights, however, there is evidence to suggest that much of Native American poverty and unemployment is due to overt discrimination, both in hiring practices and in pay scale. The existence of anti-Indian stereotypes, such as the "drunk," "incompetent" Indian or untutored ward of the federal government, has historically been used to justify discriminatory treatment.

I have dealt with this question for the San Carlos Reservation in Arizona, showing that supposed Indian incompetence is a social myth, that underdevelopment, government mismanagement, private sector exploitation and racism are the chief obstacles.[48] Stillwaggon found private sector employment literally closed to the Utes of Utah: "Utes face racial prejudice when they seek work with white employers. . . . Rather than work in a racist environment, no Utes are currently seeking work in the private sector."[49] Instead, 89 percent of employed Utes work for the tribe and its business operations.

Private business has a poor affirmative action record, even when the industries are located close to reservations and an Indian labor pool is readily available. One of the few studies of job discrimination is Leubben's 1953 investigation of Navajo miners.[50] In "Carbonate City," an off-reservation mining community where Navajos constituted 35 percent of the population, Anglos were nonetheless always hired by the company in preference to Navajos. Furthermore,

> Navajos were nearly always hired as helpers, the lowest grade, regardless of economic conditions . . . , mining capabilities, and previous experience . . . . Generally they did not hold any of the other skilled or supervisory positions, even though qualified . . . promotion was slower than for Anglos.[51]

In 1973 the U.S. Commission on Civil Rights investigated the murder of a Papago miner and uncovered relevant information on the copper mining activites in Ajo, Arizona, by the Phelps Dodge Corporation. Only ninety-six out of 1,258 of the workers were Papago, although the mine was located directly adjacent to the reservation. When asked in a commission hearing why Phelps Dodge had such a poor record of Papago employment, the company's representative replied lamely that recruiting Indians was difficult. The commission's counsel countered with, "In other words, you are telling us that your company has been in Ajo for 40 years and still has not learned how to deal with people who've lived there for several hundred years?"[52] The U.S. Equal Opportunity Commission later charged the company with "racist practices in hiring and advancement."[53] Moreover, documents seized in the

1972 takeover of the BIA offices in Washington by the Indian Trail of
Broken Treaties Caravan "disclosed that Phelps Dodge was one of the
major U.S. corporations that cheated Indians to obtain mining rights,
involving pay-offs to state legislators and U.S. Congressmen for illegal
purchase of Indian mining rights."[54]

In their study of Oklahoma Cherokee assimilation, Wahrhaftig and
Thomas found that the full-blooded Cherokee were at the bottom of
the employment pyramid in that state: "In some areas, Cherokees live
in virtual peonage; in others, straw bosses recruit Cherokee laborers for
irregular work at low pay."[55] An investigation by the U.S. Commission on Civil Rights tended to support these earlier findings:

> Many witnesses testifying . . . also felt that employment dis-
> crimination against Indians by private businesses and industries
> was widespread in Oklahoma. Several witnesses stated that Indi-
> ans applying for employment are usually told that the "job has
> been filled" when, in fact, it has not. The excuse employers usu-
> ally give for not hiring Indians . . . is that they are social mis-
> fits, or that they drink too much. . . . Indians are often paid
> lower wages than white workers for the same kind of work.[56]

A U.S. Commission on Civil Rights investigation of Montana and
North and South Dakota, a region containing nineteen Indian reservations, found a very high unemployment rate and widespread discrimination in both federal and private employment.[57] Like the Oklahoma
Indian population, a larger proportion of Indian workers in the private
sector were blue-collar workers compared to non-Indians. Witnesses
charged that discrimination by private business and industry was a
major factor, and that many companies doing business with the federal
government were not in compliance with their contracts concerning
equal employment requirements.

Less data are available on urban Indian populations, but both the
Oklahoma and Northern Plains Civil Rights Commission hearings
showed widespread discrimination in urban employment. In the Twin
Cities of Minnesota, "virtually no progress is evident."[58] Cities with
relatively large Indian populations have extremely high unemployment rates; for example, an estimated 40 percent of Indians in the Minneapolis-St. Paul metropolitan area were unemployed in 1975.[59]

More than for any other minority group, much of the racial discrimination in employment for Native Americans derives from federal
agencies. The Bureau of Indian Affairs and the PHS-Indian Health
Service are the largest single employers of Native Americans. This is
due to the land-owning, reservation and treaty status of Native Americans as indigenous minorities.[60] The 1970 Census listed 24 percent of
Native Americans nationally, and 32 percent of rural/non-farm Indi-

ans, as "government workers."[61] The problem, therefore, is that the Indian employee is locked in grade. The U.S. Civil Rights Commission report for the Northern Plains found that although 7.7 percent of the federal work force in that region was Indian, "the majority . . . were located in the lower grade and wage board levels, with over 80 percent of all the Indian GS employees at or below the GS-8 grade level."[62] The *Southwest Indian Report* disclosed that in Arizona, Indians comprised 81.2 percent of all personnel in grades 1 through 5, but white personnel constituted only 7.3 percent of employees in those grades.[63]

One reason for the high number of Indian employees in the BIA and the Indian Health Service is the federally-mandated Indian Preference Clause. Yet this applies only to these two agencies: no more than one-half of one percent of all federal jobs are subject to Indian preference. Other federal agencies consistently fail to employ Indians in proportion to their share of the population. In 1973 a coalition of Native American organizations in the San Francisco Bay area charged thirty-two federal agencies with discrimination in employment. The class-action civil complaint calculated that if given equal employment opportunity in federal agencies, "the American Indian community would earn an additional $150 million per year or $1.5 billion over the next decade."[64]

Shirley Hill Witt suggests that the low level of education of Native Americans contributes significantly to their underemployment in federal agencies.[65] The average educational level for Indians under federal supervision is five years, with only 18 percent having attended college and only 3 percent having graduated. The BIA federal boarding school is the main agent of education for reservation Indians. It operates to discriminate especially against Indian women, according to Witt's explanation, because only two vocational channels are open—domestics and secretarial work—and they represent exceedingly narrow and sexist choices. Witt, an Indian anthropologist, finds that "most employed women are domestics, whether in private homes, in janitorial positions, or in hospitals," and that "Native women in the BIA provide a veritable army of clerks and secretaries. They are concentrated, of course, in lower GS ratings, powerless and vulnerable."[66]

Unionization

Insufficient information exists on Native American union membership and affiliation. It has been supposed that a high proportion, especially in rural and reservation areas, are not organized. Many tribes in the past have barred unions from their reservations, but this is now beginning to change. The Navajo Nation, for example, which outlawed unions in 1958, by the end of the 1970s had 6,600 union members, about 12 percent of the work force, and an Office of Navajo Labor Relations.[67] About three hundred Navajos were joining building trade unions each year.

It would appear that Native Americans are more often members of craft unions than industrial unions. In 1974 the Equal Employment Opportunity Commission took a survey of minorities and women in referral unions.[68] Referral unions are those with hiring halls or which select individuals for apprenticeships and membership. All those with one hundred or more members were surveyed. It was found that "American Indian representation in referral union membership was three times greater than their incidence in the civilian labor force."[69] American Indians also have a much higher proportion of workers in building trade unions in comparison to the non-building trades than any other minority—79.5 percent of unionized Indian workers are in the building trades in contrast to 67.4 percent for whites and 42.6 percent for blacks.[70]

Indians are best represented in the ironworkers, roofers and laborers unions, although high percentages are also found in the plumbers, elevator constructors, asbestos workers and plasterers. Table 8 gives this information by percentage. Indians do not fall below parity in any building trade union. Unlike members of other oppressed minority groups, who are found principally in the low-paying trades, Indian workers are about equally represented. In the non-building trades, however, "Indians did not achieve parity with their share of the labor force in 12 of the 27 internationals . . ."[71] Almost half of the Indians in non-building trade unions are Teamsters.

Indian women, on the other hand, are represented most heavily in the non-building trades (87.8%), particularly in the Hotel and Restaurant Employees (31.9%), but also in the Teamsters (15.5%).[72] These percentages are much higher than for any other minority group or for whites. Women generally suffer the largest gap in referral union membership; they composed nearly 40 percent of the civilian labor force in 1974, but only about 12 percent of all referral union members.

TABLE 8

DISTRIBUTION OF INDIAN WORKERS IN BUILDING AND
NON-BUILDING TRADES UNIONS

Union	Percent of Indian per Building Trade
Laborers	26.8
Carpenters	16.9
Iron Workers	12.2

Plumbers	11.8
Operating Engineers	10.9
Electrical Workers	7.8
All Other Building Trades	13.7

Union	Percent of Indian per Non-Building Trade
Teamsters	46.5
Hotel & Restaurant Employees	14.6
Meat Cutters	6.9
Machinists	5.7
Stage and Moving Picture Operators	5.6
All Other Non-building Trades	20.6

American Indians in states where their population is highest tend to predominate in one or two trades and, in some instances, form a significant percentage of the overall state membership in referral unions.[73] For example, in Alaska they comprise 13.1 percent of referral union membership, mainly as carpenters and laborers. (Of course, this may have been during the construction of the Alaskan pipeline, a peak period of employment.) In Montana, 5.3 percent of all membership is Indian; in New Mexico, 7.1 percent; in Oklahoma, 9.4 percent. Of all the plumbers in the six Oklahoma locals reporting, 12.8 percent are Indian. In some cases, even non-Indian states have relatively high percentages. In Florida, of the three roofers' locals reporting, 27.7 percent of the members are Indian; and in Indiana, of the four plasterers' locals reporting, 16.5 percent of the membership is Indian.

The fact is, of those Native Americans in labor unions, an unusually high proportion are found in crafts. This finding has apparently gone unnoticed in the academic literature, but it is borne out by personal accounts. For example, an Indian friend from Texas told me that there were twelve members of his extended family who are plumbers. Most had taken part in job actions and were valued members of their respective locals, although—in a note of racism—every one of them was always called "Indian Joe" by his white fellow workers.

Craft workers, until recently, have probably been urban and small town residents, but with the increased energy exploitation of reservations during the last decade or so, a growing number of Native Americans have joined construction, mining and laborers unions. This development apparently hit its peak in the Navajo Nation, as Robbins' data indicate, and is shown in Table 9:[74]

TABLE 9

NAVAJO UNION MEMBERSHIP—SUMMER 1977 ESTIMATES

Union	Navajo Membership
Operating Engineers	450
Building Crafts and Skills Unions	2000
(Trainees)	(500)
(Apprentices)	(150)

United Mine Workers	950
Laborers Union	1600
Railway Workers	<u>1600</u>
TOTAL	6600

Source: Lynn Robbins, "Navajo Workers and Labor Unions," *Southwest Economy and Society*, III: 3(1977).

Robbins contends that a labor-Indian alliance operates for the Navajo against exploitative energy corporations and in a way in Arizona politics which has been quite effective.[75]

In 1969 a transnational electronics firm, Fairfield Corporation, opened a plant at Shiprock on the Navajo Nation. It employed twelve hundred workers, mostly women, whom the company exploited by using an Indian wage differential: during 1974 a thousand Navajo employees received a payroll of about $1 million—an average of $1,000 each—while the top twenty-three officers and directors of the corporation received salaries of $1,588,792.[76] This led the Navajo workers to try to organize a union, which led to layoffs, an occupation of the plant by the workers and community people, and the revelation that the company planned to close and transfer operations to its plants in Third World countries where it paid even poorer wages in order to maximize its profits. This is the kind of "industrialization" reservation Indians experienced in the 1960s and 1970s and which, at least in the Navajo case, led to an attempt to unionize.

Conclusions and Policy Implications

Jorgensen is correct when he contends that Indian reservations are fully integrated into the U.S. political economy.[77] Indian underdevelopment, unemployment and poverty are due not so much to rural isolation and aboriginal values as to the way the "urban centers of finance, political influence and power have grown at the expense of rural areas."[78] This is the metropolis-satellite thesis: the "urban" metropolis dominates the "rural" satellite. In my view, it is within this theoretical context that one must analyze the question of the Indian working class, the special niche within the larger class system that Native Americans occupy and the racism that has historically been directed toward them as indigenous peoples.[79]

Most Native American communities have been a part of the economic class system in the United States for many decades. I have analyzed this in the San Carlos Apache case, in which it becomes evident that in economic boom periods, Indian workers pick up their lunch pails and join the ranks of other blue-collar workers; at other times they are thrown on the ash heap of the permanently unemployed. For example:

> The San Carlos Apaches . . . were the backbone of the eastern Arizona labor force in the early decades of this century. They built many of the railroads, dams and highways, and after World War I, they worked in Arizona's mines as well. The Depression drove them from the labor force, and they did not re-enter the job market until World War II. After the war the majority of Apache workers were again consigned to capitalism's reserve army of unemployed or underemployed labor.[80]

Similarly, the Indians of British Columbia have apparently been an integral part of the Canadian work force. In reviewing a book on Indian labor in that province during the years 1858 to 1930, Weil states: "Rather than becoming isolated and internally colonized on government-administered reserves, they were drawn into virtually every economic activity of the society that engulfed them," and that "wage labor and small commodity production for cash became prevalent soon after contact."[81] This, one suspects, has been the experience for many if not the majority of Native American peoples in the United States, who neither lack the capacity nor the desire to participate in the national economy when it is in their interest to do so.

Aberle documents this for the Navajo. During World War II, in the labor shortage of the wartime economy, the Navajo like other Indians went to work in industrial plants:

> This is a phenomenon to be stressed: when the economic situation was advantageous, when jobs with good pay were abundant, Navajos who were, on the average, of lower educational attainment than is the present Navajo population, could be induced to do wagework off reservation and could perform successfully.[82]

And occasional references in other contemporary ethnographic literature implicitly state the importance of wage labor. Edward Spicer, for example, says about Lakota Sioux of North and South Dakota: "About one-fifth raise cattle, and a much smaller number dry farm some land. The majority, some 60 percent, work for wages in nearby towns, for neighboring white farmers and Sioux stockraisers, or in BIA operations."[83]

Weiss has demonstrated quite convincingly how outside merchant and, later, industrial capital penetration led the Navajo economy to change from a natural mode of production (pre-capitalist) to a modern class structure consisting of an impoverished proletariat and a very small petty and industrial bourgeoisie.[84] Aberle makes the point that the Navajo no longer have a subsistence economy. In 1958 he found that "only 10 percent of income came from livestock and agriculture;

only 1 percent from arts and crafts; *68 percent from wages;* 5 percent from mineral leases . . ." and "16 percent from railroad retirement, social security, welfare, etc."[85] (Emphasis added.) But one should not be misled by the fact that many Navajo workers or their extended families continue to value, and find time for, subsistence herding activities. The medium-size herder never lost his land as did the European peasantry in an earlier century; *the Navajo are a land-based proletariat,* as Weiss shows.

One suspects this is also the case for many of the larger Native American populations: they are a land-based if not a land-oriented proletariat with the land holding both a religious and a cultural, if not a economic, significance as well.[86] Like the Navajo worker (at least until the mining and construction "boom" of the 1970s), they go to and from their reservations seeking work when and where it is available. But as indigenous minorities they are still territorially based. Even the "urban" Indian relates to the land in that the ties to "kith and kin" at the reservation level and to one's native homeland are strong in most instances.

Where, then, do these economic processes lead? What are the prospects for the future in terms of the Native Americans' relationship to the work force?

A report by the U.S. Commission on Civil Rights in the late 1970s suggests that employment and income rates may have improved in the late 1960s and early 1970s.[87] If so, this is probably due to mining and construction associated principally with coal and uranium extraction, and related construction of gas-fired electrification plants in the Southwest. An analysis of the 1980 Census data should give a definitive answer. But any interpretation of 1980 data must take into account the economic recession of 1981-82 and its disastrous effects on Indian country. Furthermore, the military budget priorities of the Reagan administration exacerbated that economic crisis and drove Indian workers into further deprivation from which they have yet to recover.

In 1981 about 40 percent of Native Americans were officially jobless, and by mid-1984 the corresponding figure had reached 80 percent. The 1981-82 cuts in federal programs for the poor, such as welfare, food stamps and job training, affected Indian people disproportionately because of their low per capita income. And the across-the-board cuts in health, education and housing programs were ten times higher for Indians than for others in the general population.[88] Allocations for federal programs affecting Native Americans were cut in the 1982 fiscal year by 34 percent, and by another 31 percent in 1983.[89]

This reduction in federal Indian programs came at a time when the country was in the grips of an economic recession, when close to 11 percent of the national work force was officially unemployed. The few industries on which Indian workers and their families depend, such as mines and lumber mills, largely closed, and without federal programs to act as an economic cushion, the corporate tribal councils became severely strapped economically. Even if general economic conditions improve, as mainstream economists now maintain, it is doubtful that the immediate impact on Indian country will be significant.

In the Navajo Nation, which has the nation's largest unionized Indian work force, unemployment in 1983 stood at almost 80 percent, according to new reports. Thousands of Navajo miners were without work, and the Reagan administration's budget cuts eliminated thousands of federal jobs held by Indians. The Navajo Nation lost $152 million in federal aid during 1982, and it was estimated that only seventeen thousand of their eighty-three thousand workers would have jobs in 1983. At the same time the media reported the pronouncement by then-Secretary of the Interior James Watt, the government's chief land and resources manager, that the "Indian problem" is due to "socialistic government policies"! This was a new twist in blaming-the-victim theories.

Native American organizations correctly countered by pointing out that treaties and laws obligate the federal government to ensure health, welfare and the development of reservations in exchange for the hundreds of millions of acres of Indian lands ceded in the past. Over one hundred treaties pledge the federal government to furnish physicians, teachers and nurses; others pledge annual food rations, grain and farming implements. *Because such a high proportion of Indian labor depends upon tribal and federal Indian agency jobs associated with these treaty-mandated trust responsibilities and services, Indian tribes need an increase, not a decrease, in federal program spending during times of economic adversity*—just the opposite of what, in fact, has taken place.

We are seeing in the United States today the most concerted disintegration of Native American economic rights since the termination period of the 1950s. Yet, as I discussed in *Roots of Oppression*,[90] with ample federal spending or capital and imaginative social policies, many reservations could become completely self-supporting because of abundant timber, mineral and water resources. And there is a ready labor pool available, much of it experienced and skilled.

Short of bold new Indian policies and national economic recovery and development, much could be done immediately concerning affirmative action for Native American federal workers, whether rural or urban. The American Indian Policy Review Commission recommended that Congress amend the 1934 Indian Reorganization Act to make Indian preference applicable to all federal agencies administering Indian programs, and not just to the BIA and Indian Health Service as is done at present.[91] The 1977 AIPRC report found that Indian-owned resources directly supported some 120,000 jobs by both Indian and non-Indian workers: "This amounts to 20 percent of the entire Indian service population recognized by the BIA. A long step toward self-sufficiency would be taken if all these jobs were held by Indians—the owners of the resource."[92]

Interestingly, this recommendation was one of the key points of the tribal election platform of Russell Means, American Indian Movement (AIM) leader and candidate for Oglala tribal president on the Pine Ridge Reservation in the 1984 election campaign.[93] Much of the land on that reservation has either passed into non-Indian ownership or is leased out by the BIA to white ranchers, often without the permission of the Indian landowners. The traditional Indian platform of AIM, on which Means ran, advocates suspending the leases pending an investigation of their circumstances. The idea is to increase employment and economic viability by returning the land as a resource to the control of the Indian landowner.

The traditional Indian movement, in fact, is very dubious about the so-called economic development and jobs programs promoted during the 1960s and 1970s by the "partnership" of corporate tribal councils, private business and the federal government. It has witnessed the failure of industrialization attempts, discrimination in employment by the private sector employer, and the refusal by and large of the "feds" to do anything about it; and now it is experiencing possibly the most severe economic disaster of any racial or ethnic group in the 1980s.

It is understandable that politically-conscious, grassroots Indian leaders are disenchanted with the capitalist system and what they mistakenly see as the "working class model" of U.S. citizenship, rather than job development under their own Indian sovereignty. Laguna Pueblo miners are not only largely unemployed, but the community itself is radioactive from the uranium mining activities in the region. There was a serious radioactive spill on the Navajo Nation in 1979 when a containment dam burst, and Navajo miners, who formerly had a zero base rate of cancer, are now dying from the disease.[94] What is so wonderful about being part of the American work force anyway, according to this view, if your land is contaminated and you die early from cancer? The Lakota Sioux already have a serious health problem at Pine Ridge, which they believe due to previous uranium exploration, mining and milling.[95] The radioactivity level of the water at Pine Ridge is at least three times the federal standard. Given the small Lakota gene pool, Indians like Russell Means believe that their people face a serious problem of genocide from capitalist "development."

For these and other reasons the Indian movement appears to be increasingly exploring alternative and less exploitative kinds of energy development—truck gardening, cooperative ranching, sun power technology and other modified, traditional economic activities. An article in a 1978 issue of the Indian newspaper, *Akwesasne Notes*, argues that "appropriate technology is 'appropriate' to Native people only if it returns to them control over their lives. What Native people need to develop are technologies appropriate to the exercise of sovereignty."[96]

To conclude: Native Americans are today very much part of the U.S. working class, but now that they have been "kicked in the teeth" by the recent recession and have bitterly experienced employment discrimination from both the public and private sectors, will they return, "business as usual," to the labor force when economic conditions improve—if they improve? This, in my view, is the key question facing policymakers.

NOTES

[1]Stephen A. Lagone, "A Statistical Profile of the Indian: The Lack of Numbers," *Towards Economic Development for Native American Communities*, Vol. II (Washington, D.C.: U.S. Government Printing Office, 1969), pp. 1-18.

[2]Steve Talbot, *Roots of Oppression: The American Indian Question* (New York: International Publishers, 1981), pp. 5-6.

[3]David R. Wrone and Russell S. Nelson, Jr., eds., *Who's The Savage? A Documentary History of the Mistreatment of the Native North Americans* (Greenwich, Conn.: Fawcett, 1973).

[4]Howard M. Bahr, Bruce A. Chadwick and Robert C. Day, eds., *Native Americans Today: Sociological Perspectives* (New York: Harper & Row, 1972).

[5]John A. Price, *Native Studies, American and Canadian Indians* (New York and Toronto: McGraw-Hill Ryerson Ltd., 1978).

[6]Jack O. Waddell and O. Michael Watson, eds., *The American Indian in Urban Society* (Boston: Little, Brown & Co., 1971).

[7]Joseph G. Jorgensen, "Indians and the Metropolis," in Waddell and Watson, op. cit., pp. 67-113.

[8]Robert S. Weppner, "Urban Economic Opportunities: The Example of Denver," in Waddell and Watson, op. cit., pp. 244-273.

[9]David F. Aberle, "A Plan for Navajo Economic Development," in *Towards Economic Development for Native American Communities*, Vol. I, op. cit., pp. 223-276.

[10]Richard O. Clemmer, "Hopi Political Economy," *Southwest Economy & Society*, II: 1(1976): 4-33; "Black Mesa and the Hopi," in Joseph G. Jorgensen, et al., eds., *Native Americans and Energy Development*, (Cambridge, Mass.: Anthropology Resource Center, 1978), pp. 17-34.

[11] Jorgensen, op. cit., "Indians and the Metropolis"; *The Sun Dance Religion: Power for the Powerless* (Chicago: University of Chicago Press, 1973); "A Century of Political Effects on American Indian Society, 1880-1980," *The Journal of Ethnic Studies*, VI: 3(Fall 1978): 1-82.

[12] Lynn Robbins, "The Navajo Nation and Industrial Development," *Southwest Economy & Society*, II: 3(1976): 47-70; "Energy Developments and the Navajo Nation," in Jorgensen, et al., *Native Americans and Energy Development*, op. cit., pp. 35-48; "Navajo Workers and Labor Unions," *Southwest Economy & Society*, III: 3(1977): 4-23.

[13] Raymond B. Pratt, "Tribal Sovereignty and Resource Exploitation," *Southwest Economy and Society*, IV: 3(1978): 38-74.

[14] Steve Talbot, "The Myth of Indian Economic and Political Incompetence: The San Carlos Case," *Southwest Economy and Society*, II: 3(1976): 3-46; *Roots of Oppression*, op. cit.

[15] Phillip Reno, "The Navajos: High, Dry and Penniless," *The Nation* (March 29, 1975): 359-363.

[16] Lorraine Turner Ruffing, "The Navajo Nation: A History of Dependency and Underdevelopment," *The Review of Radical Political Economics*, XI: 2(Summer 1979): 25-37; "The Role of Policy in American Indian Mineral Development," Occasional Paper, Development Series (Albuquerque, N.M.: Native American Studies Center, University of New Mexico, 1980).

[17] Eileen M. Stillwaggon, "Economic Impact on Uintah and Curay Indian Reservation on the Local Non-Indian Economy," (Ph.D. Dissertation, The American University, 1979).

[18] Lawrence David Weiss, "The Development of Capitalism in the Navajo Nation," (Ph.D. Dissertation, State University of New York-Binghamton, 1979).

[19] Talbot, *Roots of Oppression*, op. cit.

[20] The U.S. Bureau of the Census, *Subject Report, American Indians*, 1970 Census of Population PC(2)-1f (Washington, D.C.: Government Printing Office, 1973).

[21] U.S. Bureau of the Census, "Race of the Population by States: 1980," PC80-S1-3 (Washington, D.C.: Government Printing Office, 1980); U.S. Department of Commerce, "Two-Thirds of American Indians, Eskimos, Aleuts Live in 10 States Census Shows," *U.S. Dept. of Commerce News*, (May 27, 1981).

[22] Talbot, *Roots of Oppression*, op. cit., pp. 22-23.

[23] U.S. Bureau of the Census, *Subject Report, American Indians*, op. cit.

[24] This figure is reproduced from a brochure by the League of Women Voters Education Fund, *Indian Country* (Washington, D.C.: League of Women Voters, 1976).

[25] Albert J. Szymanski and Ted George Goertzel, *Sociology: Class, Consciousness and Contradictions* (New York: D. Van Nostrand Co., 1979).

[26] U.S. Bureau of the Census, *Subject Report, American Indians*, op. cit.

[27] Bureau of Indian Affairs, "Estimates of Resident Indian Population and Labor Force Status; By State and Reservation" (Process, March 1973).

[28]Talbot, *Roots of Oppression*, op. cit., p. 179.

[29]Pratt, op. cit., p. 74.

[30]Fund appeal letter of January 18, 1983, from Russell Means.

[31]U.S. Bureau of the Census, *Subject Report, American Indians*, op. cit.

[32]David Blanchard, "High Steel! The Kahnawake Mohawk and the High Construction Trade," *The Journal of Ethnic Studies*, XI: 2(Summer 1983): 41-60.

[33]American Indian Policy Review Commission, *AIPRC, Final Report*, Vol. I (Washington, D.C.: Government Printing Office, 1977).

[34]U.S. Equal Employment Opportunity Commission, "Minorities and Women in Private Industry, 1975: An Analysis of OEE-1 Employment," *Research Report No. 54*, prepared by Kathleen A. McMillan (Washington, D.C.: 1977). Tables 3-6 are drawn from data contained in this same report.

[35]Ibid., pp. 12-13.

[36]Alan L. Sorokin, "Trends in Employment and Earnings of American Indians," in *Towards Economic Development for Native American Communities*, Vol. I, op. cit., pp. 107-118.

[37]Ibid., p. 116.

[38]League of Women Voters, op. cit., p. 21.

[39]U.S. Commission on Civil Rights, *Social Indicators of Equality for Minorities and Women* (Washington, D.C.: August 1978).

[40]Ibid., p. 52.

[41]Joan Kleinfeld and John A. Kruse, "Native Americans in the Labor Force: Hunting for an Accurate Measure," *Monthly Labor Review*, 105: 7 (July 1982): 47-51.

[42]Ibid.

[43]Ibid., p. 48.

[44]Ibid., p. 49.

[45]Stillwaggon, op. cit., p. 111.

[46]See Elizabeth Almquist and J. Wehrie-Einhorn, "Double Disadvantaged Minority Women in the Labor Force," in Ann H. Stromberg and Shirley Harkness, eds., *Women Working* (Palo Alto, Cal.: Mayfield Publishing, 1978), p. 6

[47]For example, Price, op. cit.; Waddell and Watson, op. cit.

[48]Talbot, "The Myth of Indian Economic and Political Incompetence: The San Carlos Case," op. cit.

[49]Stillwaggon, op. cit., p. 96.

[50]Ralph Leubben, "Prejudice and Discrimination Against Navajos in a Mining Community," in Bahr, Chadwick and Day, op. cit., pp. 89-101.

[51]Ibid., p. 92.

[52]In the Indian newspaper, *Akwesasne Notes*, 5: 4(Early Winter: Mohawk Nation at Rooseveltown, 1973).

[53]In the Indian newspaper, *Wassaja* (September 1973: American Indian Historical Society, San Francisco, California).

[54]Ibid.

[55]Albert L. Wahrhaftig and Robert K. Thomas, "Renaissance and Repression: The Oklahoma Cherokee," in Bahr, Chadwick and Day, op. cit., pp. 80-88.

[56]U.S. Commission on Civil Rights, *Indian Civil Rights Issues in Oklahoma*, Oklahoma State Advisory Committee (Washington, D.C.: January 1974).

[57]U.S. Commission on Civil Rights, *Indian Civil Rights Issues in Montana, North Dakota, and South Dakota*, Montana-North Dakota-South Dakota Joint Advisory Committee (Washington, D.C.: 1974).

[58]U.S. Commission on Civil Rights, *Bridging the Gap: A Reassessment*, Minnesota Advisory Committee (Washington, D.C.: January 1978).

[59]Ibid., p. 2.

[60]See Talbot, *Roots of Oppression*, op. cit., Chapters 1 and 2.

[61]U.S. Bureau of the Census, *Subject Report, American Indians*, op. cit.

[62]U.S. Commission on Civil Rights, *Indian Civil Rights Issues in Montana, North Dakota, and South Dakota*, op. cit.

[63]U.S. Commission on Civil Rights, *The Southwest Indian Report* (Washington, D.C.: U.S. Government Printing Office, May 1973).

[64]Talbot, *Roots of Oppression*, op. cit., p. 179.

[65]Shirley Hill Witt, "Native Women Today, Sexism and the Indian," *Civil Rights Digest*, 6: 3(Spring 1974): 29-35.

[66]Shirley Hill Witt, "Native Women in the World of Work," in U.S. Department of Labor Women's Bureau, *Native American Women and Equal Opportunity* (Washington, D.C.: 1979), pp. 8-15.

[67]Robbins, "Navajo Workers and Labor Unions," op. cit.

[68]U.S. Equal Employment Opportunity Commission, "Minorities and Women in Private Industry," op. cit.

[69]Ibid., p. 12.

[70]Ibid., p. 4.

[71]Ibid., p. 12.

[72]Ibid.

[73]Ibid., Table 12.

[74]Robbins, "Navajo Workers and Labor Unions," op. cit., p. 18.

[75]Ibid.

[76]Bruce Johansen and Roberto Maestras, *Wasi'chu: The Continuing Indian Wars* (New York and London: Monthly Review Press, 1979), p. 228.

[77]Jorgensen, "Indians and the Metropolis," op cit.; *The Sun Dance Religion*, op. cit.; "A Century of Political Effects," op. cit.

[78]Jorgensen, "Indians and the Metropolis," op. cit., p. 85.

[79]See Steve Talbot, "American Ethnocide: Native Americans and Racial Discrimination in the United States," n.d., manuscript, 42 pp.

[80]Talbot, *Roots of Oppression*, op. cit., p. 181; see also Talbot, "The Myth of Indian Economic and Political Incompetence: The San Carlos Case," op. cit.

[81]Jim Weil, review of *Indians at Work: An Informal History of Native American Labour in British Columbia 1858-1980*, by Rolf Knight, *American Anthropologist*, 84: 4(December 1982): 905-906.

[82]Aberle, op. cit., p. 233.

[83]Edward H. Spicer, *The American Indians, Dimensions of Ethnicity* (Cambridge & London: Belknap Press of Harvard University Press, 1982), pp. 105-106.

[84]Weiss, op. cit.

[85]Aberle, op. cit., p. 233.

[86]See Steve Talbot, "Desecration and American Indian Religious Freedom," in Karl Schlesier, ed., *Action Anthropology* (Frankfurt: Syndikat Publishers, in press), and also in a forthcoming article in *The Journal of Ethnic Studies* under the same title.

[87]U.S. Commission on Civil Rights, *Social Indicators*, op. cit.

[88]Council for Indian Awareness, "Impact Federal Budget Cuts Have On Indian Programs" (Tucson, Arizona: April 24, 1981).

[89]From the news wire service, June 18, 1984. Hearings held by the Presidential Commission on the Economic Development of Indian Reservations set up in 1983.

[90]Talbot, *Roots of Oppression*, op. cit.

[91]American Indian Policy Review Commission, *AIPRC Final Report*, Vol. 1, op. cit., p. 21.

[92]Ibid., p. 319.

[93]International Indian Treaty Council, *Treaty Council News*, V: 3(March 1984).

[94]Talbot, *Roots of Oppression*, op. cit., pp. 168-169.

[95]Amelia W. Irvin, "Energy Development and the Effects of Mining on the Lakota Nation," *The Journal of Ethnic Studies*, X: 1(Spring 1982): 89-101.

[96]Quoted in David Murray, *Modern Indians: Native Americans in the Twentieth Century*, Pamphlet 8, British Association for American Studies (England: 1982), p. 41

THE LABOR MARKET STATUS OF AMERICAN JEWS: PATTERNS AND DETERMINANTS*

Barry R. Chiswick

University of Illinois at Chicago

Introduction

Among the mosaic of racial and ethnic minorities that constitute the population of the United States, most are defined in terms of their race or ancestors' country of origin. Some are defined, however, on the basis of their religious identity or ancestry. The latter category includes American Jews.

Jews are a small minority in the United States, comprising about 2.5 percent of the population, yet they have had a major impact on the economic, political and cultural life of this country, in part because of their high level of schooling and occupational attainment, and in part because of their entrepreneurial activities.

Jews have been a successful minority in America, but also a troubled one. They are a religiously-based ethnic group in a period in which religious practice is on the wane. Their high level of income and education has been both a cause and a consequence of very low fertility rates. In addition, there has been an increase in intermarriage by Jews, in part reflecting their increasing level of education and the greater number of generations since immigration to the United States.[1] These trends suggest that the Jewish population may decline in absolute numbers as well as proportionately.[2] If so, the Jewish ethnic group may fall a victim to its own success.

*I am indebted to Gary S. Beker, Carmel U. Chiswick, Lawrence Fuchs, VictorFuchs, Milton Himmelfarb, Soloman Polachek, David Singer, Thomas Sowell and Teresa Sullivan for numerous insightful comments, and to Rosemary Rees and Suchittra Chamnivickorn for their research assistance. I am, however, solely responsible for the contents of this chapter, an earlier version of which was read at the Fourth Annual Green Bay Colloquium on Ethnicity and Public Policy, Green Bay, Wisconsin, May 1983, sponsored by the American Ethnic Studies Coordinating Committee, University of Wisconsin System.

The purpose of this chapter is twofold. First, it will present a comparative analysis of Jews with non-Jews in the U.S. labor market. Basic quantitative documentation of the labor market status of many racial and ethnic minorities is abundant, but this is less so for Jews. Second, it will consider why Jews have been so successful and explore alternative hypotheses. The latter analysis may prove to be of considerable importance not merely for understanding the labor market adjustment of Jews, but also for the insights applicable to other racial and ethnic minorities, including those who have been less successful. This analysis uses the methodology of social science research. Hypotheses are developed on the basis of analytical reasoning, and then they are tested with data. Hypotheses that are not consistent with the data are rejected, while hypotheses found to be consistent with the data are retained for further analysis. This methodological approach helps focus the discussion and analysis, and is essential for identifying substantive relationships among variables.

The next section of this chapter provides some brief background material on American Jews. In the third section contemporary data are considered regarding the schooling and income of Jews in comparison with other Americans. The fourth section looks backward at turn-of-the-century data to discern the patterns existing at that time, and the fifth considers alternative explanations for the success of American Jews. The concluding section places the Jewish experience in the United States in perspective, and suggests reasons for the differential success among America's racial and ethnic minorities.

Background

Why the Interest?

Studies of the labor market status of Jews are warranted for two fundamental reasons. The first is interest in the status of Jews per se. Jews are one of America's minority groups, and their labor market status is a key element in understanding their experiences in this country and their role in American history. Group specific studies are also relevant for the planning and coordinating activities of the social, cultural and political organization of the ethnic group.

We are also interested in the insights to be gained regarding the determinants of success among racial and ethnic minorities, and hence the operation of the American labor market. By almost any criterion, as a group Jews have been highly successful in the United States. This result arose in spite of a foreign origin, a non-English "mother tongue," and discrimination in access to schooling, in the labor market, in the financial market and in the public sector. By learning more about successful minorities, we may obtain insights regarding general principles for group success, particularly in the face of discrimination. These insights may help us better understand the circumstances of less successful minorities and ultimately may generate sounder policies to aid the disadvantaged.

Historical Background

Jews have played a role in American life since the earliest period.[3] The first American Jews were Sephardics, that is, of Spanish and Portuguese origin, who, after finding shelter from the Inquisition by settling in Dutch-controlled Brazil, fled to Dutch New Amsterdam when the Portuguese displaced the Dutch in 1654. Jews served the new republic during the American Revolution, and participated in the nineteenth-century westward expansion and the growth of the manufacturing and service industries in the nineteenth and twentieth centuries. Discriminated against in the large corporate sectors, Jews were most successful in small businesses and in the light manufacturing and service sectors.

Jewish immigration, however, and hence the Jewish population, was very small until the 1880s. American Jews were primarily of Sephardic and German origins until large-scale immigration began in the 1880s from Eastern Europe. The already established German Jews, some of whom were quite successful in commerce, were at first perturbed by the immigration of their more numerous "poor cousins" from Eastern Europe, who worked in sweatshop conditions and lived in slums.

The mass immigration was disrupted by World War I and was brought to a virtual halt by the "national origins" quota system introduced in the 1920s to curtail immigration from Eastern and Southern Europe. Jews fleeing the persecutions in Europe in the 1930s were largely turned away, but the immigration of some "displaced persons" was permitted after World War II. In more recent years, Jewish emigration from the Soviet Union to the United States has received the most attention.

In the century prior to World War II, overt anti-Semitism limited the opportunities of Jews. Discrimination against Jews in access to higher education was widespread, and discrimination in employment varied by the sector of the economy. Heavy industry, banking, insurance and finance appeared to have the greatest difficulty accepting Jews. In other sectors, however, Jews became industry leaders (e.g., garment manufacturing and entertainment). "Gentlemen's agreements" in employment and "restrictive covenants" in housing were mechanisms for excluding Jews. It would appear that most of these explicit and overt barriers to full Jewish participation in the nation's educational, economic, cultural and political life have disappeared, although it is less obvious that more subtle forms of anti-Semitism do not persist.

Data Availability

There has been relatively little systematic quantitative research on the labor market experiences of American Jews, as distinct from the qualitative treatment in most historical studies. In contrast, during the past three decades there have been numerous quantitative studies of disadvantaged minorities, namely blacks and, more recently, Hispanics. This emphasis has arisen, in part, because the problems of the disadvantaged minorities appear to be the more pressing social issue. However, it has also arisen because of the scarcity of appropriate quantitative information on American Jews.

The major sources of data for studies of the labor market status of minority groups have been the decennial Census of Population and the periodic and special household surveys conducted by the U.S. Bureau of the Census. With the exception of one survey, however, the Census Bureau has not asked religion.[4] As a result, indirect procedures have been used to identify Jews in the U.S. Census data, such as persons of Russian origin or with a Jewish "mother tongue."[5] Other household survey data, generally privately collected, sometimes include a question on religion, but given the high cost of survey research these samples are not large and the sample size for Jews tends to be very small.[6]

There have, however, been surveys that focused exclusively on Jews, such as the 1971 National Jewish Population Survey and the 1981-82 National Survey of American Jews.[7] These surveys are useful for comparisons among Jews and for testing the reliability of alternative methods for identifying Jews in general data. But, as with surveys limited to any one group, comparisons with other census or survey data are fraught with difficulty because of differences in survey methodology, questionnaire design and coding procedures.[8]

The analyses for contemporary American Jews discussed in this chapter are based on two data sources. One is the March 1957 Current Population Survey (CPS), a probability sample of about thirty-five thousand households in which questions were asked regarding the schooling, income, religion and other demographic characteristics of all persons aged fourteen and over.[9] Of these households, 1,100 had a Jewish head.

The March 1957 CPS data suffer from several deficiencies. First, the tables related by the Census Bureau provide limited cross-tabulations, but in the absence of Public Use Sample (micro-data tape) this is the best information available from this source. Second, the absence of data on nativity and year of immigration for the foreign born is a severe limitation. It is known, for example, that, other things being equal, second-generation white male Americans earn 5 percent more than those with native-born parents, and that immigrants in the United States earn less than do comparable native-born men during their first few years in this country, reach earnings parity at about ten to fifteen years of residence, and have higher earnings than the native born if they have been in the United States for more than fifteen years.[10] Since Jews are disproportionately first- and second-generation Americans, immigrant generation may be responsible for some of the income advantages.[11] Finally, it is now the mid-1980s, and much could have happened since the March 1957 CPS.

The other data source is the 1970 Census of Population *15 Percent Questionnaire.* It is the most recent data file that provides a large sample, a mechanism for identifying Jews and non-Jews, and a statistical control for immigrant generation. Among adult, native-born white men with a foreign-born parent (i.e., second-generation Americans), those who reported their mother tongue to be Yiddish, Hebrew or Ladino are classified as Jews, while those with a different mother tongue are classified as non-Jewish.[12] It is estimated that this procedure permits the identification of about 60 percent of second-generation American Jews, and that fewer than 5 percent of those identified as non-Jewish are actually Jews with a non-Jewish mother tongue.[13] Tests suggest that the procedure does not generate biases in means or in the partial effects of explanatory variables (regression coefficients). The procedure was limited to second-generation Americans to avoid confounding the findings by the experiences of immigrants in their country of origin, and because of the substantial loss of the Jewish mother tongues among American Jews with both parents born in the United States.

Income and Its Determinants

The data from the March 1957 Current Population Survey (CPS) indicate that American Jews have a higher level of income than the other major religious groups (Table 1). Among men aged fourteen and over with income, Jews received $4,900, 36 percent more than the overall median and 24 percent more than the next highest group, Roman Catholics. Jewish women also had higher incomes than the other women, 45 percent more than the overall median and 13 percent more than Roman Catholic women.

TABLE 1
MEDIAN INCOME OF PERSONS AGED 14 AND OVER WITH INCOME, BY RELIGION, 1956

	All Persons		Employed Persons in Urban Areas— Standardized by Occupation[b]	
Religion	Male	Female	Male	Female
Jewish	$4,900	$1,660	$4,773	$2,352
Protestant	3,463	1,040	3,780	2,031
White	3,728	1,198	4,553	2,263
Non-white	2,005	776	3,038	1,831
Roman Catholic	3,954	1,470	4,509	2,282
TOTAL	3,608[a]	1,146[a]	4,472[c]	2,255[c]

Source: U.S. Bureau of the Census, "Tabulations of Data on the Social and Economic Characteristics of Major Religious Groups, March 1957," unpublished tables, no date, Table 18.

[a]Includes persons with other religion, no religion and religion not reported.

[b]Within each sex, standardized by major occupation group for the urban employed in the three major religions.

[c]For the three major religious groups.

To some extent the high income of Jews may be related to their place of residence. Reported incomes are lower in rural areas in part because of a lower cost of living (e.g., shelter), and in part because more income is received "in-kind" through own-production (particularly for farmers). American Jews are less likely than others to live in rural areas or to be employed in agriculture.[14]

Another measure of labor market outcome is occupational status. American Jews are more likely to be employed in higher-status occupations such as professional and managerial jobs (see Table 2 on p. 102). In 1957, one-fifth of the employed male Jews were professionals compared with about one-tenth for other whites; over three-tenths of the Jews were managers and proprietors, also more than double the proportion for other whites. Jews were three times more likely to be craftsmen, foremen or operatives, one-third as likely to be in service occupations, and one-tenth as likely to be laborers (non-farm); Jews were even more scarce in agricultural jobs.

TABLE 2

OCCUPATIONAL DISTRIBUTION OF EMPLOYED MALES
AGED 18 AND OVER BY RELIGION, 1957 (PERCENT)

Occupation	Religion						Ratio Jewish to Total[b]
	Jewish	Protestant			Roman Catholic	Total[a]	
		Total	White	Black			
White Collar							
Professional, Technical and Kindred	20.3	9.9	10.9	2.6	8.9	9.9	2.1
Managers and Proprietors (Except Farm)	31.1	12.6	14.1	2.2	12.5	13.3	2.3
Clerical	8.0	6.5	6.8	4.1	8.4	6.9	1.2
Sales	14.1	5.3	6.0	0.5	4.8	5.4	2.6
Blue-Collar, Farm and Services							
Craftsmen and Foreman	8.9	19.8	21.2	9.7	22.5	20.0	0.4
Operatives	10.1	20.5	19.7	27.0	22.4	20.9	0.5
Service	2.3	5.5	4.3	14.1	7.7	6.1	0.4
Agricultural[c]	0.2	11.9	11.7	13.4	5.5	9.8	0.02
Laborers (Except Farm)	0.8	8.0	5.4	26.4	7.4	7.7	0.1
TOTAL	100.0	100.0	100.0	100.0	100.0	100.0	

Source: U.S. Bureau of the Census, "Tabulations of Data on the Social and Economic
    Characteristics of Major Religious Groups, March 1957," unpublished tables,
    no date, Table 15.

[a]Includes persons not reporting the three major religious groups.

[b]Ratio of Jewish to total.

[c]Includes farmers, farm managers, foremen and farm laborers.

Although income and occupation are both measures of labor market
status (or success), it is useful to investigate whether the income differences among the three major religious groups reported in columns (1)
and (2) of Table 1 are due to differences in occupational attainment.
Columns (3) and (4) in Table 1 consider only employed persons in urban areas, thereby controlling for group differences in the proportion
living in urban and rural areas. In addition, the median income data
control for group differences in occupational status by standardizing
for this variable.[15] These two modifications substantially narrow
group differences in median incomes. Among adult males the ranking
changes as white Protestants now have slightly higher incomes than
Roman Catholics. The Jewish income advantage, however, is 6.7 percent overall, 5.9 percent compared to Catholics, and 4.8 percent compared to white Protestants. Thus, on average, among urban men in the

same major occupational category, Jews had higher incomes than other white men.

To what extent is the high income of Jews due to their level of schooling? The data from the March 1957 CPS indicate that for all persons aged twenty-five and over, and among employed men, the median schooling of Jews is 1.5 years more than the overall median and one year more than white Protestants (Table 3). Among men living in urban areas, there is little difference in earnings between Jews and other men for those with less than eight years of schooling (see Table 4 on p. 104). Among those with twelve years of schooling, the median Jewish income exceeded the overall median by 7.7 percent, and among those with sixteen or more years of schooling the Jewish median is 30.1 percent higher. Compared to white Protestants, the Jewish earnings advantage is 4.9 percent and 26 percent, respectively, for those with twelve and sixteen or more years of schooling. Thus, at the median schooling level Jews earn more than other white men, and their earnings advantage is greater the higher the level of schooling.

TABLE 3

MEDIAN YEARS OF SCHOOLING COMPLETED BY RELIGION,
MARCH 1957

Religion	Persons Aged 25 and Over	Employed Persons Aged 18 and Over	
		Male	Female
Jewish	12.3	12.7	12.6
Protestant	10.7	11.2	12.1
White	11.3	11.7	12.3
Nonwhite	Under 8	8.0	8.8
Roman Catholic	10.4	11.3	12.1
TOTAL[a]	10.6	11.2	12.1

Source: U.S. Bureau of the Census, "Tabulations of Data on the Social and Economic Characteristics of Major Religious Groups, March 1957," unpublished tables, no date, Tables 2 and 12.

[a]Includes persons with other religion, no religion and religion not reported. For persons aged twenty-five and over the median for "Other Religion" is 8.9 years, and for "No Religion" it is 8.6 years.

TABLE 4

MEDIAN INCOME OF URBAN MEN
AGED 14 AND OVER BY RELIGION AND EDUCATION, 1956

Years of Schooling Completed	Jewish	Protestant Total	Protestant White	Protestant Black	Roman Catholic	Total[a]
0-7	$2,609	$2,558	$2,812	$2,249	$2,819	$2,654
8	3,844	3,582	3,712	2,864	3,729	3,631
9-11	4,672	3,639	4,850	2,849	4,170	3,858
12	4,913	4,628	4,684	3,092	4,567	4,563
13-15	5,026	4,529	4,712	b	4,361	4,526
16	8,041	6,049	6,375	b	5,727	6,179

Source: U.S. Bureau of the Census, "Tabulations of Data on the Social and Economic
   Characteristics of Major Religious Groups, March 1957," unpublished tables,
   no date, Table 19.

[a]Includes persons with other religion, no religion and religion not reported.

[b]Sample size too small for the reporting of medians.

TABLE 5

MEANS OF VARIABLES FOR SECOND-GENERATION ADULT
WHITE MEN, BY RELIGION, 1970

Variable	Jewish[a]	Non-Jewish	Total
Earnings ($)	16,176	10,431	10,781
Age (years)	49.2	47.2	47.3
Schooling (years)	14.0	11.7	11.8
Residence			
Rural (percent)	2.2	16.7	15.8
Southern (percent)	10.5	9.7	9.7
Population (percent)	6.1	93.9	100.0

Source: U.S. Bureau of the Census, *1970 Census of Population, Public Use Sample, 15
   Percent Questionnaire*, (data tape, one-in-a-hundred sample, 1973).

[a]Persons who reported Yiddish, Hebrew or Ladino as their mother tongue.

Similar patterns emerge in the analysis using the 1970 Census of
Population data. Among second-generation American men, the Jews
had 55 percent higher earnings, 2.3 more years of schooling, and were
more likely to live in urban areas, but had a similar proportion living in
the South (Table 5).[16] The higher earnings of Jews is in part attributable to their higher level of schooling and urban residence. Using multi-
ple regression analysis to control statistically for schooling and demographic variables (age, martial status, place of residence), Jews have a
statistically significant 16 percent higher earnings than second-generation white, non-Jewish American men of British parentage (Table 6).
Earnings of other non-Jewish men do not differ from those of British
origin, except for those of Mexican and French-Canadian parentage
who have lower earnings.[17,18]

TABLE 6

PARTIAL EFFECT OF BEING JEWISH AND PARENT'S COUNTRY OF BIRTH FOR NON-JEWS ON EARNINGS FOR NATIVE-BORN ADULT MEN WITH FOREIGN-BORN PARENTS, 1970[a]

Origin	Percent Difference in Earnings	t-ratio
British Isles	—	—
Jewish[b]	16.0	12.41
Western Europe	-0.9	-0.95
Southern Europe	-1.0	-1.12
Central Europe	-0.2	-0.16
U.S.S.R.	5.8	4.63
Balkans	2.1	1.34
Canada	-3.9	-3.33
Mexico	-21.5	-14.68
Other Latin America	-0.6	-0.14
Asia/Africa	-0.5	-0.22

Source: Barry R. Chiswick, "The Earnings and Human Capital of American Jews," *Journal of Human Resources*, XVIII:3(June 1983): 313-336.

[a]British Isles is the benchmark. Controlling for schooling, labor market experience, marital status, and urban/rural, South/non-South residence. Country categories are defined by parent's country of birth for non-Jews.

[b]Persons who reported Yiddish, Hebrew or Ladino as their mother tongue.

As indicated above, a person's occupation, as well as earnings, can be thought of as an outcome of the human capital investment and labor market processes. Yet, it is instructive to determine whether the higher earnings level of Jews is attributable to their higher occupational status.[19] Controlling for the major occupational categories reduces the earnings advantage of Jews from 16 percent to 10 percent. That is, one-third of the higher earnings of Jews of the same schooling, age, marital status and area of residence as non-Jews is due to their higher occupational status.

About half of American Jews live in the urban areas of New York, New Jersey and Connecticut.[20] This is the residence of about one-fifth of non-Jews. Could the higher earnings of Jews be attributable to their disproportionate residence in these high-income northeastern states? Even when the census data are limited to urban areas in these three states, Jews have a statistically significant 8 percent higher earnings than other native-born white men.

The census data on American Jews can also be used to compare the schooling and earnings of native-born American Jews with native-born members of other racial and ethnic groups (see Table 7 on p. 106).[21] In these data Jewish men have higher earnings than any other group. Native-born Chinese and Japanese men (primarily second-generation Americans) have earnings similar to foreign-parentage white men, and all three have earnings greater than white men with native-born parents (third- and higher-generation Americans). The disadvantaged minorities, as measured by their earnings, are the Mexican Americans, blacks, Filipinos and American Indians. The ranking by educational attainment is similar to that of earnings, the main exception being that Chinese and Japanese men have a higher schooling level than do white men.

TABLE 7

CHARACTERISTICS OF ADULT NATIVE-
BORN MEN BY RACE AND ETHNIC GROUP, 1970[a]

Race and Ethnic Group	Earnings ($)	Age (years)	Schooling (years)	Partial Effect of Schooling on Earnings[b] (percent)	Sample Size[c]
White					
All	9,653	42.7	11.9	7.0	33,878
Native-Born Parents	9,441	41.7	11.9	6.9	27,512
Foreign-Born Parents	10,567	47.1	11.9	7.2	6,366
Jewish[d]	16,176	49.2	14.0	8.0	3,719
Non-Jewish[d]	10,431	47.2	11.7	6.8	57,351
Mexican-Origin[e]					
All	6,330	39.5	9.3	5.2	4,949
Native-Born Parents	6,602	38.8	9.7	5.0	2,724
Foreign-Born Parents	6,664	40.3	8.9	5.7	2,225
Black (Urban)					
All	6,126	42.0	9.9	4.4	26,413
Native-Born Parents	6,110	42.0	9.9	4.4	26,137
Foreign-Born Parents	7,719	39.0	11.8	6.8	276
Japanese	10,272	43.4	12.7	6.5	2,063
Chinese	10,406	41.4	13.1	6.7	627
Filipino	7,173	37.3	11.3	4.5	335
American Indians[f]	5,593	40.0	9.9	5.4	1,894

Source: Barry R. Chiswick, "Differences in Educational Attainment Among Racial and Ethnic Groups: Patterns and Hypotheses Regarding the Quantity and Quality of Children" (Mimeograph, University of Illinois at Chicago: 1983).

[a]The data are for men aged twenty-five to sixty-four in 1970 who worked and had non-zero earnings in 1969. Earnings are defined as wage, salary and self-employment income. The Asian data exclude men in the armed forces in 1970; the Jewish/non-Jewish data exclude persons enrolled in school.

bCoefficient of schooling from the linear regression of the natural logarithm of earnings in 1969 on schooling, experience, experience squared, marital status dummy variable, geographic distribution, and for some regressions, weeks worked. Geographic distribution is urban/rural and South/Non-South, except for the Asian analysis in which it is Hawaii/California/South/Other Non-South and urban/rural.

cThe sampling fractions are 1/1,000 for white men, 1/100 for the Mexican, Jewish/non-Jewish and black men, and 2/100 for Asian and American Indian men.

dThe Jewish/non-Jewish data are for native-born men of foreign parentage (one or both parents foreign born), where Jews are defined as those reporting Yiddish, Hebrew or Ladino as their mother tongue (language other than or in addition to English spoken in the home when the respondent was a child).

eThe Mexican analysis is for Spanish-surnamed men living in the five southwestern states with either an English or Spanish mother tongue and with parents born in the United States or Mexico. Although the data are limited to whites, over 95 percent of the Mexican-origin population was classified as white in the 1970 Census. The schooling coefficient is 4.9 percent for those with a Spanish mother tongue.

fExcludes men living in Alaska.

It was noted previously (Table 4) that in the 1957 data the ratio of the earnings of Jews to non-Jews increased with the level of schooling. The same pattern emerges in the 1970 Census data. The partial effect of an extra year of schooling on earnings (from a regression equation) is higher for Jews than for any other group (Table 7). This finding is quite robust; it persists even after holding constant occupational attainment or residence in the New York metropolitan area. The larger effect of schooling on earnings implies that Jews receive a higher rate of return on this investment than do others. The greater profitability of schooling for Jews may explain their higher level of investment.

Jews in America at the Turn of the Century

The majority of adult, native-born American Jews in the post-World War II period are the descendants of immigrants who came to the United States from Eastern Europe during the period from 1880 to World War I. It is useful to examine the labor market status of turn-of-the-century Jewish immigrants to ascertain the foundation from which the contemporary Jewish labor market achievements emerged.

The turn-of-the-century data suggest two conclusions. One is that the skill level of turn-of-the-century Jewish immigrants enabled them to close the earnings gap with the native born and immigrants from Northern and Western Europe. The other is that a comparison of the relative labor market status of American Jews from the turn of the century to the post-World War I period indicates a steeper rate of increase in occupational status and earnings for Jews than for non-Jews.

Arcadius Kahan has written, "While the Jewish immigrants from Eastern Europe brought along little money or physical assets, their value for the U.S. economy and the source of their expected incomes consisted of their skill endowment and their ability to employ their skills gainfully."[22] Data on the occupational distribution of pre-World War I Jewish immigrants prior to their arrival indicate that nearly two-thirds had been employed in manufacturing (of whom half were in clothing manufacturing), about one-quarter were in commerce, and relatively few were laborers, agricultural workers or professionals.[23] Turn-of-the-century Jewish social welfare agencies facilitated the improvement in the economic status of Jewish workers by providing them with training opportunities and assistance in finding work.

Kahan indicates that Jewish immigrants were earning about the same as other immigrants in the same industry.[24] This implies they were earning more than other Eastern and Southern European immigrants, but less than those from Northern and Western Europe. He also concludes that each cohort of Jewish immigrants caught up to the earnings of native-born American workers of the same age and occupation within ten to fifteen years of residence in the United States. These achievements are attributed to the high proportion of skilled workers among the Jews, and their urban residence.[25]

The Dillingham Immigration Commission, established to study the condition of European immigrants in the United States and to propose immigration reform, conducted a survey of about one-half million workers in mining and manufacturing in 1909. The commission's report, published in 1911, included detailed cross-tabulations that have recently been used by social scientists to study turn-of-the-century immigrants. Robert Higgs reports data on adult men for the weekly earnings, English-speaking ability, literacy and duration of U.S. residence of thirty-five white foreign-born groups, including Russian Jews and other Jews, and the native-born (Table 8).[26]

The Jewish immigrants, whether of Russian or other origin, had higher weekly earnings than the foreign born. The earnings advantage over the white foreign born was 8 percent for Russian Jews, 22 percent for other Jews and 11 percent when the Russian and other Jews were combined. To some extent the high earnings of Jews is attributable to the larger proportion of Jews who could speak English (76 percent compared to 64 percent) and who were literate (93 percent compared to 86 percent). Although the proportion residing in the United States

TABLE 8

EARNINGS AND OTHER CHARACTERISTICS OF ADULT MALE WORKERS IN MINING AND MANUFACTURING, 1909

Group	Average Weekly Earnings ($)	Percent Speaking English	Percent Literate[a]	Percent Residing In U.S. for Less Than Five Years
Foreign Born				
All[b]	11.81	63.6	85.6	38.1
Jewish[c]	13.16	76.0	93.2	38.4
Russian Jews	12.71	74.7	93.3	42.9
Other Jews	14.37	79.5	92.8	26.2
Native Born				
White	14.37	(d)	98.2	(d)
Black	10.66	(d)	76.4	(d)

Source: Robert Higgs, "Race, Skills, and Earnings: American Immigrants in 1909," *Journal of Economic History*, XXXI: 2(June 1971): 420-428.

[a]Able to read a language.

[b]Weighted average for thirty-five foreign-born groups from Europe, Canada, Turkey and Syria, including the two Jewish categories.

[c]Weighted average. Sample size was 3,177 for Russian Jews and 1,158 for other Jews. Jews were 3.2 percent of the sample.

[d]Not reported. Assumed to be 100 percent for the native born.

for fewer than five years was the same for Jews and non-Jews (38 percent), a larger proportion of the Russian Jews and a smaller proportion of other Jews were recent immigrants. Controlling for these determinants of earnings, the Jews had 3 to 5 percent higher earnings than other foreign-born men, but the difference is not statistically significant.[27]

Compared to the white native born, the turn-of-the-century Jewish immigrants had 8 percent lower earnings, that is, 12 percent lower earnings for Russian Jews and no difference for other Jews. If the Jews had the same proportion in the United States for five or more years as the white native born (100 percent), with no change in literacy, the earnings disadvantage of the Jews would disappear (1 percent lower earnings for all Jews, 3 percent lower earnings for Russian Jews and 5 percent higher earnings for other Jews).

The comparison of the Dillingham Commission data with the 1957 CPS and 1970 Census data suggests that, both overall and when other variables are the same, the relative earnings of Jewish men have improved dramatically over the period.

Alternative Explanations

The high level of schooling and earnings of contemporary American Jews appears to be unique. What factors can account for this impressive economic performance? Over the years, several explanations have been advanced. These include a cultural preference for education, a history of education and labor market discrimination, a history of persecution, and greater productivity in acquiring or implementing education. This section considers these explanations, which are not necessarily mutually exclusive.

Cultural Preferences for Education

Jews are sometimes referred to as the "People of the Book," but this is in reference to the Bible rather than a commentary on contemporary educational levels. As a group, Jews do apparently have a keen interest in learning. In Europe, especially Eastern Europe, learning to read Hebrew and studying the "Torah" (the first five books of the Bible) and the commentaries were prized in a son or son-in-law. This "love of learning" in European Jewry may well have been translated into a thirst for secular education in twentieth-century America. For example, in their discussions of the higher level of education of American Jews, Alice Kessler-Harris and Virginia Yans-McLaughlin wrote: "Religious tradition and community approval encouraged the Jew in America to invest in education and correspondingly to increase his upward mobility. No other group had this advantage . . . Jews came to America with a tradition of such sacrifice."[28] And, "when choices had to be made, such groups as Italians, Irish and Poles would sacrifice the educational interests of their young, withdrawing them from school, sending them to work, and absorbing their earnings. Such decisions increased present earnings at the expense of future skills. Jews do not seem to have made similar compromises."[29]

This explanation suggests that Jews value education for far more than just its monetary benefits; part of the benefit is fulfilling cultural and peer group expectations. As a result, Jews would be expected to continue their schooling for longer than is warranted by purely pecuniary reasons. This is consistent with the high level of schooling, and a high level of schooling would account for high earnings. It also implies an over-investment in schooling, that is, a lower rate of return. This arises from acquiring schooling even if it is not financially profitable. Expressed in a different manner, it implies that at each level of schooling Jews would have a lower average level of ability and lower earnings than non-Jews.

Empirically, however, Jews have higher earnings than non-Jews at each level of schooling (beyond eight years) and a higher rate of return from schooling. This suggests that if Jews do have a cultural thirst for education, it is not the cause of their high level of education. Rather, it may be a consequence of either the education itself or whatever it is that generates the large investments in education.

Discrimination

American Jews have experienced discrimination in the labor market and in access to higher education. While overt discrimination has diminished in recent decades, there is no doubt as to its presence when the cohort of adults in the 1957 or 1970 data discussed previously was of school age and making investment decisions.[30] One would expect discrimination to result in a lower rate of return from schooling, unless discrimination is much more intense against those with lower levels of schooling. Indeed, for most disadvantaged groups, labor market and educational discrimination are offered as important explanations for their lower levels of earnings and educational attainment, and smaller rate of return from schooling. Yet, American Jews apparently have a higher level of schooling and higher rates of return from schooling.

It might be said, however, that discrimination spurred the American Jews on to do better. This raises two questions: Why did it spur them to do *even* better than non-Jews? Why did other groups who experienced discrimination not respond in the same manner (except possibly for the Chinese and Japanese)? A more compelling explanation, however, is that the Jews were successful despite, rather than because of, the discrimination. If so, their labor market achievements in the United States would have been even more impressive if not for anti-Semitism.

Persecution

It is useful to distinguish between discrimination and persecution. Under discrimination, a person may be denied access to a job or entry into a particular school. Discrimination is passive. Persecution, on the other hand, is more active—one fears for one's life and property. Persecution, in addition to discrimination, in Eastern Europe from the 1880s was instrumental in generating a massive emigration of Jews, mostly to North America, but with smaller streams settling in Western Europe and Palestine, among other places. The "pogroms" were part of a long chain of persecutions that had periodically driven Jews back and forth across Europe since the early Middle Ages. Well imprinted in the subconscious and culture of European Jews was that, because of anti-Semitism, no place was secure, no tolerance could be guaranteed to last.[31]

The appropriate response to such externally-generated insecurity is to avoid investments that are "geographic specific," that is, investments that are productive in one location but not in other locations. "Human capital" is embodied in the person and therefore it is portable. Hence, European Jews would have an incentive to invest in human capital rather than other assets. Given the intensity of the past persecution, this view was imprinted on the subconscious and culture of American Jews. The tendency could only have been encouraged by the continued persecutions of other Jews in Europe and elsewhere, and by the anti-Semitism experienced in the United States. Thus, persecution encouraged Jews to tilt their investments in favor of schooling.[32]

There are several problems with this hypothesis. Although human capital is embodied in the person, it is not obvious that this form of capital is always more transferable than non-human assets. Properly specified, the hypothesis suggests that persecuted groups would invest in transferable and liquid assets rather than assets that are merely portable. Legal training, for example, is highly portable, but unlike medicine, for institutional and other reasons, the skills are not transferable across geographic areas. One test of the hypothesis is whether American Jews have a stronger preference for medicine than for law. Relative to other second-generation white American men, Jews do not show a preference for medicine over law.[33]

The hypothesis also implies a substitution away from other investments in favor of education. It is not obvious that Jews have made smaller investments in other assets, other things the same. In addition, the implication of over-investing in education because of its portability or transferability would be a lower monetary rate of return on the investment. Yet, as indicated above, Jews appear to have a higher rate of return than any other group.

While undoubtedly a history of persecutions has implications for the subconscious and culture of a group, and hence the group's behavior, the process is undoubtedly complex, and persecution appears to be inadequate for explaining the high level of education, earnings and rate of return from schooling among American Jews.

High Productivity of Education

The apparently higher rate of return from schooling for Jews is consistent with the hypothesis that Jews are more productive in converting education into earnings. This may arise because Jews acquire a higher quality (or more units) of human capital in a year of schooling or because they are more effective in using their human capital in the labor market.[34] The higher rate of return would encourage greater investments in human capital and result in a higher schooling level and higher occupational status.[35] These differences may be the result of investments made by parents in their children's human capital prior to and concurrent with schooling.[36]

Parents may be viewed as making rational decisions regarding the "number" and "quality per child" of their children.[37] While "number" is relatively easy to measure, investments in "child quality," the value of the time and other resources parents devote to their children, are not easily measured. Racial and ethnic groups may differ in their optimal combination of the number and quality of children because they face different opportunities or "relative prices." Fertility is higher where contraception is more expensive because of cultural or religious proscriptions, it is higher in rural areas where space is cheaper and children can do productive work at an earlier age, and it is higher among women who have less schooling or who for other reasons have poorer labor market opportunities. Higher levels of fertility imply lower investments of parental time and other resources per child, and hence lower child quality.[38]

American Jews are a predominantly urban population that, in general, does not have religious prohibitions on contraception. American Jewish women have a high level of education. These considerations, by themselves, would lead one to expect a lower fertility rate among American Jewish women.

Jewish women apparently do have lower fertility rates (see Table 9 on p. 114).[39] Among urban women aged fifteen to forty-four years in March 1957, standardizing for age, there were 1.2 children ever born per Jewish woman compared with 1.5 overall and for Protestants and Catholics. The Jewish/non-Jewish differential is slightly larger for ever-married women in urban areas, 1.6 children for Jewish women and 2.0 for all Protestant and Catholic women.[40] The data for women under age forty-five, however, may be reflecting their own high

TABLE 9
MEDIAN NUMBER OF CHILDREN EVER BORN PER
1,000 WOMEN BY RELIGION, MARCH 1957

Panel A: Women 15 to 44 years, Standardized by Age[a]

Religion and Race	Women of All Marital Classes		Ever-Married Women	
	U.S.	Urban	U.S.	Urban
Total[b]	1,677	1,504	2,188	2,009
Protestant	1,733	1,541	2,206	1,992
Roman Catholic	1,610	1,493	2,210	2,093
Jewish[c]	1,184	1,184	1,598	1,598
Non-White[d]	1,990	1,642	2,653	2,220

Panel B: Ever-married Women, Age 45 and Older

Detailed Religion	Children Ever Born
Total	2,798
Protestant	2,753
Baptist	3,275
Lutheran	2,382
Methodist	2,638
Presbyterian	2,188
Other Protestant	2,702
Roman Catholic	3,056
Jewish	2,218
Other, none and not reported	2,674

Source: U.S. Bureau of the Census, "Tabulations of Data on the Social and Economic
   Characteristics of Major Religious Groups, March 1957," mimeo, no date, Ta-
   bles 1, 6 and 10; and U.S. Bureau of the Census, *Statistical Abstract of the United
   States: 1958* (Washington, D.C.: 1958), Table 40, p. 41

[a]Standardized by age of all ever-married women, 1950.

[b]Includes persons of other religion, no religion and religion not reported.

[c]Although urban data for Jews are not shown separately in the source, 96 percent of Jews
age fourteen and over live in urban areas. The U.S. rate is used in urban areas for Jews for
purposes of comparison.

[d]Includes persons of all religions. Ninety percent of nonwhite wives are Protestant.

education and the high level of the education and earnings of their husbands. More compelling are the data on number of children ever born
for women aged forty-five and older. These women have completed
their fertility and these decisions were made on the basis of the relative
economic opportunities available in earlier decades. Among older ever-
married women, Jews had 2.2 children per woman, compared with 2.8
overall and for Protestants, and 3.1 for Catholics. Each of the major
Protestant denominations, with the exception of the Presbyterians,
had higher fertility rates than Jews.[41]

The lower fertility rate among American Jews is not reflecting a recent U.S. phenomenon.[42] The limited data on European Jewish fertility in the nineteenth century suggest that it was lower than the fertility

rate of non-Jews. In this country, various sources also suggest lower fertility at the turn of the century and throughout the twentieth century. For example, the Rhode Island State Census of 1905 indicated that the average family size for native-born Jewish women was 2.3, compared to an average of 2.5 for native-born Protestants and 3.2 for native-born Catholics.[43]

Labor force participation rates of women vary systematically by economic and demographic characteristics. They tend to be higher for women in urban areas, with higher levels of education and with fewer children, particularly young children. For these reasons, one would expect Jewish women to have higher labor force participation rates than other women.[44] The data, however, indicate just the opposite. The 1957 Current Population Survey data indicate that in each broad age group, married Jewish women have lower labor force participation rates than Protestant or Catholic women. By implication, the Jewish women are more likely to be staying home and providing care to their smaller number of children prior to and concurrent with schooling.

TABLE 10
LABOR FORCE PARTICIPATION RATES FOR MARRIED WOMEN, SPOUSE PRESENT, BY RELIGION, MARCH 1957

Group	Total[a]	Protestant Total	White	Non-White	Roman Catholic	Jewish
Total	29.6	30.7	29.6	40.4	27.3	27.8
Age						
Under 35	27.7	29.2	28.5	34.4	24.6	21.7
35-44	35.7	37.8	36.1	51.1	31.5	24.5
45-64	32.3	32.9	31.6	45.0	30.9	30.6
65 and Over	6.4	6.0	6.2	—	6.7	—
Presence of Children						
No Children Under 18	35.6	35.7	34.1	47.7	36.6	30.0
With Children 6-17, None Under 6	36.7	37.5	36.2	52.6	35.3	28.6
With Children Under 6	17.0	18.9	18.2	23.6	13.2	11.8
Urban Areas—Age						
Total	31.2	33.1	31.5	43.6	28.5	24.8
Under 35	30.2	32.7	31.6	39.2	26.3	21.8
35-64	34.9	36.9	35.1	49.0	32.2	28.2
65 and Over	6.1	5.8	5.7	—	6.2	—

Source: U.S. Bureau of the Census, "Tabulations of Data on the Social and Economic Characteristics of Major Religious Groups, March, 1957," no date, Table 13.
[a]Includes persons with other religion, no religion and religion not reported.

Thus, the high labor market productivity of Jewish men may be a consequence of their having had fewer siblings with whom to compete for parental time and other resources. This may have arisen in part because of a lower cost of contraception and a higher cost of additional children. In addition, Jewish children may benefit from the greater parental input of resources, family size held constant, as is suggested by the lower Jewish female labor force participation rate.[45]

Investments in child quality are facilitated by stable family living arrangements. More parental time and other resources can be invested if both parents are available. Thus, lower rates of out-of-wedlock births and of divorce, separation and desertion would be associated with higher child quality. In addition, a lower frequency of "deviant behavior" on the part of parents would also tend to improve child quality. In an essay on motivation among American Jews, Nathan Hurvitz cites studies showing lower rates among Jews of divorce, separation and desertion, juvenile delinquency, adult crime, alcoholism, psychoses, suicide and deaths from violent causes. He concludes that studies of marital instability and deviant behavior "associated with disorganized family life therefore indicate that American Jews may have greater family solidarity and stability."[46]

Concluding Remarks

This chapter has considered both the patterns and the determinants of the labor market status of American Jews. Data from the March 1957 Current Population Survey and the 1970 Census of Population indicate that American Jewish men have higher levels of schooling and labor market earnings, and a higher rate of return from schooling than men of other racial and ethnic groups. This does not mean that there is no poverty among Jews, as there is a large variation in circumstances within any racial and ethnic group. It does mean, however, that as a group Jews have been perhaps the most successful minority. Comparisons of turn-of-the-century data with contemporary data suggest that American Jews have experienced a steeper rise in occupational attainment and earnings than other white men. This is most impressive given the recent arrival in the United States of the bulk of the Jewish population, their foreign "mother tongue," and the past discrimination against American Jews in the labor market and in access to education.

The higher rate of return from schooling may be causing the high level of investment in education and hence the high earnings. But what explains the high rate of return? American Jews may be more productive than others not because of genetic differences, but because of greater parental investments of their own time and other resources in each child. These greater investments are possible because of a substitution of higher "child quality" for a greater number of children. The fertility rate of Jewish women has been substantially below that of other women. This substitution in favor of child quality for Jews was undoubtedly encouraged by the (virtual) absence of religious prohibitions on fertility control, residence in urban areas, and the high level of schooling of Jewish mothers.

In addition, in the past Jewish women had very low rates of labor force participation even though their urban residence, education level and number of children should suggest high participation rates. Apparently, Jewish mothers are more likely to be providing child care to their smaller number of children prior to and concurrent with schooling.

Alternative explanations that appear in the literature are inconsistent with the data. Some suggest that the Jewish "thirst for education" is the direct causal factor, but this is merely describing the outcome of the process that generates the high level of education. The spur of anti-Semitism to do even better is sometimes suggested, but does not explain why Jews became so successful, and why many other groups that experienced discrimination in the United States are much less successful than average. The insecurity of location-specific assets for a persecuted minority implies investments in transferable and liquid human and non-human assets, but only some of the types of schooling (e.g., medicine rather than law) in which Jews have made large investments satisfy this requirement. Other persecuted groups do not seem to have attained a similar level of success. These alternative hypotheses all predict a lower rate of return from schooling for American Jews than the majority white population. The data indicate, however, that the rate of return from schooling is greater for Jews than for the majority white population and other racial and ethnic minorities.

This hypothesis regarding the trade-off of quantity and quality of children offers a compelling framework for analyzing group differences in labor market status. But it is a hypothesis that requires more investigation. To what extent is there an independent Jewish effect encouraging more of a preference for quality over quantity of children than would exist for other groups, even if all other factors were the same? Did the Jewish culture and experience help influence a pattern of behavior that results in the economic betterment of the average member of the group, while at the same time tending to reduce the size of the group? Will increased "Americanization" of the American Jewish culture alter behavior patterns and reduce their relative labor market success? To what extent can this approach provide insights into the poorer labor market performance of the less successful racial and ethnic minorities?

If nothing else, the analysis suggests that Jewish mothers, though much ridiculed by Jewish writers and entertainers, and Jewish fathers played key roles in the economic success of their children, in large measure, by making rational choices in favor of quality of child rather than quantity of children.

NOTES

[1] Bernard Lazerwitz, "Jewish Christian Marriages and Conversions," *Jewish Social Studies*, XLIV:1 (Winter 1981): 31-46.

[2] For a discussion of these concerns see Calvin Goldscheider, "Demography and American Jewish Survival" in Milton Himmelfarb and Victor Baras, eds., *Zero Population Growth—For Whom? Differential Fertility and Minority Group Survival* (Westport, Conn.: Greenwood Press, 1978), pp. 119-148.

[3] There is a voluminous literature on the history of Jews in America. See, for example, Irving Howe, *World of Our Fathers: The Journey of the East European Jews to America and the Life They Found and Made* (New York: Harcourt, Brace, Jovanovich, 1976) and Ande Manners, *Poor Cousins* (Greenwich, Conn.: Fawcett Crest Books, 1973). For a set of essays on the economic history of Jews, see Nachum Gross, ed., *Economic History of the Jews* (New York, Schocken Books, 1975).

[4] The exception is the *Supplement* to the March 1957 *Current Population Survey*. Although some tables have been released, the Census Bureau has not made available a public use sample (microdata file). The Census Bureau has recently introduced a question about ethnic ancestry into its censuses and surveys, but the question does not permit identification of religiously-based ethnic groups such as Jews.

[5] See, for example, Barry R. Chiswick, "The Earnings and Human Capital of American Jews," *Journal of Human Resources*, XVIII:3 (June 1983): 313-336, and Erich Rosenthal, "The Equivalence of United States Census Data for Persons of Russian Stock or Descent with American Jews: An Evaluation," *Demography*, 12:2 (May 1975): 275-290.

[6] The data include the National Opinion Research Center General Social Survey, the Princeton Fertility Sample, the National Bureau of Economic Research-Thorndyke Sample, and the National Academy of Sciences Twin Sample. See, for example, Jere R. Behrman, et al., *Socioeconomic Success* (Amsterdam: North-Holland, 1980); David Featherman, "The Socioeconomic Achievement of White Religio-Ethnic Subgroups: Social and Psychological Explanations," *American Sociological Review*, 36:2 (April 1971): 207-222; Galen L. Gockel, "Income and Religious Affiliation: A Regression Analysis," *American Journal of Sociology*, 74:6 (May 1969): 632-646; and Andrew M. Greeley, *Ethnicity, Denomination and Inequality* (Beverly Hills: Sage Publication, 1976). These studies also show higher levels of schooling, occupational attainment and income for Jews, but the Jewish samples are small.

[7] See, for example, Fred Massarik and Alvin Chenkin, "United States National Jewish Population Study: A First Report," *American Jewish Year Book, 1973* (New York: American Jewish Committee, 1973), pp. 264-308; Fred Massarik, "National Jewish Population Study: A New United States Estimate," *American Jewish Year Book, 1974-75* (New York: American Jewish Committee, 1974), pp. 299-300; and Steven Martin Cohen, "The 1981-82 National Survey of American Jews," *American Jewish Year Book, 1983* (New York: American Jewish Committee, 1983), pp. 89-111.

[8]For an interesting comparative analysis based on data from several contemporary sources, see Erich Rosenthal, "The Jewish Population of the United States: A Demographic and Sociological Analysis," in Bernard Martin, ed., *Movements and Issues in American Judaism* (Westport, Conn.: Greenwood Press, 1978), pp. 25-62.

[9]The question on religion in the special *Supplement* was, "What was your religion—Baptist, Lutheran, etc.?" The data are described in U.S. Bureau of the Census, "Religion Reported by the Civilian Population of the United States: March 1957," *Current Population Reports, Population Characteristics*, P-20, No. 79, (Washington, D.C.: February 2, 1958).

[10]See Barry R. Chiswick, "Are the Sons of Immigrants At An Earnings Disadvantage?", *American Economic Review*, 67:1 (February 1977): 376-380, and Barry R. Chiswick, "The Economic Progress of Immigrants: Some Apparently Universal Patterns," in William Fellner, ed., *Contemporary Economic Problems 1979* (Washington, D.C.: American Enterprise Institute, 1979), pp. 359-399.

[11]Immigrant generation of persons aged twenty-five to sixty-four (percent):

Generation	Jews[a]	White Males[b]
First (foreign born)	14	5
Second (foreign-born parents)	63	18
Third and higher (native-born parents)	23	77
TOTAL	100	100

The data are from Massarik and Chenkin, op. cit., Table 4, p. 276, and U.S. Bureau of the Census, *1970 Census of Population, Public Use Sample, 15 Percent Questionnaire* (data tape, one-in-a-hundred sample of the population, 1973).
[a]Jewish household heads.
[b]Includes Jews.

[12]A person has a non-English mother tongue if there was a language other than or in addition to English spoken in the home when the person was a child. Ladino is the language of Sephardic Jews.

[13]The procedure is implemented in Chiswick, "The Earnings and Human Capital of American Jews," op. cit. The procedure cannot be applied to more recent data, such as the 1976 Survey of Income and Education and the 1980 Census of Population, because the Census Bureau has dropped its questions on parent's nativity and mother tongue. The procedure can be applied to the 1920 and 1940 censuses as they included the questions on nativity, parent's nativity and mother tongue. Public use samples from these censuses are being produced.

[14]Proportion living in a rural area (aged fourteen and over) and proportion of employed men aged eighteen and over in agriculture, by religion in March 1957 (percent):

	Jewish	Protestant			Roman Catholic	Total[a]
		Total	White	Black		
Rural	3.9	44.4	44.8	33.9	21.2	36.1
Agriculture[b]	0.2	11.9	11.7	13.4	5.5	9.8

The data are from U.S. Bureau of the Census, "Tabulations of Data on the Social and Economic Characteristics of Major Religious Groups, March 1957," Tables 1 and 15 (Mimeograph, no date).

[a]Includes persons with no religion, other religions and religion not reported.

[b]Farmers, farm managers, farm laborers and foremen.

[15]The income data are standardized by the occupational distribution of the three major religious groups.

[16]Second-generation Americans are less likely to be rural and southern than those with native-born parents.

[17]The significant effect of U.S.S.R.-origin parents in Table 6 results from the large proportion of non-identified Jews in this category.

[18]Higher earnings, overall and other things the same, have also been reported for Jews in Canada and the U.S.S.R. For Canada, see Nigel Tomes, "The Earnings of Jews in Canada: Notes on Earnings Regressions," Department of Economics, University of Western Ontario (Mimeograph, 1982). Gur Ofer (Hebrew University, Jerusalem) reported in a personal conversation (April 1983) that his comparative study of retrospective data on Russian Jewish emigrants in Israel and data from Soviet sources revealed 8 percent higher earnings for Soviet Jews, other things the same.

[19]Indeed, in the 1970 Census data 27 percent of the Jewish men are professionals, compared to 15 percent for non-Jews. Medicine and law alone account for 9.7 percent of the Jews, compared to 2.1 percent of the non-Jews. Jews are also more likely to be nonfarm managers (26.5 percent compared to 13.4 percent) and in sales occupations (19.7 percent compared to 7.0 percent). The proportion in clerical jobs is similar (about 8 percent). A smaller proportion of Jews are in the lower-skilled occupations: 18.3 percent of the Jews and 56.2 percent of the non-Jews are in blue-collar, farm and service occupations. See Chiswick, "The Earnings and Human Capital of American Jews," op. cit., Table 4.

[20]See Alvin Chenkin, "Jewish Population in the United States in 1972," *American Jewish Year Book*, 1973, op. cit., pp. 307-309.

[21]These data are limited to persons born in the United States to avoid confounding the patterns by the characteristics of immigrants. For this reason, the sample sizes for those of Puerto Rican and Cuban origins are too small for inclusion in the table.

[22]Arcadius Kahan, "Economic Opportunities and Some Pilgrims' Progress: Jewish Immigrants from Eastern Europe in the U.S., 1890-1914," *Journal of Economic History*, XXXVIII: 1 (March 1978): 237.

[23]A symbiotic relationship developed between Jewish workers and entrepreneurs and the clothing industry. The Jewish experience in this industry in Eastern Europe, combined with the rapid growth of factory-made clothes for men and especially ready-made clothes for women, was clearly beneficial to the growth of the industry and the Jewish community. Ibid., p. 237.

[24]Ibid., pp. 250-251.

[25]In a study published in 1919, Paul Douglas also notes the high skill level of Jews compared to other Eastern and Southern European immigrants. See Paul H. Douglas, "Is the New Immigration More Unskilled than the Old?", *Journal of the American Statistical Association*, XVI: 126 (June 1919): 393-403. See also Simon Kuznets, "Immigration of Russian Jews to the United States: Background and Structure," *Perspectives in American History*, 9 (1975): 34-124.

[26]Robert Higgs, "Race, Skills and Earnings: American Immigrants in 1909," *Journal of Economic History*, XXXI: 2 (June 1971): 420-428.

[27]With the natural logarithm of average weekly earnings as the dependent variable, the weighted regression equations for adult white foreign-born men in mining and manufacturing (1909) are:

Explanatory Variable	Regression Equations		
	(1)	(2)	(3)
Jewish	0.0516	0.0311	0.0436
	(0.68)	(0.41)	(0.55)
Percent Literate	0.0089	0.0083	0.0085
	(5.93)	(4.88)	(4.94)
Percent in United States	0.0019	—	0.0012
5 or More Years[a]	(2.26)		(0.75)
Percent Speaking English[a]	—	0.0019	0.0009
		(2.24)	(0.54)
Constant	1.5729	1.6246	1.6014
N (groups)	35	35	35
R_2	0.76	0.75	0.76
R (adj.)	0.73	0.73	0.72

Note: t-ratios in parentheses designate variable not entered. Computed from the data reported in Higgs, ibid.

[a]Highly correlated variables.

[28]See Alice Kessler-Harris and Virginia Yans-McLaughlin, "European Immigrant Groups," in Thomas Sowell, ed., *American Ethnic Groups* (Washington, D. C.: Urban Institute, 1978), p. 120.

[29]Ibid., p. 114.

[30]See, for example, Armen A. Alchian and Reuben A. Kessel, "Competition, Monopoly and the Pursuit of Pecuniary Gain," in H. G. Lewis, ed., *Aspects of Labor Economics* (Princeton, N.J.: Princeton University Press 1962), pp. 170-171; Benjamin R. Epstein and Arnold Forster, "*Some of My Best Friends. . .*" (New York: Farrar, Straus and Cudahy, 1962); Joe R. Feagin, "Jewish Americans," *Racial and Ethnic Relations* (Englewood Cliffs, N.J.: Prentice Hall, 1978), pp. 148-187; A. C. Ivy and Irwin Ross, "Discrimination in College Admissions," in Milton A. Baron, ed., *American Minorities* (New York: Alfred A. Knopf, 1958), pp. 133-144; and Marcia Graham Synnott, *The Half-Opened Door: Discrimination and Admissions at Harvard, Yale and Princeton, 1900-1970* (Westport, Conn.: Greenwood Press, 1979). See also Lois Waldman, "Employment Discrimination Against Jews in the United States— 1955," *Jewish Social Studies*, XVIII: 3 (July 1956): 208-216.

[31]The author recalls a moving talk by a Nobel Laureate on the occasion of his seventieth birthday. The speaker recalled that among his earliest memories were those of his father in pre-World War I Europe telling him that some day he would have to leave Hungary because the Austro-Hungarian Empire would no longer be safe for Jews.

[32]This hypothesis is often referred to as the Kessel Hypothesis. For a recent exchange on the hypothesis and its applicability to Palestinian Arabs as well as Jews, see Reuven Brenner and Nicholas Kiefer, "The Economics of the Diaspora: Discrimination and Occupational Structure," *Economic Development and Cultural Change*, 29: 3 (April 1981): 517-533, and Eliezer Ayal and Barry R. Chiswick, "The Economics of the Diaspora Revisited," *Economic Development and Cultural Change*, 31: 4 (July 1983): 861-875.

[33]Using the 1970 Census procedures discussed above for identifying Jews, the proportion of adult white men in medicine and law are:

	Medicine[a]	Law[a]	All Professions
Jews	6.10	3.58	27.2
Non-Jews	1.35	0.72	15.3
Ratio (Jews/Non-Jews)	4.50	5.00	2.8

Source: U.S. Bureau of the Census, *1970 Census of Population, 15 Percent Questionnaire*, op. cit.

[a]Medicine includes doctors, dentists and related health professionals with doctorate degrees. Law includes lawyers and judges.

[34]A pre-World War I study of Jews noted: "In the struggle for life, besides intellectual gifts, the industry, versatility, and powers of adaptation of the Jew stand him in good stead. . . . Appreciation of the value of learning and study is a tradition among Jews to an extent unequalled perhaps by any other people." See Arthur Ruppin, *The Jews of To-Day* (New York: Henry Holt and Company, 1913).

[35]Additional evidence on this point is found in data on the college performance of Jews and in their productivity within occupations. Despite the fact that a larger proportion of Jewish youths go to college, Jewish college students have higher high school grades, perform better in college, and go to higher quality institutions. Among academics, on average, Jews are in higher quality institutions, publish more books and articles, and have higher academic rank and salaries in spite of being younger and having parents who were less likely to be college graduates or teachers. See Seymour Martin Lipset and Everett C. Ladd, Jr., "Jewish Academics in the United States: Their Achievements, Culture and Politics," *American Jewish Year Book, 1971* (New York: American Jewish Committee, 1971), pp. 98-107, and Seymour Martin Lipset and Everett C. Ladd, Jr., "The Changing Social Origins of American Academics," in Robert H. Merton, James S. Coleman and Peter H. Rossi, *Qualitative and Quantitative Social Research* (New York: Free Press, 1979), pp. 319-338.

[36]In an essay on Jewish educational attainments, Leonard Dinnerstein wrote: "Basically [East European Jews] agreed upon the importance of education in the development of a full human being. From their earliest days children imbibed this attitude, first unconsciously, later with more awareness. . . . In the home children learned to venerate books, to remain quiet while father studied, and to treat learned guests with great respect. . . . The Jewish immigrants who came to this country in the 1880's and after brought these values and traditions with them." Leonard Dinnerstein, "Education and the Advancement of American Jews," in Bernard J. Weiss, ed., *American Education and the European Immigrant, 1840-1940* (Urbana, Ill.: University of Illinois Press, 1982), pp. 44-60, quotation from p. 45.

[37]For a recent development of this approach, see Gary S. Becker, *A Treatise on the Family* (Cambridge, Mass.: Harvard University Press, 1981). For its application to racial and ethnic groups, see Barry R. Chiswick, "Differences in Educational Attainment Among Racial and Ethnic Groups: Patterns and Hypotheses Regarding the Quantity and Quality of Children" (Mimeograph, University of Illinois at Chicago: 1983).

[38]There appears to be an inverse relation, across the racial and ethnic groups in the United States, between family size and the educational attainment of the children. Among the native born, in addition to Jews, the Chinese and Japanese have high levels of education and come from small families. This is in contrast to the large families and low schooling level of the U.S.-born Fili-

pinos, Mexicans, blacks and American Indians. A notable exception are Mormons who have both large families and children with high levels of education. See Chiswick, "Differences in Educational Attainment," op. cit., and Bernard Berelson, "Ethnicity and Fertility: What and So What," in Himmelfarb and Baras, op. cit., pp. 100-107.

[39]Analyses of the data from the 1973 and 1976 National Surveys of Family Growth also show lower fertility for Jews than for both white Protestants and non-Hispanic white Catholics, overall and after controlling for age, education and area of residence. The differences are smaller for "wanted pregnancies" than for "total births expected" or "children ever born." See William D. Mosher and Gerry E. Hendershot, "Religion and Fertility Reexamined" (Mimeograph, National Center for Health Statistics. Presented at Population Association of America, Pittsburgh, 1983.) These findings suggest that Jews are more successful in controlling fertility either because they are more efficient in contraception or because additional children are perceived as being more costly.

[40]In all age groups for those twenty-five to sixty-four years, Jewish women have a higher proportion never married than white Protestants and a smaller proportion never married than Roman Catholics. U.S. Bureau of the Census, "Tabulations of Data . . . Major Religious Groups . . . 1957," op. cit., Table 5.

[41]A completed fertility rate of about 2.1 per adult woman is needed to maintain a stable population. This requires a higher completed fertility rate for ever-married women. The Jewish fertility rate is below these levels.

[42]See, for example, Becker, op. cit., p. 110; Calvin Goldscheider, "Fertility of the Jews," Demography (1967): 196-209; Sidney Goldstein, "Jews in the United States: Perspectives from Demography," American Jewish Year Book (New York: American Jewish Committee, 1981), pp. 3-39; Jacques Silber, "Some Demographic Characteristics of the Jewish Population in Russia at the End of the Nineteenth Century," Jewish Social Studies, XLII: 314 (Summer/Fall 1980): 269-280; and John S. Billings, "Vital Statistics of the Jews in the United States," Census Bulletin, No. 19 (Washington, D.C.: December 1889), pp. 4-9.

[43]Goldstein, op. cit.

[44]The higher income of their husbands would be an offsetting factor.

[45]Preliminary analyses by the author using the 1970 Census of Population suggest that, other things the same, the presence of a child under age six in the household has a greater depressing effect on adult female labor force participation rates for Jewish than for non-Jewish women.

[46]Nathan Hurvitz, "Sources of Motivation and Achievement of American Jews," Jewish Social Studies, XXIII: 4 (October 1961): 217-234.

THE POLISH IMMIGRANTS AND THEIR DESCENDANTS IN THE AMERICAN LABOR FORCE

Helena Znaniecka Lopata

Loyola University of Chicago

Many factors affect the rate and the form of assimilation of immigrants in any society. Few peoples forming a numerical minority can isolate themselves from the dominant society and its culture sufficiently to retain their native culture. In addition, few immigrant groups have been able to reproduce their home society in a way that would make possible a miniature sub-society. Certainly most groups who have migrated to the United States in modern times with mass communication have, sooner or later, left behind most of their home culture in a process of acculturation that has fitted them into the American social structure.[1] The factors influencing acculturation, and whether or not relatively complete assimilation takes place, include: the time of migration, the size of the migrant group, the composition of the waves, the manner of settlement, the ability to create institutional completeness with community boundaries, the relations with the home country, the use of the dominant society's means of social mobility and, of course, the attitudes of both groups toward each other and toward other cultural and/ or racial groups. The degree of divergence between the immigrant group and the dominant ones in terms of physical and cultural characteristics, and the ease with which these differences are decreased, are, naturally, extremely important components of the process.[2]

This chapter is devoted to a partial analysis of one segment of an immigrant group's relations with the dominant society—its position in the labor force. The group in question is that of Polish immigrants, and the society is the American.

Historical Background

Many historians of Polish settlement in America and of Polonia as an ethnic community begin by telling of the fifty glass, pitch and tar workers who conducted the first labor strike on this side of the ocean in Jamestown in 1619.[3] Mention is also made of, or chapters written about, Pulaski and Kosciuszko, Polish officers who fought in the American Revolutionary War.[4] However, the majority of Polish immigrants entered America only after 1880.[5] There are considerable problems in estimating the numbers of Polish immigrants and their descendants, one of which is the inconsistency with which the U. S. Bureau of Immigration classified immigrants over the years.[6] Changes in policy affected the recording of Polish immigration in several ways. Poland did not exist as a political state from 1795 until 1918, having been subdivided and occupied by Russia, Prussia and Austria. People coming from that area could identify themselves with the Polish national culture society, with smaller regional units, with one of several minorities contained within the territory, or with the occupying power. This made classification of immigrants difficult, and the U.S. Bureau of Immigration was not sure how to identify them. In addition, the bureau shifted several times from classifying all immigrants by country of "origin" to the use of "races" or "peoples."

The first method of classification resulted in great losses of numbers of Polish immigrants. The bureau representatives were forbidden for some years from recording anyone by that nationality as Polish, listing only the political state from which he/she came. A further complication arose from the fact that many people traveled back and forth during these years, having never planned to remain in America longer than necessary to acquire sufficient capital to buy property and in general raise their status back home. Others, although initially declaring themselves as immigrants, went back to Poland to arrange for the immigration of relatives or for political reasons. Poland was in constant turmoil prior to World War I and the time surrounding World War II.[7] Governments were formed in exile and political leaders frequently came to America for varying periods of time. Monies were needed to maintain the governments and rebuild the nation when it acquired political independence. Extensive efforts were made to develop and increase nationalism among the Polish Americans, many of whom came from villages with limited area identification. The efforts were mainly successful, as evidenced by the fact that Polonia raised a division of twenty-eight thousand men who trained in Canada and joined the Polish forces in France during World War I.[8] Millions of dollars were raised on this side of the ocean for political causes as well as for medicines, food, clothing and other supplies which went to the Poles in the country and in exile.

Although much of what Americans know about Polish immigrants comes from Thomas and Znaniecki's classic, *The Polish Peasant in Eu-*

rope and America, over the years Polonia as a community contained
many members of the intelligentsia, a broad stratum of Polish society,
and other members of the middle classes.[9] Over 1,300 different newspapers, journals and special interest periodicals were started in the Polish-American community (Polonia) in the years between 1842 and
1966 alone. A vast superstructure of voluntary associations pulled together people in the same locality, and into larger regional and nationwide communication and activity, each with its own publications, con-
gresses and traveling representatives. Several of these started out as
mutual aid groups and developed the strong economic foundations of
life insurance and banking firms.[10]

All in all we can identify 1,443,473 immigrants classified as Poles by
"race or people" entering America during the years from 1899 to 1932.
Since 294,824 left this country during the same time period, a total of
1,148,649 additions were made to the population.[11] Poland as "country of birth" was listed by 664,971 people in the years from 1885 to
1898, 1933 to 1946, and 1947 to 1978. Subtracting 22,766 who left during those years, we come to a total of 642,205. The grand total then
comes to 1,790,854. However, these figures are deceptively precise
since some people went back and forth several times, and others declared different identities when entering this country. In addition,
these figures end in 1972, and we know that there has been a recent
influx of Polish immigrants.

The Polonian community itself classifies its members as belonging to
one of two or three emigrations. *Stara emigracja* (old emigration) consisted of all those people who migrated before the 1920s, at which time
the United States imposed its quota system that cut the flow to a
trickle. The people who came during those years, and who remained in
the United States in spite of their original determination to return to
Poland once it regained its political independence, were primarily former peasants who then settled in industrialized and urbanized areas.[12]
At the turn of the century a third of the immigrants were illiterate and
most were young males. Families came later, especially after World
War I.[13] The characteristics of the immigrants prior to World War I
are exemplified by those entering in the fiscal year ending in June 30,
1909, who listed themselves as Polish. Three-fourths were farm laborers, unskilled workers or servants. "There was only sixty-six professionals," others were "skilled workers" typical of village economies;
blacksmiths, carpenters, locksmiths, miners, dressmakers, shoemakers
and tailors.[14] The U.S. Immigration and Naturalization Service
recorded more detailed information about the immigrants as the society was worried about their ability to support themselves. We thus
know that only 3 percent of the Polish immigrants of that year had

fifty dollars or more with them at entrance. However, that was quite a sum of money since, at the same time, workers in Chicopee, Massachusetts mills worked long hours for two dollars a week.[15] Only one-fourth had the cost of transportation covered by other people. Most of the Poles were joining relatives, with only 14 percent being headed toward friends or employers. Immigrants of later years reflected the changing nature of Polish society. By 1924 only 3 percent were illiterate.[16]

The *nowa emigracja* (new emigration) consisted mainly of refugees and "displaced persons" who had survived the Nazi and Soviet invasions but were moved out of their home territory by the war, boundary changes and similar events, and did not want to return to a communist-controlled Poland. The American government passed special bills allowing more than 164,000 refugees to enter between 1946 and 1969. This population was much more heterogeneous in background, but with a higher proportion of better-educated, urbanized people. For example, only 7 percent of those entering in 1949 gave their occupation as operatives, household workers, non-household service workers, farm laborers or laborers.[17] One-quarter had been farmers (i.e., owners of farms), or farm managers, professionals, sales or clerical workers and craftsmen. One-half declared themselves as having "no occupation" and these were wives, children and older parents. Mostwin found the new emigration more dispersed in residence and occupation than the first generation of the *stara emigracja*.[18] Being better educated, they more quickly acculturated and adjusted to the new society. Many had previously lived in England and learned the language. On the other hand, respondents to Mostwin's mailed questionnaire showed a decline in status if they had been in the higher layers of social stratum in Poland prior to World War II. Doctors, lawyers and many writers were unable to retrain and obtain equivalent positions in the new land. Many had spent years in foreign countries, often all over the world, before finally coming to America. An interesting norm developed among the Poles of the *nowa emigracja*. Social status and companionate relations revolved around former status and behavioral evidence of membership in the "intelligentsia," regardless of current occupation, income and residence. Thus, manner, knowledge of Polish culture, ability to carry forth an intellectual conversation, and the general "national character" traits idealized in the Polish gentry became the means by which even those in blue-collar jobs could retain their emotional and social life-style.[19]

Communist-controlled Poland fell behind the "iron curtain" in the postwar years; emigration stopped entirely and contact with Western cultures was brought to a minimum. It is only during the recent years that Poland has allowed its citizens to leave the country, often for a limited time and without their families, kept as a form of hostage to ensure return. The actual numbers of post-1956 immigrants to America are hard to determine since many entered as visitors and remained, not wishing to return but working as illegal aliens. They are unable to obtain a "green card" because of their illegal status, and are thus open to exploitation. Those who entered several years ago are eagerly awaiting a change in United States immigration policy which would give them amnesty.

The post-World War II Polish emigrants appear to be highly divided in social class background. The least-educated segment includes such persons as "cleaning and charwomen" working not only in private homes, but also in offices as night cleaners in an effort to obtain as much money as possible without needing to learn English, desiring then to return to Poland. The immigrants also include the political emigrés who intend to remain in America as long as Poland has a communist regime. Gross[20] combines all World War II and immigration thereafter into waves:

> The first wave of World War II, during the decade of 1939-1950, is that of emigrants from the "Second Republic," still nurtured in the traditions and environment of an independent Poland in the period between the wars.[21]

It is this wave which was studied by Mostwin in *The Transplanted Family.*

> The second wave of World War II emigrants are the refugees, escapees and emigrants of the 1950's to the mid 1960's. This is also a primarily political emigration, but of people who left a country which had been for more than a decade under Communist rule . . . many belonged to the intelligentsia with professional training.

> The third wave of this period is far more complex. The composition of this generation includes arrivals from about 1965 to the present day.[22]

Gross finds this wave to contain skilled workers who find employment easily, and "appreciate their good salaries, comfort and personal freedom." Another group contains onetime communists who have now moved away from identification with the party or the ideology. The third group includes scholars affected by the 1968 antiliberal and "anti-Zionist" (anti-Jewish in fact) actions of the government. Most have been able to locate in similar positions in the United States. Finally, there are the young students who have no knowledge of prewar Poland and who are not interested in the virulently anti-communist Polonian community. Because of the tremendous differences among these three waves of emigrants, there has been a great deal of friction within the loosely formed community and its voluntary associations, as well as a tendency for mutual exclusivity.[23]

One additional fact needs to be known before we examine the occupational distributions of people who can be identified as Poles or Polish Americans. Polish culture on all of its class levels contains a strong tendency toward status competition within varying size areas. Individualistically based, a person's reputation in his or her *okolica*, defined by Thomas and Znaniecki as the area within which this reputation is contained, is based on material possessions, personal abilities and family status.[24] The competition results in shifts of status vis-à-vis others in the *okolica*, which can be as broad as the nation itself.

Although the intelligentsia valued highly the personal knowledge and skills brought about by education and artistic training, the broad strata of the peasantry who emigrated brought to America an anti-intellectual bias and a dislike for any but a minimal education. Thus for the members of the *stara emigracja*, and even for the second—sometimes even the third—generation who came from peasant stock, the criteria for status were similar to those in the country of emigration: land, houses and other permanent material objects, money and individual skills, to which was added organizational honor through offices and special symbols. Families removed children from schools as soon as possible in order that they could be sent to work to improve the family's financial status, at first for bare survival, but later in competition with other families. This characteristic of the culture increased antagonism between this stratum of the community and those who identified themselves as the intelligentsia, who use different personal criteria.

Poles and Polish Americans in the American Labor Force

Keeping in mind the wave of emigration and the generation of settlement in the United States, we can now turn to whatever evidence is available as to the distribution of Poles and Polish Americans in the American economy, especially in its labor force.

Old Emigration, First Generation

According to Pinkowski, some of the early Polish immigrants turned to farming, taking advantage of the vastness of land in the United States. Although they also spread out to Wisconsin, Texas and Oklahoma, many settled in the Connecticut valley, first as farm laborers and then as owners.[25] Abel found native farmers highly prejudiced against the Polish immigrants, whom they found working so hard as to sacrifice many of the "niceties of life" in an effort to obtain land.[26] Most of the

Polish immigrants, however, did not turn to farming. Lacking a knowledge of English, the men and women who sought employment were dependent upon occupations and industries in which bilingual foremen and other connecting links were present. As Golab and Pinkowski document and Thomas and Znaniecki discuss at great length, emigrants follow the steps of previous immigrants in residence and employment.[27]

Pinkowski presents data about the occupational distributions of Polish-born immigrants and their children in 1900. It is hard to determine with exactness the employment of the women at that time, since seasonal part-time and occasional employment were relatively frequent. Women who contributed to the family income often did so by keeping boarders and lodgers. The largest reported employment of women was as servants and waitresses. Service in private households was soon replaced by work in the cotton mills, especially by still unmarried Polish women.[28] The males employed in service industries worked mainly as laborers or, to a lesser extent, as bartenders.[29] Those located in trade and transportation industries were limited to retail trade, often as hucksters and peddlers, or salesmen and managers of small stores in the Polish neighborhoods. Many worked "in various capacities on railroads."[30] Mining and the production of iron and steel products drew Polish men to manufacturing operations; the women generally sticking to textile production. Table 1 contains the summary statistics on the ten leading occupations of Polish male immigrants and their sons in the United States in 1900.

The first generation of male immigrants was disproportionately involved in work as leather curriers and tanners, charcoal, coke and lime burners, wireworkers, tailors, chemical, iron and steel workers, meat packers, fruit canners, and hat and cap makers. The second generation was more dispersed but mainly too young to be counted.

> Polish wage earners were at one time or another the leading immigrant group in the slaughtering and meat-packing industry, carpet manufacturing, car building and repairing, lock making and brass hardware, zinc smelting and refining, glass manufacturing, agricultural implement and vehicle manufacturing and a number of other industries.[31]

The proportion of Polish workers who were employed in professional services was relatively low. Teachers, including teaching nuns and college professors, clergymen and musicians, represented professional categories most frequently.

Parot found Polish married women in Chicago to be almost 100 percent unemployed in 1900.[31] On the other hand, over 74 percent of the unmarried females were working for pay, many in sweatshops in the

TABLE 1
TEN LEADING OCCUPATIONS OF POLISH MALE IMMIGRANTS
AND THEIR SONS IN THE UNITED STATES IN 1900

Occupation	Number	Percent Distribution	Rank of Occupation	
			1st Generation	2nd Generation
First Generation				
TOTAL	183,055	100.0		
Laborers (Not Specified)	53,232	29.1	1	2
Miners and Quarrymen	14,024	7.7	2	4
Iron and Steel Workers	12,060	6.6	3	5
Farmers	10,480	5.7	4	3
Tailors	8,621	4.7	5	10
Farm Laborers	7,795	4.3	6	1
Merchants (Except Wholesale)	7,428	4.1	7	9
Textile Mill Operatives	5,731	3.1	8	21
Steam Railroad Employees	3,919	2.1	9	17
Hucksters and Peddlers	3,197	1.7	10	27
All Other Occupations	56,568	30.9		
Second Generation				
TOTAL	25,925	100.0		
Farm Laborers	4,729	18.2	6	1
Laborers (Not Specified)	4,081	15.7	1	2
Farmers	1,389	5.3	4	3
Miners and Quarrymen	1,292	5.0	2	4
Iron and Steel Workers	1,049	4.0	3	5
Salesmen	959	3.7	17	6
Clerks and Copyists	750	3.0	28	7
Carpenters and Joiners	591	2.3	12	8
Merchants (Except Wholesale)	524	2.0	7	9
Tailors	476	1.8	5	10
All Other Occupations	10,095	38.9		

Source: Edward Pinkowski, "The Great Influx of Polish Immigrants and the Industries They Entered," in Frank Mocha, ed., *Poles in America* (Stevens Point, Wis.: Worzalla Publishing, 1978), p. 357.

garment trades. Looking at a particular area of Chicago which was highly congested, with an unusually high birth rate, he concludes:

. . . it is likely that marriage may indeed have been used as an avenue of escape from the squalor, exploitation and boredom of the sweatshop. Moreover, when one correlates this "escape factor" to the high fertility rate in Polonia . . . , one might even hazard the interpretation that Polish women viewed each pregnancy as some sort of "guarantee" against ever again returning to the sweatshops.[33]

Occupational Persistence

A number of observers of ethnicity in American society have pointed to
the tendency of younger generations of Polish Americans to remain not
so much in the same occupations, but on the same occupational level,
as their parents and even grandparents.[34] Hutchinson compared the
Poles to other immigrants and their children and found a strong pattern of occupational inheritance. Many were still in steel mills, stock-
yards, mines and automobile assembly work. As late as the 1960s various sociologists interested in the mobility of ethnic groups compared
education, occupation and income of Americans of foreign origin.
Lieberson found the Poles below other groups in intergenerational mobility.[35] Duncan and Duncan found the Poles in the 1962 U.S. Census
sample not so much behind in education, but "their occupational success falls short of the American average for men of similar social origin
and educational qualification."[36] Greeley and his colleagues at the National Opinion Research Center of the University of Chicago used a
composite sample from seven NORC surveys in which both religious
and national background questions were asked.[37] The studies took
place in the years between 1963 and 1972 and the Polish sub-sample is
small. Furthermore, the span of nine years tends to camouflage a
change which apparently was taking place. However, it is one of the
few sources for comparative data on American ethnic groups on a national level, so some of its findings will be used.

Table 2 contains demographic data on the various groups. It shows
that people identified as Poles or Polish Americans tended to be older
than the American mean and to have a relatively large family size in
terms of the number of children. The rather high mean age may account for the other characteristics. Previous comments as to the neglect of advanced education among Polish-American families are supported by the fact that they had achieved almost a year less schooling
than the national median in those years. Their occupational prestige
was one of the lowest of all groups; only blacks were lower. However
their median income was higher than several other groups, reflecting
persistence in blue-collar jobs, but movement into higher levels within
such categories.

An indication that the Polish Americans are changing their attitudes toward higher education is contained in Table 3 (see p. 134). This
development possibly has been occasioned by the increasing embrace-
ment of such by the third generation and post-World War II emigrés.
One observes here that the Poles aged thirty-five and over had completed only 10.9 years of schooling, only the Spanish and Italians

TABLE 2

DEMOGRAPHIC INFORMATION ON AMERICAN RELIGIO-ETHNIC GROUPS
(BASED ON SEVEN NORC SURVEYS)

Religio-ethnic Group (Number in Sample)	Years of Education	Average Age[a]	Occupational Prestige	Percent White Collar	Number of Children[b]	Family Income	Percent of Population
Protestant							
British (1303)	11.9	47.5	3.98	53	2.3	$ 8,309	13.6
German (1205)	11.0	45.8	3.46	40	2.5	7,858	12.6
Scandinavian (359)	11.3	45.1	3.38	42	2.7	7,869	3.7
Irish (530)	10.6	46.2	3.17	38	2.7	7,022	5.5
Other (1883)	10.5	45.5	3.33	41	2.6	7,275	19.7
Catholic							
Irish (328)	12.2	44.5	4.27	49	2.8	9,255	3.4
German (342)	11.3	44.4	3.88	45	3.1	8,903	3.6
Italian (346)	10.7	44.6	3.48	39	2.8	7,979	3.6
Polish (136)	10.0	45.1	2.69	34	2.9	7,940	1.4
Slavic (237)	10.4	45.0	3.48	31	2.3	7,693	2.5
French (156)	10.4	43.9	3.30	25	2.8	7,478	1.6
Spanish-speaking (122)	9.3	38.2	3.10	24	3.1	6,145	1.3
Other (609)	11.0	41.1	3.46	38	2.7	8,105	6.4
Jewish							
German (30)	12.9	48.0	5.36	57	2.3	9,326	0.3
East European (160)	13.3	45.0	4.77	79	1.7	11,114	1.7
Other (50)	13.3	43.6	4.38	73	2.0	11,218	0.5
Blacks (1285)	9.7	43.3	2.47	18	2.9	5,425	13.4
Oriental (20)	11.6	42.0	2.60	35	2.6	7,918	0.2
No Religion (304)	12.0	41.7	3.49	45	1.9	9,046	3.2
Other (150)	11.2	45.2	3.72	44	2.3	7,654	1.6
AMERICAN MEAN	10.9	44.8	3.42	39	2.6	7,588	100.0

Source: Andrew M. Greeley, *Ethnicity in the United States* (New York: John Wiley & Sons, 1974), pp. 42-43.
[a]Adults over 18.
[b]Percent ever married.

TABLE 3
HIGHEST GRADE OF SCHOOL COMPLETED BY PERSONS 25 YEARS OLD AND OVER, BY ETHNIC ORIGIN
(1969)

Origin	Total (Thousands)	Percent Distribution by Years of School Completed						Median School Years Completed	1972*
		0-7	8	9-11	12	13-15	16 or More		
All 25 years & Over	106,281	13.8	13.4	17.6	33.9	10.3	11.0	12.2	12.2
25 to 34 years old	23,882	4.5	4.8	17.4	43.5	14.7	15.2	12.5	12.6
English	2,301	4.3	4.6	15.5	41.2	16.8	17.6	12.6	12.9
German	2,848	1.6	4.1	14.8	47.4	14.6	17.5	12.6	12.7
Irish	1,670	2.6	3.7	18.8	45.1	15.9	13.9	12.6	12.6
Italian	902	5.3	3.3	16.3	50.4	12.7	11.9	12.5	12.6
Polish	503	1.3	3.0	10.6	53.8	15.1	16.2	12.7	12.8
Russian	209	0.7	0.7	3.7	24.7	17.7	52.5	16+	16.0
Spanish	1,239	19.2	10.0	23.5	32.2	9.8	5.3	11.7	11.3
Other	11,625	3.6	4.4	17.5	43.3	15.6	15.6	12.6	12.6
Not Reported	2,585	6.2	7.2	20.3	43.6	10.9	11.8	12.4	12.4
35 years and over	82,399	16.5	15.9	17.6	31.1	9.1	9.8	12.0	12.1
English	9,698	11.9	13.7	17.8	31.7	11.1	13.6	12.2	12.4
German	9,977	10.6	22.0	16.1	34.2	8.6	8.5	12.0	12.1
Irish	6,960	14.3	16.3	18.8	32.9	8.4	9.3	12.0	12.1
Italian	3,780	23.5	17.7	20.0	27.6	5.2	5.9	10.3	11.1
Polish	2,266	18.5	19.0	19.2	30.9	5.2	7.2	10.9	11.2
Russian	1,375	10.8	12.1	11.9	35.1	11.7	18.4	12.4	12.6
Spanish	2,576	43.0	14.4	14.9	17.5	5.7	4.5	8.5	8.2
Other	37,661	16.5	14.3	17.8	31.1	9.9	10.4	12.0	12.0
Not Reported	8,106	20.4	17.3	17.6	30.0	7.4	7.4	11.1	11.1
*NORC Polish Catholics	137		30.9	20.6	33.1	10.3	5.1		

Sources: U.S. Bureau of the Census, *Population Characteristics, Ethnic Origin and Educational Attainment* (November 1969), Series P-20, No. 220, April 1971.

*Andrew Greeley, *Perspectives on American Ethnicity* (New York: Wiley-Interscience, 1974), Chapter 7.

achieving less. However, the younger Polish Americans, that is, those between ages twenty-five and thirty-four, had already outdistanced all the ethnic groups except the Russian, which is heavily represented by Jewish immigrants with a recorded proclivity toward education.[38] Of course, some of the young people identified as Polish may also be of Jewish background. Greeley found that the young Polish scientists specializing in physical sciences and engineering, rather than in social sciences and humanities, do not expect to reach as high a salary within six years as do other scientists.[39] The latter finding is not unexpected in view of the recency of higher education in many Polish-American families, especially those of the "old emigration."

Greeley concluded that the Poles deviated 15 percent from the average percentage of male white-collar workers in urban, non-South, America, if they were aged forty or over, and only 4 percent if under age forty.[40] This substantiates our earlier observation that the Polish Americans are shifting away from a heavy dependence on blue-collar jobs, which had been due to the tradition of occupational inheritance and the avoidance of higher education. However, the American movement between 1950 and 1960 toward professional or management jobs was not yet reflected in the occupations of Polish Americans, only 20 percent of each cohort being so located. Greeley believes that:

The Polish Catholic performance . . . indicated a slow upward movement of the Polish population—though the number of respondents is sufficiently low to merit caution in appraising it. The three oldest age cohorts of Poles were beneath the national mean for their age cohorts in both the 1950s and the 1960s, though they improved their relative position somewhat during the two decades. Cohort II (born 1931-1940) was the first Polish cohort to be above the national mean, though its relative advantage slipped somewhat from the 1950s to the 1960s. Polish Catholics, then, seem to be improving their relative position in American society, but far more slowly than the earlier Catholic immigrant groups.[41]

The special census of 1969, which asked for ethnic origin, produced the next evidence as to the occupational distribution of the Polish Americans.[42] Table 4 (see p. 136) presents the data on men; Table 5 (see p. 137) on women of Polish-American ethnic origin and other groups. One observes here that 30 percent of the Polish-American men are found in professional, technical and managerial occupations. The Russians far outdistance them; the English are somewhat higher but are above the average in such occupations. Again, we do not know how many of the Poles are of Jewish background. Few Polish men are in clerical or sales jobs, but a quarter are in crafts and a fifth work as

TABLE 4

EMPLOYMENT STATUS AND MAJOR OCCUPATION GROUP OF THE MALE POPULATION 16 YEARS OLD AND OLDER, BY ETHNIC ORIGIN (NUMBERS IN THOUSANDS)

(1969)

Subject	NATIONAL ORIGIN							
	English	German	Irish	Italian	Russian	Spanish	Polish	Polish-1972*
Males 16 Years and Over	6,615	7,595	4,697	2,710	895	2,491	1,549	—
Civilian Labor Force	5,197	6,203	3,712	2,149	672	2,022	1,284	—
% in Labor Force	76.6	51.7	79.0	79.3	75.1	81.2	82.9	—
% Unemployed	2.1	1.6	2.3	1.7	1.8	5.1	2.3	—
Males Employed-Total	5,088	6,102	3,630	2,112	656	1,919	1,252	—
Percent by Occupation								
Professional, Technical and Like Workers	16.7	14.8	14.1	13.5	27.1	7.9	14.5	18.1
Farmers, Farm Managers	4.4	6.7	3.6	0.4	0.3	0.6	1.6	0.9
Managers, Officers and Proprietors (Non-farm)	16.9	15.4	15.5	14.9	29.3	7.4	15.2	12.9
Clerical and Like Workers	7.3	5.8	8.5	9.1	8.7	6.7	8.8	7.9
Sales Workers	6.0	6.1	6.3	5.2	12.8	3.3	6.2	6.3
Craftsmen, Foremen and Like Workers	19.9	21.7	20.8	22.7	9.6	18.5	24.4	23.3
Operatives and Like Workers	17.8	18.2	17.9	20.0	9.3	28.6	19.6	18.3
Private Household Workers	0.1	—	—	—	—	—	0.1	—
Service Workers (Non-household)	5.0	4.7	6.0	7.5	1.8	10.5	3.0	7.7
Farm Laborers and Foremen	1.2	1.6	1.0	0.2	—	4.8	0.6	0.4
Laborers (Non-Farm, Non-Mine)	4.9	4.9	6.1	6.4	1.1	11.8	6.1	4.3

Source: U.S. Bureau of the Census, *Current Population Reports*, Series P-20, No. 221, "Characteristics of the Population by Ethnic Origin, November, 1969" (Washington, D.C.: Government Printing Office, 1971).

*Thomas Sowell, ed., *Essays and Data on American Ethnic Groups* (Washington, D.C.: The Urban Institute, 1978), p. 378.

TABLE 5

EMPLOYMENT STATUS AND MAJOR OCCUPATION GROUP OF THE FEMALE POPULATION 16 YEARS OLD AND OVER, BY ETHNIC ORIGIN (NUMBERS IN THOUSANDS)

(1969)

Subject	NATIONAL ORIGIN							
	English	German	Irish	Italian	Russian	Spanish	Polish	Polish-1972*
Females 16 Years and Over	7,841	7,753	5,586	2,882	923	2,822	1,676	—
Civilian Labor Force	3,170	3,301	2,324	1,213	350	1,146	740	—
% in Labor Force	40.4	42.6	41.6	42.1	37.9	40.6	44.2	—
% Unemployed	2.9	3.7	4.1	4.5	4.9	7.5	4.1	—
Females Employed	3,076	3,175	2,224	1,155	330	1,060	710	—
Percent by Occupation								
Professional, Technical and Like Workers	16.6	16.6	14.9	9.7	23.0	8.6	13.1	14.1
Farmers, Farm Managers	0.4	0.4	0.2	—	—	—	—	0.1
Managers, Officers and Proprietors (Non-farm)	6.1	4.1	6.0	4.5	10.6	1.7	3.4	4.9
Clerical and Like Workers	34.9	33.6	35.6	39.4	43.6	25.6	35.6	36.0
Sales Workers	8.4	7.6	7.0	7.4	8.8	5.0	8.5	8.0
Craftsmen, Foremen and Like Workers	1.3	0.9	0.9	2.2	2.1	1.1	1.1	1.2
Operatives and Like Workers	13.4	13.0	13.1	25.3	6.7	32.8	19.2	16.8
Private Household Workers	3.9	4.5	3.6	0.9	0.9	6.4	2.1	1.7
Service Workers (Non-household)	13.5	15.9	16.9	10.4	3.9	17.1	15.5	15.1
Farm Laborers and Foremen	1.3	2.9	1.2	0.2	0.3	0.8	1.3	1.3
Laborers (Non-farm, Non-mine)	0.2	0.3	0.6	0.2	—	0.8	0.3	0.9

Source: U.S. Bureau of the Census, *Current Population Reports*, Series P-20, No. 221, "Characteristics of the Population by Ethnic Origin, November, 1969" (Washington, D.C.: Government Printing Office, 1971).

*Thomas Sowell, ed., *Essays and Data on American Ethnic Groups* (Washington, D.C.: The Urban Institute, 1978), p. 378.

TABLE 6

OCCUPATIONAL COMPOSITION OF POLES IN THE LABOR FORCE, 1951-71

Occupation	1951 Male Number	1951 Male %	1951 Female Number	1951 Female %	1961 Male Number	1961 Male %	1961 Female Number	1961 Female %	1971 Male Number	1971 Male %	1971 Female Number	1971 Female %
All Occupations	78,780	100.0	20,408	100.0	96,100	100.0	34,870	100.0	95,770	100.0	52,510	100.0
Managerial, Administrative	4,433	5.6	569	2.8	8,813	9.2	1,202	3.5	3,375	3.5	750	1.4
Occupations in Natural Sciences, Engineering, Mathematics, Social Sciences; Religion; and Artistic, Literary, Recreational	1,608	2.0	244	1.2	4,890	5.1	664	1.9	5,880	6.1	1,135	2.2
Teaching	307	0.4	442	2.2	776	0.8	1,156	3.3	1,805	1.9	2,585	4.9
(University)	(38)	(0.1)	(2)	(0.0)	(95)	(0.1)	(18)	(0.0)	(300)	(0.3)	(85)	(0.2)
(Other)	(269)	(0.3)	(440)	(2.2)	(681)	(0.7)	(1,138)	(3.3)	(1,505)	(1.6)	(2,500)	(4.7)
Occupations in Medicine and Health	280	0.3	577	2.8	863	0.9	1,248	3.6	1,170	1.2	3,555	6.8
(Doctors)	(156)	(0.2)	(17)	(0.1)	(502)	(0.5)	(64)	(0.2)	(415)	(0.4)	(80)	(0.2)
(Nursing)	(8)	(0.0)	(485)	(2.4)	(69)	(0.1)	(931)	(2.7)	(425)	(0.4)	(2,775)	(5.3)
(Other)	(116)	(0.1)	(75)	(0.3)	(292)	(0.3)	(253)	(0.7)	(330)	(0.3)	(705)	(1.3)
Clerical Occupations	2,553	3.2	4,247	20.8	4,962	5.2	8,235	23.6	6,190	6.5	14,905	28.4
Sales Occupations	2,033	2.6	1,850	9.1	3,698	3.8	2,409	6.9	6,740	7.0	4,010	7.6
Service Occupations	4,314	5.5	5,653	27.7	6,971	7.3	9,442	27.1	8,955	9.3	10,385	19.8
Farming	18,434	23.4	1,166	5.7	13,468	14.0	3,287	9.4	8,675	9.1	3,185	6.1
Fishing, Forestry and Mining	4,342	5.5	3	0.0	3,423	3.6	6	0.0	2,385	2.5	35	0.0
Processing and Machining	10,085	12.8	1,482	7.3	13,919	14.5	2,245	6.4	11,565	12.1	1,580	3.0
Product Fabricating	6,268	8.0	2,941	14.4	8,184	8.5	2,787	8.0	9,830	10.3	3,310	6.3
Construction	5,635	7.1	26	0.1	6,149	6.4	12	0.0	9,815	10.2	110	0.2
Transport	5,403	6.9	30	0.1	4,276	4.4	25	0.1	4,105	4.3	110	0.2
Materials Handling; Other Crafts & Equipment Operating; and Occupations N.E.S.	12,252	15.6	961	4.7	13,018	13.5	1,114	3.2	7,735	8.1	1,610	3.1
Occupations Not Stated	833	1.1	217	1.1	2,695	2.8	1,038	3.0	7,545	7.9	5,245	10.0
Summary Table												
"White Collar" Occupations	6,628	8.4	1,882	9.0	15,342	16.0	4,270	12.3	12,230	12.8	8,025	15.3
Service Occupations	8,900	11.3	11,750	57.6	15,626	16.2	20,086	57.6	21,885	22.9	29,300	55.8
Primary Occupations	22,776	28.9	1,169	5.7	16,891	17.6	3,293	9.4	11,060	11.5	3,220	6.1
Manufacturing & Construction	39,643	50.3	5,440	26.6	45,546	47.4	6,183	17.7	43,050	45.0	6,720	12.8
Not Specified	833	1.1	217	1.1	2,695	2.8	1,038	3.0	7,545	7.8	5,245	10.0
TOTAL	78,780	100.0	20,408	100.0	96,100	100.0	34,870	100.0	95,770	100.0	52,510	100.0
Population, Age 15+	89,743		73,335		117,736		101,767		123,700		116,265	
Participation Rate	87.8		27.8		81.6		34.3		77.4		45.2	
Canadian Participation Rate	83.8		24.1		77.7		29.5		75.1		38.7	

Source: Rudolf K. Kogler, "Occupational Trends in the Polish Canadian Community: 1941-71," in Frank Renkiewicz, ed., *The Polish Presence in Canada and America* (Toronto: Multicultural History Society of Ontario, 1982), p. 222

operatives. Most have stayed away from farm ownership or hired labor, and few are in private service or other service occupations.

Polish-American women are about average in the frequency with which they are in paid employment. Only 13 percent are in professional and technical jobs and few are managers. They are less likely than Russian women to be in clerical positions, and more apt to be in operative and non-household service jobs. This distribution reflects the continued unwillingness of Polish Americans to educate their daughters beyond the minimal schooling required by law. However, they have definitely moved out of personal service jobs.

Kogler found the Polish males in Canada still highly concentrated in manufacturing and construction in 1971, while the women remained in non-household service jobs to a great extent (see Table 6).[43] However, when compared to the national composition, in 1971 the Polish Canadians deviated much less in their labor force composition than they did in 1941. According to the Index of Dissimilarity, the Polish ethnic group's males deviated 13.7 and the females 12.4 from the national average in 1941, and only 6.7 for the males and 5.2 for the females in 1971.[44] The Italians deviated the most at both times, and the German males showed the greatest rate of improvement:

TABLE 7
INDEX OF DISSIMILARITY, SELECTED ETHNIC GROUPS,
1941 AND 1971

Ethnic Group	1941		1971	
	Male	Female	Male	Female
British	5.7	4.2	4.1	5.5
French	4.4	8.4	3.5	5.6
German	20.0	7.8	8.4	5.1
Italian	25.5	23.3	19.5	26.8
Polish	13.7	12.4	6.7	5.2
Ukrainian	21.7	14.0	5.9	7.8

Source: Rudolf Kogler, "Occupational Trends in the Polish Canadian Community: 1941-1971," in Frank Renkiewicz, ed., *The Polish Presence in Canada and America* (Toronto: The Multicultural History Society of Ontario, 1982), p. 215.

Although it is hard to compare the Canadian and American figures, it does appear that the Poles in Canada work more frequently in sales and service jobs, and much less frequently in managerial occupations, than in the United States (see Tables 4, 5 and 6).

Babinski used the United States census to trace the "Occupational Mobility of Polish Americans in Selected U.S. Cities after World War Two."[45] His conclusions, which apply to the years 1950 to 1970 and to selected cities, include:

Polish Americans in these cities move upward in average occupational position in a manner and rate similar to other ethnic groups. Changes of America's Polonia are neither slower nor different than changes in other groups.

When age is held constant, the index of occupational dissimilarity between second-generation Polish Americans and all Americans of native, of foreign, or mixed parentage is low. This index also gives a low score for Polish second generation compared with the American population as a whole. But one has to be aware that the scale of occupations used in the census is not very precise and distinguishes only the major occupational categories.[46]

Babinski documents these conclusions, depicted in Table 8, which shows, for example, that both the men and the women identified as Polish American of foreign stock (foreign born or of mixed or foreign-born parents), age twenty-five to forty-four, have entered professional and technical occupations to an extent commensurate with the American population as a whole, thus pulling themselves up to that level at a rate higher than the total.[47] This is especially true of the men, who are more apt to be professionals than are the males of the nation as a whole. Both the men and the women are still unlikely to be in managerial positions and to be overrepresented in operative jobs.

Summary and Conclusions

The attempt to discover as much as possible about Polish and Polish-American workers in this country leads to several conclusions. The first is that the different immigrations contained a variety of types of Poles in terms of social class, education, occupation, family composition, knowledge of Polish, interest in assimilation to America and so forth. The social class and interest differences contributed both to the building of a complex ethnic community and to internal strife, accentuated by the status competition. The mass of "old emigration" consisted of former peasants who settled in urban areas and at the low end of industrial jobs. They are the best known of the Polish immigrants to America, the other strata often keeping apart from them, hoping for political changes in the home country and oriented toward a different kind of life here. The great gap between the peasant and the gentry strata, the latter of which identified with the intelligentsia, traditionally led to distrust and dislike of education by the former peasants, even in their settlement in America.

TABLE 8

OCCUPATIONAL DISTRIBUTION OF POLISH AMERICAN AND NATIVE BORN, 1950-1970, AGE GROUP 25-44 (PERCENTAGE)

Occupation	Men 1950		Men 1970		Women 1950		Women 1970	
	U.S.	Polish	U.S.	Polish	U.S.	Polish	U.S.	Polish
Professional and Technical	9.8	7.3	21.9	24.3	11.0	7.0	19.7	19.4
Managers and Administrators	12.7	9.3	14.3	13.3	4.5	3.6	4.1	3.7
Sales Workers	15.1	12.8	7.8	7.9			6.8	6.5
Clerical Workers	21.3		7.6	8.2	40.5	30.7	41.1	42.1
Craftsmen	23.6	23.6	21.0	21.0	2.1	2.7	1.7	1.7
Operatives, Except Transport	23.6	23.6	10.0	11.7	27.6	42.4	11.8	14.4
Transport Equipment Operatives			5.1	4.5			0.5	0.4
Laborers, Except Farm	6.0	6.9	4.0	3.3	0.8	1.3	0.7	0.8
Farmers and Farm Managers	4.7	1.8	1.3	0.6	0.2	0.2	0.1	0.1
Farm Laborers and Farm Foremen	1.5	0.8	0.8	0.2	1.5	0.7	0.4	0.1
Service Workers, Except Domestic	4.7	4.3	6.2	5.1	8.8	9.2	12.2	10.4
Domestic Workers	—	—	—	—	1.8	1.5	0.8	0.4
Index of Occupational Dissimilarity: U.S. vs. Polish	12		5		16		3	

Source: Grzegorz Babinski, "Occupational Mobility of Polish Americans in Selected U.S. Cities After World War II," in Frank Renkiewicz, ed., The Polish Presence in Canada and America (Toronto: The Multicultural History Society of Ontario, 1982), pp. 229-239.

As a result of the fact that education was not a criterion for social status in the non- and anti-intellectual levels of Polonian life, there was a relative lack of intergenerational occupational mobility, though median family income increased as the lower-level unskilled jobs were dropped in early years. However, there appears to be a change in the attitudes of second- and third-generation Polish Americans toward higher education, so that parents are allowing and even encouraging their young to get more schooling. This trend is beginning to be reflected in the occupational distribution of younger people who still identify their national or ethnic origin as Polish. At least the second-generation Polish Americans are apparently moving away from industrial jobs and into ones requiring higher levels of education.

NOTES

[1] Milton Gordon, *Assimilation in American Life* (New York: Oxford University Press, 1964).

[2] Fredrik Barth, ed., *Ethnic Groups and Boundaries* (Boston: Little, Brown, 1969); Raymond Breton, "Institutional Completeness of Ethnic Communities and the Personal Relations of Immigrants," *American Journal of Sociology*, LXX:2 (September 1964): 193-205; Helena Znaniecka Lopata, *Polish Americans: Status Competition in an Ethnic Community* (Englewood Cliffs, New Jersey: Prentice Hall, 1976).

[3] See W. S. Kuniczak, *My Name is Million* (Garden City, New York: Doubleday, 1978) and *The Silent Emigration* (Chicago: Polish Arts Club, 1968); and Arthur L. Waldo, *True Heroes of Jamestown* (Miami: American Institute of Polish Culture, 1977).

[4] Mieczyslaw Haiman, *Historia Udzielo Polakow w Ameryhskiej Wojnie Domowej* (Chicago: Dziennik Zjednoczenia, 1928); *Polacy w Ameryce* (Chicago: Polish Roman Catholic Union Press, 1930); *Polacy w Walce o Niepodleglosci Ameryki* (Chicago: Dziennik Zjednoczenia, 1930); *Kosciuszko in the American Revolution* (New York: Polish Institute of Arts and Sciences in America, 1943); *Kosciuszko, Leader and Exile* (New York: Polish Institute of Arts and Sciences in America, 1946); and Kuniczak, *My Name is Million*, op. cit.

[5] Helena Znaniecka Lopata, "Polish Immigration to the United States of America: Problems of Estimation and Parameters," *The Polish Review*, 21:4 (November 1976): 85-108; and Lopata, *Polish Americans, op. cit.*

[6] Lopata, "Polish Immigration," ibid.

[7] Jan Szczepanski, *Polish Society* (New York: Random House, 1970).

[8] Lopata, *Polish Americans*, op. cit.

[9] W. I. Thomas and Florian Znaniecki, *The Polish Peasant in Europe and America* (New York: Alfred Knopf, 1918-1920); Lopata, *Polish Americans*, op. cit.; Helena Znaniecka Lopata, "Widowhood in Polonia," *Polish American Studies*, 34:4 (Autumn 1977): 7-25; Helena Znaniecka Lopata, "Funcia Stowarzyazen Dobrowolnych w Polonijney Wspolnocie Etnicznej," *Studia Polonijne* 2 (Lublin, Poland: 1978): 83-112; Helena Znaniecka Lopata "The

Double Bind of Emigre Intelligentsia: The Polish Case," presented at the Midwest Sociological Society Meetings (Milwaukee, 1980).

[10]See Helena Znaniecka Lopata, "The Function of Voluntary Associations in an Ethnic Community: Polonia," in Ernest W. Burgess and Donald J. Bogue, eds., *Contributions to Urban Sociology* (Chicago: University of Chicago Press, 1964) and Lopata, "Funcja Stowarzyazen Dobrowolnych," op. cit., for a description of Polonia.

[11]Lopata, "Polish Immigration," op. cit., p. 21.

[12]Haiman, op. cit., and Koniczak, *My Name is Million*, op. cit.

[13]Lopata, "Polish Immigration," op. cit.

[14]U.S. Immigration and Naturalization Service, 1909, as listed in Lopata, *Polish Americans*, op. cit., p. 40.

[15]Edward Pinkowski, "The Great Influx of Polish Immigrants and the Industries They Entered," in Frank Mocha, ed., *Poles in America: Bicentennial Essays* (Stevens Point, Wis.: Worzalla Publishing Co., 1978), p. 336.

[16]Lopata, "Polish Immigration," op. cit., and *Polish Americans*, op. cit.

[17]Lopata, *Polish Americans*, op. cit., p. 41.

[18]Danuta Mostwin, "Post World War II: Polish Immigrants in the United States," *Polish American Studies*, 26:2 (Autumn 1969): 5-14; and *The Transplanted Family: A Study of Social Adjustment of the Polish Immigrant Family to the United States After the Second World War* (Ann Arbor, Mich.: University Microfilms, 1971).

[19]See Jan Szczepanski, "The Polish Intelligentsia, Past and Present," *World Politics*, XVI: 3 (April 1962): 406-420; Szczepanski, *Polish Society*, op. cit.; Lopata, *Polish Americans*, op. cit.; and Lopata, "The Double Bind," op. cit.

[20]Felix Gross, "Notes on the Ethnic Revolution and the Polish Immigration in the USA," *The Polish Review*, XXI:3 (August 1976): 149-176.

[21]Ibid., p. 161.

[22]Ibid., p. 162.

[23]Stanisalwu A. Blejwus, "Old and New Polonias: Tensions within an Ethnic Community," *Polish American Studies*, XXXVIII:2 (Autumn 1981): 55-83; Mostwin, "Post World War II," op. cit.; Mostwin, *The Transplanted Family*, op. cit.

[24]Thomas and Znaniecki, op. cit.

[25]Pinkowski, op. cit.

[26]Theodore Abel, "Sunderland: A Study of Changes in the Group-life of Poles in New England Farming Community," in Edmund De S. Brunner, ed., *Immigrant Farmers and Their Children* (Garden City, N. Y.: Doubleday, 1919), pp. 213-243.

[27]Caroline Golab, *Immigrant Destinations* (Philadelphia: Temple University Press, 1977); Pinkowski, op. cit.; Thomas and Znaniecki, op. cit.

[28]Pinkowski, op. cit., p. 338.

[29]Ibid., p. 334.

[30]Ibid., p. 345.

[31]Ibid., p. 359.

[32]Joseph J. Parot, "The 'Serdeczna Matki' of the Sweatshops: Marital and Family Crises of Immigrant Working-Class Women in Late Nineteenth-Century Chicago," in Frank Renkiewicz, ed., *The Polish Presence in Canada and America* (Toronto: The Multicultural History Society of Ontario, 1982), pp. 155-182.

[33]Ibid., p. 163.

[34]Beverly Duncan and Otis Dudley Duncan, "Minorities and the Process of Stratification," *American Sociological Review*, 33:2 (June 1968): 356-364; Andrew Greeley, *Ethnicity in the United States* (New York: Wiley and Sons, 1974); Edward Hutchinson, *Immigrants and their Children: 1850-1950* (New York: John Wiley & Sons, 1956); Stanley Lieberson, *Ethnic Patterns in American Cities* (New York: The Free Press, 1963); and Lopata, *Polish Americans*, op. cit., pp. 94-95.

[35]Lieberson, op. cit., p. 189.

[36]Duncan and Duncan, op. cit., p. 363.

[37]Greeley, *Ethnicity in the United States*, op. cit., p. 35.

[38]Ibid.; Thomas Sowell, ed., *Essays and Data on American Ethnic Groups* (Washington, D.C.: The Urban Institute, 1978).

[39]Andrew Greeley, "The Ethnic and Religious Origins of Young American Scientists and Engineers: A Research Note," *International Migration Review*, 6:3 (Fall 1972): 282-287.

[40]Greeley, *Ethnicity in the United States*, op. cit.

[41]Ibid., p. 86.

[42]U.S. Bureau of the Census, *Current Population Reports*, Series P-20, No. 221, "Characteristics of the Population by Ethnic Origin, November, 1969" (Washington, D.C.: U.S. Government Printing Office, 1971), pp. 220, 221, 249.

[43]Rudolf Kogler, "Occupational Trends in the Polish Canadian Community: 1941-1971," in Renkiewicz, op. cit., p. 222.

[44]Ibid., p. 215.

[45]Grzegorz Babinski, "Occupational Mobility of Polish Americans in Selected U.S. Cities after World War II," in Renkiewicz, op. cit., pp. 229-239.

[46]Ibid., pp. 234-235.

[47]Ibid., p. 236.

ALTERED STATES: CHICANOS IN THE LABOR FORCE

Lionel A. Maldonado

University of Wisconsin-Parkside

Introduction

This chapter reviews the experience of the Mexican-origin population in the work force of the United States. The 135 years that Mexicanos have been in the United States are divided into eras or periods. These periods illustrate changed economic and social conditions; each mirrors an altered economic niche of Mexican Americans. The more recent years, since 1970, are accorded greater detailed attention. The chapter concludes that the experiences of Mexican Americans in the United States economy have been, and will continue to be, significantly different from those of other groups. This distinctiveness stems from two sources: (1) the historical legacy of discrimination bestowed upon Chicanos and (2) factors associated with immigrant status among Mexicans now arriving in the United States.

Historical Background

Introduction

Chicanos, like blacks and Native Americans, were involuntarily incorporated into American society. This involuntary incorporation of Chicanos was through military conquest. The United States fought its first war of imperialism, with Mexico, from 1846 to 1848. The spoils of this action were the addition of over one million square miles of what is now known as the American Southwest, an addition which increased the size of the United States by fully one-third its present size (Acuña, 1981; Barrera, 1979; Estrada, et al., 1982; McWilliams, 1968). In addition to territorial expansion and the abundant natural resources that came with it, the United States also acquired the Mexican population that elected to remain on its conquered land. Estimates of this population place it between eighty-six thousand and 116,000 around the time hostilities ceased, and suggest that it had increased by more than four-fold by the turn of the century (Martinez, 1975).

The population, with roots extending to the days of Spanish coloni-zation, represented the full range of the class structure. There was an upper class that was largely a landed aristocracy, whose social position was based on large holdings acquired through Spanish and Mexican land grants. Typically, this group had ties to other economic activities such as finance and, later, the developing railroad lines. It was also the dominant political force. The middle class consisted of artisans, small-scale landowners, vaqueros and merchants in assorted business and commercial activities. The largest proportion of the class pyramid was of individuals principally in farm labor, as tenant farmers and as un-skilled workers in the town economies. The growth and development of the mining (copper, silver and gold) and lumber industries, along with the railroads, expanded Mexicans' occupational opportunities as wage laborers in the latter part of the nineteenth century.

In their first fifty years as U. S. citizens, the newly incorporated Mexicans were affected by two powerful forces which radically altered their social structure. One was the *dispossession* of real property hold-ings. Wholesale transfers of land from Mexican to Anglo ownership took place between 1848 and 1900 and shortly thereafter. Force, coer-cion, intimidation and outright fraud were common means to achieve this end. Land courts and commissions established by the American state provided the legal sanctions and justifications for the process of dispossession, ultimately transferring better than two-thirds of the Mexicans' land holdings to Anglos.

The second social force that operated on the Mexican population was that of class *displacement*. The decades from the Mexican War's end to the turn of the century were marked by a steady growth in the proportion of Mexicans in manual occupations, and a concomitant de-crease in the numbers who were merchants and in commercial pursuits. New occupational opportunities developed in mining, lumber and the railroads. Here, Mexicans, both long-term native residents of the Southwest and those newly recruited from Mexico, faced a dual wage system: they received lower pay than Anglos for identical jobs. They also had to contend with the fact that jobs above a certain rank were closed to them. That category tended to be the more prestigious and rewarding skilled and supervisory jobs. The net result was a wholesale, downward shift of the class position of the majority of the Mexican population by the close of the nineteenth century (Acuña, 1981; Barrera, 1979; Estrada, et al., 1981; Griswold del Castillo, 1979; Camarillo, 1979).

The role of the American state during this period was clear and consistent. It was instrumental in the initial marshalling of military forces to conquer an area rich in natural resources with a plentiful source of labor. The legal system also functioned to undermine the social, economic and political status of the group as it was subordinated and rendered impotent. Mexicans were reduced to landless wage laborers who, in times of economic hardship, filled the ranks of the unemployed as a reserve labor pool. Original settlers and those more recently recruited to till the soil, work the mines and help build the railroads were held together by a common bond imposed upon them: rigid segregation and discrimination best described as a state of conflict with the dominant society. This state of affairs had its ideological justification in the racism inherent in the national theme of Manifest Destiny. This ideological baggage served to justify harsh treatment and inequality before the law, conditions not restricted solely to Mexicans during these times. Parallels can be noted in the treatment of blacks, Native Americans and the Chinese (Daniels and Kitano, 1970).

The Twentieth Century

If the mode of incorporation of Mexicanos in the mid-nineteenth century was involuntary, that in the early decades of the twentieth was just the opposite. Between 1900 to 1930 there was an increased flow north across the two thousand miles of border separating the United States from Mexico. One estimate is that from 1901 to 1910 approximately 9,300 Mexicans came to the United States each year. The annual average was about 1,900 between 1911 and 1914, rising to around 2,750 persons yearly from 1915 to 1919. The third decade was one of still greater numbers moving north. Between 1920 and 1924 more than 135,000 Mexicans (i.e., about twenty-seven thousand annually) left for the United States. This figure dropped to about eighteen thousand per year between 1925 and 1930. In all, about 250,000 Mexicans arrived in the United States in the first three decades of the twentieth century (Estrada, et al., 1981; Servin, 1966).

Reasons for this northward flow are varied and complex. They include the nature of foreign investment in Mexico, which extracted wealth and helped restrict the growth and development of the nation's economy. The mechanization of agriculture served to displace Mexican peasantry, few of whom could be absorbed in the modest industrial sector. These structural strains were made worse by Mexico's very high population growth rate (for example, it increased by 50 percent between 1875 and 1910). These factors, among others, perpetuated tre-

mendous social and economic inequalities. The net result of these inequalities was the Revolution of 1910 (Barrera, 1979; Acuña, 1981;
Stavrianos, 1981).

The lack of opportunities in Mexico was more than made up by
those in the United States. The Southwest's economy was developing
and expanding. Initial labor demands were in agriculture, along with
sheep and cattle ranching. By 1900 over 1,500,000 acres had been given
over to farming. The national Reclamation Act of 1902 was significant
in further developing the highly labor-intensive agricultural sector
with the building of dams and reservoirs that transformed the desert
into a highly fertile region. This also helped spread the cultivation of
cotton west from the South, to the point that cotton became an important commodity in every state of the Southwest. World War I began in
1914 and served as an added impetus for the expansion of the agricultural economy in the Southwest. It led to the introduction and cultivation of still other commodities necessary to feed and clothe the armies
in Europe.

The expanding agricultural economy, of course, helped create other
industries for processing, canning, packing and crating these products.
Railroad construction for transporting goods to market increased
greatly at this time. Sheep and cattle ranching continued, thereby creating new industries in meat processing and shipping. Mining gained
momentum also. Manufacturing of machines for the extraction of ore
and its processing was in demand. Labor was needed first for copper
mining in Arizona and New Mexico, then quartz in Nevada, Colorado
and Arizona. Petroleum in Texas and California soon came into its own
importance. Housing needs helped stimulate the lumber industry, and
it became a major force in Texas, California, Arizona and New Mexico.
Processing and distribution needs in this industry also created still
other work opportunities.

The expanding economy was highly labor-intensive. Mexicans filled
this need. (Europeans were being absorbed in the industrial economies
of the Northeast and Midwest; relatively few got very far west.) The
evidence is fairly consistent that the economic niche of Mexicans who
made their way north (through kinship networks or active recruitment
by U.S. companies) united them with their native-born Chicano counterparts. The work was often seasonal in nature. In agricultural and
related industries, they were pressed into the dual wage system. Their
ethnic and national origins barred them from supervisory positions.
Conditions in mining and related industries were scarcely better
(Briggs, Fogel and Schmidt, 1977; Acuña, 1981; Barrera, 1979).

Urban centers in the Southwest were developing into larger concentrations during this time. In most instances, these were expanded ver-

sions of earlier Mexican towns. Mexicans and Chicanos overwhelmingly were concentrated in the lower reaches of the urban occupational structure. Wage differentials common to the rural sectors persisted in urban areas, but were not quite as pronounced. Access to particular occupations and industries, however, was limited. Mobility rates were very low out of the unskilled and semiskilled positions in which Chicanos and Mexicans found themselves. They formed a reserve labor pool to be called upon as the situation dictated. Contractions of the economy quickly relegated them to the ranks of the unemployed.

Mexicans and Chicanos served the industrial economy in other ways. They were often used as strikebreakers by employers, an action directly intended to undermine unionizing efforts. It is clear that this also tended to generate ethnic antagonism between working-class Mexicans and Chicanos and their Anglo counterparts (Bonacich, 1972, 1976).

Trade union practices excluded Mexicans. Some unions went so far as to support and lobby for state legislation requiring workers in various industries to be American citizens (Higham, 1955; Hutchinson, 1956). The net effect of these practices was to maintain Mexicans and Chicanos at the bottom end of the class distribution during the first three decades of the twentieth century. It also forced them to organize their own unions and associations.

There is some evidence that there was a resurgence or reemergence of a middle class among Mexicans and Chicanos at this time. Typically, these were people self-employed in small-scale service enterprises (newspapers, retail stores, etc.), with a sprinkling of "professionals"— that is as elementary and secondary school teachers. Their businesses tended to serve their own Mexican and Chicano communities (Barrera, 1979; Acuña, 1981; Meier and Rivera, 1972).

During the early 1920s Mexicans and Chicanos began to settle outside the Southwest. Many were recruited by northern manufacturing interests: meat packing plants and steel mills in the Chicago area; automobile assembly lines in Detroit; the steel industry in Ohio and Pennsylvania; and Kansas City's meat packing plants. By 1930 about 15 percent of the nation's Mexicans and Chicanos were living outside the Southwest. In addition to the recruitment from Mexico and the American Southwest by the industries listed above, many Chicanos and Mexicans chose to settle out of the principal migrant streams. Regular routes had become established connecting South Texas with the Great Lakes and plains states. Many continued their odyssey, following the crops west through the northern tier of states, finally arriving in the Northwest, then turning south again. Others journeyed from Texas to the South, then north along the Eastern seaboard. Still others went

west for agricultural work. Mexicans and Chicanos in California
worked the crops north through that state, into the Northwest, then
east through the mountain states. Many settled out of the migrant
stream in areas where they found work (Briggs, Fogel and Schmidt,
1977). These labor markets, like those in the Southwest, tended to di-
vide along ethnic lines. Mexicans were seen as workers from a nation
with a lower level of living and as competitors willing to work for less,
given their alternatives at home. Not surprisingly the outcome tended
to be the maintenance of ethnic hostility, though perhaps less harsh
than that experienced by Mexicans and Chicanos in the Southwest
(Barrera, 1979; Bonacich, 1972, 1976; Estrada, et al., 1981; Taylor,
1970).

The openly racist motivation to bar Southern, Central and Eastern
European ethnic groups' immigration in the 1920s curiously exempted
Mexicans (Handlin, 1957). This exemption, while not exactly palat-
able to many political elites (cf. Acuña, 1981; Barrera, 1979), was
firmly grounded in economic interests. The argument was perhaps
most succinctly presented before a congressional committee by John
Nance Garner, who would later become vice president under Franklin
Delano Roosevelt: "In order to allow land owners now to make a profit
of their farms, they want to get the cheapest labor they can find, and if
they get the Mexican labor it enables them to make a profit." (Cited in
Estrada, et al., 1981: 116.)

Thus concluded the first three decades of the twentieth century for
Mexicanos and Chicanos. Myrdal's "principle of cumulation" (1944:
75-78, 1065-1070) perhaps most aptly sums up the successive accumulation of socially imposed discrimination that helped solidify their social and economic disadvantages. It is clear, moreover, that both intended and unintended consequences of the policies of the emerging
modern state, as it cooperated with economic interests to provide a
labor pool, further served to solidify and preserve Mexicans' and
Chicanos' disadvantaged social and economic position in America.

The Great Depression succeeded where nativists, xenophobes and
restrictionists had failed: It halted the flow of Mexicans to the United
States. Soon enough, this immigration was turned into a mass return
exodus. Hoffman (1974: 174-175) presents the figures of those who returned to Mexico. He presents data collected by the Mexican Migration Service which show that between 1929 and 1937, nearly a half-
million persons (N = 458,039) returned to Mexico from the United
States. Thus, in somewhat less than a decade, three-quarters more
Mexicans, many with American-born children, left the United States
than had arrived in the thirty years prior to the Great Depression.

This reverse population flow was influenced by policies of the state. Then commissioner general of the Bureau of Immigration, Harry E. Hull, stated in his annual report for fiscal year 1932:

Following the procedures inaugurated in February, 1931, making operative on an intensive scale the provisions of section 23 of the immigration act of 1917, authorizing the removal of aliens to their native countries who within three years of their landing in the United States have fallen into distress or public need aid. . . . This procedure constitutes an important contribution to the relief of communities and organizations burdened with the support of these aliens, who are without employment and destitute. As recorded for the last fiscal year, many cases involved persons in the prime of life, potential workers, who will no longer be competitors for the greatly restricted employment opportunities in our communities (Hull, 1932: 72-73).

There has been a recent effort to assess the effects of this large-scale repatriation of Mexicans and their American-born children on the socioeconomic status of the Mexican-American population of the United States. A cohort analysis was done on the Bureau of the Census 1976 Survey of Income and Education (SIE). Tabulations were presented on the Mexican-origin male population, sorted into native (United States)- and foreign (Mexican)-born, who selected Mexican American, Chicano, Mexican or Mexicano as their preferred ethnic identity. Each nativity group then was stratified into age cohorts to reflect various period effects (e.g., occupational opportunities that resulted from war industries, etc.). Comparisons were then made on occupational and educational attainments. Occupation was coded in Duncan's Socio-Economic Index (SEI); education was coded in mean years attained, with a range of 0-16 years.

Table 1 (see p. 152) shows that differences between nativity groups are substantial. Mexican-born men lag behind their U.S.-born counterparts on both factors by large margins. This is the case among all cohorts. Among the Mexican-born, there is a steady, though very modest, increase in average education from one cohort to the next. Mexican-born men, who begin at a much lower level than their American-born counterparts, systematically lag behind for each and every cohort comparison.

The table also shows a corresponding trend toward increasing homogeneity in terms of education. That is, the measure of dispersion (standard deviation) systematically decreases from each older to younger cohort; these changes are more pronounced within the U.S.-born group.

TABLE 1
EDUCATIONAL AND OCCUPATIONAL ATTAINMENTS OF
MEXICAN-ORIGIN MEN, BY COHORT AND NATIVITY, 1976
(Reported in Means, SDs and Proportions)

		Native Born			Foreign Born		
		X̄	SD	Proportion[a]	X̄	SD	Proportion
Cohorts by Age (Birth Years)				Education			
25-34	(1942-51)	12.0	3.0	1.15	7.5	4.3	1.17
35-44	(1932-41)	10.4	3.6	1.23	6.4	4.2	1.04
45-54	(1922-31)	8.4	4.1	1.35	6.1	4.5	1.12
55-64	(1912-21)	6.2	4.8	1.51	5.4	4.7	2.0
65+	(Before 1912)	4.1	4.1	—	2.7	5.3	—
				Occupation[b]			
25-34	(1942-51)	33.2	21.7	1.00	21.5	16.5	1.01
35-44	(1932-41)	33.2	21.5	1.24	21.1	16.5	1.18
45-54	(1922-31)	26.6	18.6	1.16	17.8	16.6	.85
55-64	(1912-21)	22.8	18.1	1.39	20.8	19.1	1.22
65+	(Before 1912)	16.4	14.5	—	17.0	16.6	—

Source: U.S. Bureau of the Census, *1976 Survey of Income and Education*. See also L. A.
Maldonado, "Class, Ethnicity, and the State: The Case of Mexican American
Repatriation" (Paper presented at the Midwest Sociological Society meetings,
1983).

[a]Proportion is based on the cohort's mean score divided by preceding cohort's mean
score. A value of less than one means a relative decline; above one, a relative advance.

[b]See Table 2 which illustrates the correspondence between various occupations and
scores on the Duncan-Blau Index of Occupational Status.

It is clear that the greatest relative advances in education occurred
much earlier among the U.S.-born men than among those from Mexico.
Specifically, the table shows that men born in the United States between 1912 and 1921 increased their education, on average, by one-
third over what the preceding cohort had attained, to 8.4 years. The
next cohort, those born just prior to the Great Depression, attained
one-third again the number of years of education relative to their preceding cohort. Those born between 1932 and 1941 received nearly one-
fourth more education than those born between 1922 and 1931. The
youngest cohort (aged 25-34), on the average, graduated from high
school.

In contrast, the advances in education among the Mexican-born
men are more modest and began at a much lower level than their U.S.
counterparts. Their relative gains also show up much more recently
among those born after 1942. The data show that the greatest educational advances were made by cohorts of Mexican Americans born in

the United States during the Great Depression decade, who benefited from the generally expanded educational facilities during the years they were growing up, the 1940s and 1950s. In contrast, Mexican-born men lagged behind their American-born counterparts, made gains that were far more modest, and evidenced greater intra-group variation.

Table 1 also lists the mean SEI occupational scores for succeeding cohorts of each nativity group. It is clear that the oldest cohorts of each nativity group have very low occupational scores. It is also obvious that the U.S.-born groups have increased their occupational attainments more dramatically, with the greatest attainments among those born during and immediately after the Great Depression ($\overline{X}$ = 33.2 for each of the two cohorts). The table also indicates that the significant inter-cohort changes have been sustained.

Unlike the pattern shown among U.S.-born Mexican Americans, those from Mexico show only very modest gains from one cohort to the next; their scores of occupational status remain low for all groups. Indeed, the highest score among this nativity group (21.5 for men aged 25 to 34) is well below that of all except the very oldest of the U.S.-born.

With regard to the extent of occupational homogeneity among both groups, it is clear that the U.S.-born are far more similar than their Mexican-born counterparts. Moreover, there is increasing homogeneity from older to younger cohorts; it is more marked among U.S.-born Mexican-American men. The major watershed period is the rapid economic expansion that occurred with World War II.

TABLE 2
OCCUPATIONS ILLUSTRATING VARIOUS SCORES
ON THE INDEX OF OCCUPATIONAL STATUS

Score Interval	Title of Occupation (Frequency per 10,000 Males in 1960 Experienced Civilian Labor Force in Parentheses)
90 to 96	Architects (7); dentists (18); chemical engineers (9); lawyers and judges (45); physicians and surgeons (47)
85 to 89	Aeronautical engineers (11); industrial engineers (21); salaried managers, banking and finance (30); self-employed proprietors, banking and finance (5)
80 to 84	College presidents, professors and instructors (31); editors and reporters (14); electrical engineers (40); pharmacists (19); officials, federal public administration and postal service (13); salaried managers, business services (11)
75 to 79	Accountants and auditors (87); chemists (17); veterinarians (3); salaried managers, manufacturing (133); self-employed proprietors, insurance and real estate (9)
70 to 74	Designers (12); teachers (105); store buyers and department heads (40); credit men (8); salaried managers, wholesale trade (41); self-employed proprietors, motor vehicles and accessories retailing (12); stock and bond salesmen (6)

65 to 69   Artists and art teachers (15); draftsmen (45); salaried managers, mo-
              tor vehicles and accessories retailing (18); self-employed proprie-
              tors, apparel and accessories retail stores (8); agents, n.e.c.* (29);
              advertising agents and salesmen (7); salesmen, manufacturing (93);
              foremen, transportation equipment manufacturing (18)
60 to 64   Librarians (3); sports instructors and officials (12); postmasters (5);
              salaried managers, construction (31); self-employed proprietors,
              manufacturing (35); stenographers, typists and secretaries (18);
              ticket, station and express agents (12); real estate agents and bro-
              kers (33); salesmen, wholesale trade (106); foremen, machinery
              manufacturing (28); photoengravers and lithographers (5)
55 to 59   Funeral directors and embalmers (8); railroad conductors (10); self-
              employed proprietors, wholesale trade (28); electrotypers and ste-
              reotypers (2); foremen, communications, utilities and sanitary ser-
              vices (12); locomotive engineers (13)
50 to 54   Clergymen (43); musicians and music teachers (19); officials and ad-
              ministrators, local public administration (15); salaried managers,
              food and dairy products stores (21); self-employed proprietors, con-
              struction (50); bookkeepers (33); mail carriers (43); foremen, metal
              industries (28); toolmakers, die-makers and setters (41)
45 to 49   Surveyors (10); salaried managers, automobile repair services and ga-
              rages (4); office machine operators (18); linemen and servicemen,
              telephone, telegraph and power (60); locomotive firemen (9); air-
              plane mechanics and repairmen (26); stationary engineers (60)
40 to 44   Self-employed proprietors, transportation (8); self-employed proprie-
              tors, personal services (19); cashiers (23); clerical and kindred work-
              ers, n.e.c. (269); electricians (77); construction foremen (22); motion
              picture projectionists (4); photographic process workers (5); rail-
              road switchmen (13); policemen and detectives, government (51)
35 to 39   Salaried and self-employed managers and proprietors, eating and
              drinking places (43); salesmen and sales clerks, retail trade (274);
              book-binders (3); radio and television repairmen (23); firemen, fire
              protection (30); policemen and detectives, private (3)
30 to 34   Building managers and superintendents (7); self-employed proprie-
              tors, gasoline service stations (32); boilermakers (6); machinists
              (111); millwrights (15); plumbers and pipe fitters (72); structural
              metal workers (14); tinsmiths, coppersmiths and sheet metal work-
              ers (31); deliverymen and routemen (93); operatives, printing, pub-
              lishing and allied industries (13); sheriffs and bailiffs (5)
25 to 29   Messengers and office boys (11); newsboys (41); brickmasons, stone-
              masons and tile setters (45); mechanics and repairmen, n.e.c. (266);
              plasterers (12); operatives, drugs and medicine manufacturing (2);
              ushers, recreation and amusement (2); laborers, petroleum refining
              (3)
20 to 24   Telegraph messengers (1); shipping and receiving clerks (59); bakers
              (21); cabinetmakers (15); excavating, grading and road machine op-
              erators (49); railroad and car shop mechanics and repairmen (9);
              tailors (7); upholsterers (12); bus drivers (36); filers, grinders and
              polishers, metal (33); welders and flame-cutters (81)
15 to 19   Blacksmiths (5); carpenters (202); automobile mechanics and repair-
              men (153); painters (118); attendants, auto service and parking
              (81); laundry and dry cleaning operatives (25); truck and tractor
              drivers (362); stationary firemen (20); operatives, metal industries
              (103); operatives, wholesale and retail trade (35); barbers (38); bar-
              tenders (36); cooks, except private household (47)
10 to 14   Farmers (owners and tenants) (521); shoemakers and repairers, ex-
              cept factory (8); dyers (4); taxicab drivers and chauffeurs (36); at-

tendants, hospital and other institution (24); elevator operators (11); fishermen and oystermen (9); gardeners, except farm, and groundskeepers (46); longshoremen and stevedores (13); laborers, machinery manufacturing (10)

5 to 9   Hucksters and peddlers (5); sawyers (20); weavers, textile (8); operatives, footwear, except rubber, manufacturing (16); janitors and sextons (118); farm laborers, wage workers (241); laborers, blast furnaces, steel works and rolling mills (26); construction laborers (163)

0 to 4   Coal mine operatives and laborers (31); operatives, yarn, thread and fabric mills (30); porters (33); laborers, saw mills, planing mills and millwork (21)

---

*n.e.c. means "not elsewhere classified"

Sources: Peter M. Blau and Otis Dudley Duncan, *The American Occupational Structure* (New York: Wiley, 1967), pp. 122-123. This table in turn was compiled from Albert J. Reiss, Jr., et al., *Occupations and Social Status* (New York: The Free Press of Glencoe, 1961), Table B-1; and U.S. Bureau of the Census, *1960 Census of Population*, Final Report, PC(1)-1D, Table 201.

These data offer support for the observation that policies of the modern state during the depression had a direct effect on the class position of Mexican Americans. This is based on the assumption that findings from the 1976 SIE suggest that the experiences of Mexicans and Chicanos who underwent repatriation during the Great Depression would have matched those who remained: significant upward mobility. The data demonstrate that U.S.-born Mexican Americans made the most significant advances as a result of the expanded economic opportunities of the post-depression years, a time when the economy of the United States experienced major growth. The conclusion is that the state's policies, in effect, removed a significant proportion of the Mexican-American population, preventing it from being able to take advantage of the expanded economic opportunities which had a significant impact on those who did remain.

World War II had other profound effects on the Mexican-American community. The movement to the cities accelerated. Regional economic interests continued to dominate policy, particularly in the agricultural arena. The bracero program was reestablished in 1942 on the earlier 1917-1920 model. The bracero program was a bilateral agreement established between Mexico and the United States with the intent to supply labor for agriculture. The United States underwrote Mexicans' travel costs, insured a minimum wage, and guaranteed their just and equitable treatment. Agricultural interests were required to post a bond for every bracero and to abide by the negotiated agreement between the two nations. This program was, in effect, a federal subsidy of agriculture's labor needs.

The bracero program was intended to be in effect only for the duration of World War II. Its advantages to both nations became a powerful inducement for its continuation. For Mexico, it was a temporary solution to high levels of unemployment; it also made for a significant flow of capital to that nation in the form of wages earned and sent home. For U.S. interests, it provided a steady supply of labor easily controlled, minimally paid, and for whom no long-term responsibilities were assumed.

The bracero program was extended annually after World War II. Among the reasons advanced for its continuation was the labor shortage resulting from America's involvement in the Korean War. Nearly five million Mexicans came to the United States as a result of the bracero program. Peak years were from 1954 to 1962, when 70 percent of all Mexicans involved in the project were in the United States. No reliable figures have been provided on the number of laborers who returned to Mexico. The program finally was terminated in 1964 with the establishment of immigration quotas for Western Hemisphere nations set at 120,000 annually.

An unanticipated consequence of the bracero program, with far more enduring effects, is that it stimulated the parallel flow of undocumented workers. On the one hand, they generally were hired for wages substantially below the modest pay for braceros, nor was it necessary for employers to post bonds. The undocumented workers were used to undermine unionizing activities in agriculture. But there were also significant drawbacks to this labor source. It was a highly unstable labor pool, for the status of the undocumented laborers afforded them the luxury of ignoring the condition of a binding agreement to an employer. They were free to seek their highest wage (within the confines imposed by undocumented status), and they did not have to heed the formal agreement that restricted braceros to the agricultural sector.

A series of strategies was initiated by agricultural interests, in conjunction with the U.S. government, to regain control of the Mexican labor supply (see Acuña, 1981: 201-206; Estrada, et al., 1981; Galarza, 1964). The most dramatic of these efforts was Operation Wetback, a national effort launched by the Immigration and Naturalization Service (INS) in 1954. The aim was to remove the undocumented, and toward this end a total of 3.8 million presumably Mexican aliens were apprehended and expelled over the next five years. Fewer than 2 percent left as a result of formal proceedings. The vast majority were removed by threat of deportation.

In spite of the termination of large-scale guest worker programs between Mexico and the United States, and the operations by the INS to curtail the influx of the undocumented, immigration from Mexico continues to be extensive. This flow of Mexicans, legal and otherwise, shows no sign of abatement (Frisbie, 1975; Heer, 1979; Keely, 1982). It is a response to economic opportunities in the United States (even if they are in the secondary labor market, marked by its lower wages, limited fringe benefits and general instability), and the lack of such in Mexico (Portes, 1979). The periodic strategy by the INS of systematically removing large portions of the Mexican-origin population continues to affect the current status of Mexican Americans. Its long-term implications can be predicted to be negative.

In addition to the persistent influx of Mexicans to the United States, the Chicano population demonstrates a number of unique demographic characteristics important for understanding its labor force participation. One of these important factors is its *youthfulness*, with a median age seven years below that of the balance of the nation. (Estrada, et al., 1981: 125-126, summarize these factors.)

A second important trait among Chicanos is the substantial *growth* of the group over the last decade. In part, this growth can be attributed to improved methods of survey and enumeration by data-collection agencies. The greater part of the increase comes from real growth, estimated to be between 2.2 and 3.5 percent per year. This growth rate stands in stark contrast to the decreasing rates among the U.S. population, which appear to have stabilized at just above replacement levels. Factors such as early marriage and an emphasis on family account for these higher fertility rates.

The third major factor to bear in mind is the continuing dispersion of the Mexican-origin population from the Southwest. This is a movement that can be traced back to the 1920s. The current decade of the 1980s undoubtedly will see nearly half of the Chicano population living outside the five southwestern states.

It is against this combination of factors—historic, immigration-connected and demographic—that the current status of the Mexican-origin population in America's labor market must be viewed.

Current Status: Since 1970

There has been a very large and rapid growth in the research literature on Mexican Americans. In large measure, researchers have relied on census data for many macro-level analyses. This has tended to present a somewhat distorted picture of Mexican Americans to the extent that researchers have based their work on enumerations on the Spanish-surnamed, rather than exclusively on the Mexican-origin. The core of the problem lies in the fact that 40 percent of the Spanish-surnamed come from non-Mexican groups. These include Cubans, Puerto Ricans, Central Americans and South Americans, among others.

It has been demonstrated that there are significant variations between Mexican-origin and these other Hispanic groups (Garcia and Maldonado, 1982). These differences are in labor force participation factors such as education, occupational attainments, income, age, family size and growth rates. The data presented here, therefore, will be only of the Mexican-origin portion of Hispanics in the United States.

Table 3 provides a summary of selected social characteristics of the Mexican-origin population in the United States in 1970. Three generational groups within the Mexican-origin population are presented: "first generation" are those born in Mexico; "second generation" are all U.S.-born persons with at least one parent born in Mexico; and "third generation" includes U.S.-born persons of U.S.-born parents. Parameters for the first two categories are from the 15 percent sample of the 1970 Census; the third is derived from merging the 15 and 5 percent samples. Both samples were weighted to represent their actual proportions. A residual was obtained by subtracting adjusted tabulations for persons of foreign stock from adjusted tabulations of those identifying themselves as of Mexican-origin; this represents third and succeeding generations of Mexican-descent persons in the United States. It is possible that this procedure may result in added estimation errors in the native-born of the native parentage group because of sampling variability between the two files. The procedure does, however, avoid errors associated with the systematic mislabelling of both Mexican- and non-Mexican-origin persons (Garcia and Maldonado, 1982).

The gap in educational attainments between whites and Mexican Americans has been amply documented. Pachon and Moore (1981), for example, inform us that in 1980 only about one-third (34.3 percent) of the Mexican Americans completed more than a dozen years of schooling; in sharp contrast to the better than two-thirds (67.1 percent) of whites who completed that amount of education. Others, adding more refinement, have partitioned Mexican Americans into U.S.- and Mexican-born, and have then compared each nativity group to whites' educational attainments (Chiswick, 1983). Here, too, there are significant differences among the groups, with whites having the greatest attainments followed by native- and then foreign-born Mexican Americans.

Table 3 presents a still more detailed tabulation of educational attainments among Mexican Americans. There are noticeable differences among males in three groups. That is, third-generation males rank above the second, and both show markedly higher attainments

TABLE 3
SELECTED CHARACTERISTICS OF THE MEXICAN-ORIGIN POPULATION BY SEX, NATIVITY AND ORIGIN, 1970

	Sex and Generation					
	Males			Females		
Selected Characteristics	1st	2nd	3rd	1st	2nd	3rd
Education (25 years and over)						
Median Years	5.8	9.4	11.1	5.8	9.0	7.9
Percent High School Graduates	15.2	33.1	41.7	14.3	29.1	22.8
Delta[a]	51.8	20.2	—	23.5	7.2	—
Occupation[b] (16 and over)						
Higher White Collar (1)	6.5	12.0	14.2	5.8	10.3	7.5
Lower White Collar (2)	5.7	10.9	12.9	17.7	34.3	36.8
Higher Manual (3)	19.0	21.8	20.2	2.5	2.5	2.0
Lower Manual (4)	52.8	47.9	48.8	67.3	49.6	50.5
Farm (5)	16.0	7.4	3.9	7.7	3.3	3.2
Delta[a]	22.1	7.0	—	18.4	8.2	—
Family Income (Mexican-origin head of household)						
Median	$6440	$7846	$7580			
Delta[a]	11.6	4.8	—			

Source: Reproduced from Philip Garcia and Lionel Maldonado, "America's Mexicans: A Plea for Specificity," *Social Science Journal*, 19:1 (January 1982): 9-24, Table 4. This table in turn was compiled from U.S. Bureau of the Census, *Census of the Population: 1970*, "Subject Reports: Persons of Spanish Origin," PC(2)-1C and "Subject Reports: National Origin and Language," PC(2)-1A.

[a]Indices computed from detailed distributions of seven educational categories, ten occupational categories, and eleven income level categories. Delta, the index of dissimilarity, is equivalent to one-half the sum of the absolute difference between the percentage distributions of two groups. The numerical summary can be interpreted as the proportion of one group that would have to shift in order to achieve equal representation with the other.

[b]Categories aggregated in the following manner: (1) = Professional workers and managers, except farm; (2) = Sales and clerical; (3) = Craftsmen and foremen; (4) = Operatives, service workers and laborers, except farm; (5) = Farmers and farm laborers.

than immigrants. For example, it would take an upward shift of almost 9 percent to bring parity between the second- and third-generational groups with regard to the proportion completing twelve years of education; over 25 percent of those born in Mexico would have to shift upward in order to attain equality with the native-born. Few of these differences, moreover, are attributable to higher proportions of the native-born group having gone to college.

Male/female contrasts of the respective generational groups show very small differences, except among the third generation. The greatest differences between men and women are found in the native-born of native-born parentage; these are related to the greater concentrations of males in both high school and college.

Table 3 also presents a description of the occupational distribution of Mexican Americans aged sixteen years and older in 1970. The table shows a strong dichotomy between native- and Mexican-born individuals. The differences between second- and third-generation Mexican Americans are relatively slight, with only a 7 percent shift required for the two generational groups to be equal in attainments. Yet better than one-fifth of the Mexican-born men would have to move up in occupation to equal either of the native groups. The table also demonstrates that all three groups of men are not highly represented in white-collar jobs; Mexican-born men are least likely to be in these occupations. Among women, the pattern of differences among generational groups is similar to that of men. Where differences do obtain, it is an overrepresentation of immigrant females in clerical positions and as operatives that explains the differences.

The Bureau of the Census did not publish *personal* income tabulations by nativity or parentage from the 1970 Census; only *total family* income was provided. Median incomes for families headed by persons of native birth are higher than the median of $6,962 reported for the total group; these figures in turn exceed the median income for immigrant families by more than $1,000.

Table 3 also indicates that Mexican Americans have made progress from one generation to the next. Is the conclusion warranted, therefore, that the group can be expected to behave like earlier immigrant groups whose economic absorption was merely a matter of time? Will successive generations of Mexican Americans narrow the economic gap between themselves and whites in American society? Is it that the group's youthfulness has not allowed its members time to acquire the necessary experiences that lead to greater rewards in the labor market? Is it that acquiring English will also propel them toward economic assimilation? Do their present lower educational attainments account for their status?

A series of recent analyses of these and related questions indicate that they are not sufficient in themselves to explain Mexican Americans' disadvantages (see reference entries under Garcia at the end of this chapter for specific studies). These studies are based on detailed regression analyses of 1970 Census and 1976 SIE data; the equations are a composite of those specified by Chiswick (1978). The work compares Mexican Americans to whites in the adult labor force. Mexican Americans are divided into U.S.- and Mexican-born; the latter group is further subdivided in terms of when they came to the United States, as adults or as children. Those who came to the United

States as children, it is reasoned, have spent a substantial period of their formative years here and, therefore, are more like their U.S.-born counterparts.

In 1969, Chicanos' income was 66 percent of white males; the ratio dropped to .61 for each immigrant group, relative to whites. Six years later, the income ratios of all Mexican-American men had declined, with both immigrant groups suffering the greater losses. Table 4 summarizes the analyses.

TABLE 4
SUMMARY ANALYSES OF THE EFFECTS OF SOCIAL AND ETHNIC
ORIGINS ON ANNUAL WAGE ATTAINMENT: SALARIED MEXICAN-
ORIGIN MALES AGED SIXTEEN YEARS AND OVER IN 1970 OR 1976,
WITH EARNINGS OF $100 OR MORE IN 1969 OR 1975.

Ethnic Origin	Gross Effects[a]	Net Effects[b]			Residual[c]
		(1)	(2)	(3)	
1975					
Mexican-Origin Native Born	-4968	-2334	-825	-1134	-675
Mexican-Origin Child Immigrant	-6749	-3313	-1185	-1286	-965
Mexican-Origin Adult Immigrant	-6036	-1431	-640	-1845	-2120
1969					
Mexican-Origin Native Born	-3944	-1898	-182	-1039	-825
Mexican-Origin Child Immigrant	-4587	-3067	-169	-1327	-24
Mexican-Origin Adult Immigrant	-4620	-881	-86	-1730	-1923

Source: Philip Garcia, mimeo (nd), Table 3, derived from *1970 Census of the Population,*
1/1000 Sample, 5 Percent Questionnaire; 1976 Survey of Income and Education.
White tabulations based on the following ten states where 94.8 percent of the
Mexican-origin population resided in 1976: California, Texas, Arizona, Illinois,
New Mexico, Colorado, Michigan, Indiana, Washington and Ohio.

[a]Deviations from the 1969 and 1975 mean annual wages of $11,750 and $12,264 for salaried, non-Hispanic white males, aged sixteen years and over in 1970 and 1976.

[b](1) Deviations from the mean annual wage for non-Hispanic white males after statistically controlling for the independent variables specified in the wage attainment equation, minus weeks worked and the SEI score; (2) additional deviations after statistically controlling for weeks worked; (3) additional deviations after statistically controlling for the SEI score.

[c]Net deviations from the observed mean annual wages of each ethnic-origin group after statistically controlling for all the variables specified in the wage attainment equation.

Table 4 indicates that, when statistically controlling for education, occupation, work experiences and a host of other factors, Mexican Americans still lag behind white males and, further, that the gap has widened over the years between 1970 and 1976. The widened gap, moreover, is not insignificant. The data also indicate that adverse effects in the business cycle result in greater disadvantages accruing to Mexican Americans. Finally, there is also support for the notion that immigrants get lesser rewards than native-born Chicanos of similar characteristics.

Conclusion

This chapter has attempted to suggest the complexity of historical and current factors in explaining the status of Mexican Americans today. The early history saw a profound negative effect on this population from policies and practices of the state, beginning with the mode of incorporation into American society. Mexicanos' initially pyramid-shaped class structure had been radically altered by the turn of the century, relegating the conquered to a caste-like status below all whites.

Active labor recruitment by American interests during the first three decades of this century, an action with strong state support, brought in more Mexicans expressly for unskilled and semi-skilled work; they joined resident Mexican Americans at the bottom of the occupational structure. The Great Depression was a major watershed for Mexican Americans; massive numbers were returned to Mexico. This action, also sanctioned by the state, worked to further undermine the Mexican-American community.

Upturns in the American economy as a result of World War II had several effects. One was the significant occupational advancement into the semi-skilled and skilled work categories for large number of Mexican Americans. A second effect was the reactivation of the state's involvement to help provide a supply of laborers for selected industries, especially agribusiness. A concomitant effect was the stimulation of the flow of undocumented workers.

The history of Mexican Americans sets them apart from the analytic models developed to explain the experiences of white ethnics. Analyses of recent data on Mexican Americans over the recent past suggest that the experiences of Mexican Americans continue to be significantly unlike those of white ethnic groups, and that to apply theoretical models developed on others' experiences is a risky effort at best. That is, there is ample evidence that nativity and generational status have had a declining significance in white ethnic attainments as long ago as the 1950s (Garcia and Maldonado, 1982: 21 and footnote 4). This is not the case for Mexican Americans.

A second major distinction between Mexican Americans and whites is the continuing influence of immigrant status on a significant proportion of the former group. This has faded as a salient factor among white ethnics.

A third issue that restricts the application of the white ethnics' experiences to the understanding of the Mexican-American experience is best appreciated by recalling the disparities between whites and Chicanos, the latter whose roots in America go back many generations. The long-term and apparently widening differences in social rewards direct our attention to domestic factors, an important one being institutional discrimination.

Recent arguments to explain the status of Mexican Americans have tended to focus on unfair labor practices and to note that discrimination against Mexican Americans is a source of pecuniary gains for employers in that their lower wages reduce labor costs (Acuña, 1981; Barrera, 1979). Others add that small firms are inclined to rely on Mexican-American workers in order to fight rising labor costs (Portes, 1976). Still others suggest that Mexican Americans function to a greater extent as a reserve labor supply. Their employment level varies with expansions and contractions of the economy. Marginal workers are displaced from the labor force during periods of low business activity in an effort to offset some of the negative consequences of recessionary times for employers and domestic workers. In short, Mexican Americans are characterized as prime members of the secondary labor market (Pachon and Moore, 1981). It would appear that these factors, combined, offer insight for understanding contemporary Mexican Americans.

REFERENCES

Acuña, Rodolfo. *Occupied America: A History of Chicanos*, 2nd ed. New York: Harper and Row, 1981.

Barrera, Mario. *Race and Class in the Southwest*. South Bend, Ind.: University of Notre Dame Press, 1979.

Bloch, Herman D. *The Circle of Discrimination*. New York: New York University Press, 1969.

Bonacich, Edna. "A Theory of Ethnic Antagonism: The Split Labor Market." *American Sociological Review* 37(5): 547-559, October 1972.

——————. "Advanced Capitalism and Black/White Race Relations in the United States: A Split Labor Market Interpretation." *American Sociological Review* 41(1): 34-51, February 1976.

Briggs, Vernon M., Walter Fogel, and Fred H. Schmidt. *The Chicano Worker*. Austin, Tex.: University of Texas Press, 1977.

Camarillo, Albert. *Chicanos in a Changing Society: From Mexican Pueblos to American Barrios in Santa Barbara and Southern California, 1848-1930.* Cambridge, Mass.: Harvard University Press, 1979.

Chiswick, Barry R. "An Analysis of Earnings Among Mexican Origin Men." *Business and Economic Statistics,* pp. 222-231, 1977.

_____. "The Effect of Americanization on the Earnings of Foreign Born Men." *Journal of Political Economy* 86(5): 897-922, October 1978.

_____. "The Economic Progress of Immigrants: Some Apparently Universal Patterns." *In Contemporary Economic Problems 1979,* William Fellner, ed. Washington, D.C.: American Enterprise Institute, 1979.

_____. "Illegal Aliens in the United States Labor Market." Paper presented at the Sixth World Congress, International Economic Association, Mexico City, 1980.

_____. "Differences in Educational Attainments Among Racial and Ethnic Groups: Patterns and Hypotheses Regarding the Quantity and Quality of Children." Mimeographed paper. Urbana, Ill.: University of Illinois, Survey Research Laboratory, 1983.

Daniels, Roger and Harry H. L. Kitano. *American Racism: Explorations of the Nature of Prejudice.* Englewood Cliffs, N. J.: Prentice Hall, 1970.

Estrada, Leobardo, F. Chris Garcia, Reynaldo Flores Macias and Lionel Maldonado. "Chicanos in the United States: A History of Exploitation and Resistance." *Daedalus* 110(2): 103-131, Spring 1981.

Featherman, David L. and Robert M. Hauser. *Opportunity and Change.* New York: Academic Press, 1978.

Frisbie, Parker. "Illegal Migration from Mexico to the United States: A Longitudinal Analysis." *International Migration Review* 9(1): 3-14, Spring 1975.

Galarza, Ernesto. *Merchants of Labor: The Mexican Bracero Story.* Santa Barbara, Cal.: McNally and Loftin, 1964.

Garcia, Philip. "An Evaluation of Unemployment and Employment Differences Between Mexican Americans and Whites: The Seventies." *Social Science Journal,* 20(1): 51-62, January 1983.

_____. "Joblessness Among Hispanic Youth: 1973-1981." *Astlan,* forthcoming.

_____. "Dual-language Characteristics and Income Attainment Among Mexican American Men." *Social Science Research* 13(3): 221-235, September 1984.

_____. "Trends in the Relative Income Position of Mexican American Workers: The Early Seventies." *Sociology and Social Research* 66: 467-483, July 1982.

Garcia, Philip and Lionel Maldonado. "America's Mexicans: A Plea for Specificity." *Social Science Journal* 19(1): 9-24, January 1982.

Griswold del Castillo, Richard. *The Los Angeles Barrio, 1850-1890: A Social History.* Los Angeles and Berkeley, Cal.: University of California Press, 1979.

Heer, David M. "What is the Annual Net Flow of Undocumented Mexican Immigrants to the United States?" *Demography* 16(4): 417-423, November 1979.

Higham, John. *Strangers in the Land: Patterns of American Nativism, 1860-1925.* New Brunswick, N. J.: Rutgers University Press, 1955.

Hourwich, Isaac A. *Immigration and Labor,* 2nd ed. New York: Huebsch Publishing, 1922.

Hull, Harry E. *Twentieth Annual Report of the Secretary of Labor, Fiscal Year Ending June 30, 1932.* Washington, D.C.: Government Printing Office, 1932.

Hutchinson, E. P. *Immigrants and Their Children, 1850-1950.* New York: John Wiley and Sons, 1956.

Keely, Charles B. "Illegal Migration." *Scientific American* 246(14): 41-47, March 1982.

Maldonado, Lionel A. "Mexican Americans: The Emergence of a Minority." In *The Minority Report,* 2nd ed., A. G. Dworkin and R. J. Dworkin, eds. New York: Holt, Rinehart and Winston, 1982.

Martinez, Oscar J. "On the Size of the Chicano Population: New Estimates, 1850-1900." *Aztlan* 6(1): 43-67, Spring 1975.

McWilliams, Carey. *North from Mexico: The Spanish-Speaking People of the United States.* New York: Greenwood Press, 1968.

Meier, Matt S. and Feliciano Rivera. *The Chicanos: A History of Mexican Americans.* New York: Hill and Wang, 1982.

Moore, Joan W. with Harry Pachon. *Mexican Americans,* 2nd ed. Englewood Cliffs, N. J.: Prentice-Hall, 1976.

Myrdal, Gunnar with Richard Sterner and Arnold Rose. *An American Dilemma.* New York: Harper, 1944.

Pachon, Harry P. and Joan W. Moore. "Mexican Americans." *The Annals of the American Academy* 454: 111-124, March 1981.

Portes, Alejandro. "Illegal Immigration and the International System: Lessons from Recent Legal Mexican Immigrants to the United States." *Social Problems* 26(4): 425-438, April 1979.

Portes, Alejandro, Samuel A. McLead, Jr. and Robert N. Parker. "Earnings Differences Between Anglo and Mexican American Male Workers in 1960 and 1970: Changes in the Cost of Being a Mexican American." *Social Science Quarterly* 57(3): 618-631, December 1976.

Reimers, David M. "Post-World War II Immigration to the United States: America's Latest Newcomers." *The Annals of the American Academy* 454: 1-12, March 1981.

Servin, Manuel P. "The Pre-World War II Mexican-American: An Interpretation." *California Historical Society Quarterly* XLV(4): 325-338, December 1966.

Stavrianos, L. S. *Global Rift: The Third World Comes of Age.* New York: William Morrow and Company, 1981.

Taylor, Paul. *Mexican Labor in the United States*, Vols. 1 and 2. New York:
    Arno Press, 1970.

GHETTO TO SUBURBS: IRISH OCCUPATIONAL AND SOCIAL MOBILITY

Lawrence J. McCaffrey

Loyola University of Chicago

Recent research indicates that the Irish are probably the most successful white gentiles in the United States. They have traveled far since
their early nineteenth-century days as pioneers of the American urban
ethnic ghetto. Then, their alien, poverty culture frightened Anglo-
Protestant residents of East Coast cities. The Irish physical and psychological transition from rural Ireland to urban America; the struggle
to overcome the trauma stemming from Old and New World experiences, technological ignorance and the contempt of other Americans;
and successful competition for power and dignity made them arche-
types of the American urban ethnic experience. Their hazardous and
exciting pilgrimage through nineteenth- and twentieth-century American urban history has foreshadowed the adventures of other non-An-
glos who settled in the cities of the United States.

Early seventeenth-century Ireland hosted immigrants, providing land,
social status and political influence for the younger sons of the English
aristocracy and gentry and for lowland Scotch Presbyterians. At the
same time many of the Catholic upper classes displaced by English
colonialism emigrated to Continental Catholic countries to seek opportunities no longer available to them on their native soil.[1]

In the late seventeenth century, North America replaced Ireland as
the leading sanctuary for immigrants in the Western world. Many of
the new Americans came from Ireland, particularly Presbyterian
Ulster. These Scotch-Irish emigrés reacted against the privileged position of the Church of Ireland and British mercantilist restrictions on
the Irish economy. As skilled, ambitious and liberty-loving people,
they made a large contribution to an emerging nation.[2]

Most prosperous and cultured Catholics departing Ireland continued to prefer a Continental destination, but some Catholics who were
skilled craftsmen or substantial farmers decided on America. Like
Ulster Presbyterians they provided talent for a land in the process of
development. A large number of eighteenth-century Catholics also entered America as indentured servants or transported convicts, and after completing their seven- or fourteen-year indentures or sentences in
agricultural labor, they tended to establish themselves on the western
frontier of southern colonies. Since they arrived in America as ignorant, superstitious, often indifferent Catholics, and found themselves
far from the ministrations of a small, understaffed American Church,
ex-indentured servants and former convicts tended to blend into an
evangelical Protestant milieu.[3]

While most of the Irish Catholic rural masses lacked the means or
the courage to sail thousands of miles across the Atlantic, many did
cross the Irish Sea, some as seasonal harvest workers, others on a more
permanent basis. They supplied unskilled labor to advance Britain's
industrial and transportation revolutions. Irishtown ghettos magnified
the urban blight in England, Scotland and Wales.[4]

After 1815, Irish emigration, particularly among Catholics, speeded
up. An agricultural depression following the long Anglo-French conflict
encouraged a shift from tillage to pasture agriculture, promoting rural
discontent that often led to violence. Agrarian poverty and distur-
bances persuaded many tenant farmers that the United States offered
more hope than Ireland. When in the 1820s Ireland began to experience
a series of disease-caused potato crop failures resulting in famine, the
specter of starvation drove many peasants aboard emigrant ships.
Those who could afford the fares sailed directly to New York, New
Orleans or Boston; the more impoverished went to Canada. Many who
first arrived in Canada walked across the American border at locations
from Maine to Michigan. Some Irish Catholics earned enough in the
Newfoundland fisheries to travel on to Boston.[5]

By 1835 Catholic emigrants from Ireland to the United States began
to outnumber Protestants, and the Great Famine, 1845-1849, depos-
ited over a million refugees from hunger and disease on the American
shore, giving Irish America a permanent Catholic profile.[6] The United
States continued to be the main haven for post-famine Irish Catholics
unable to sustain a civilized standard of living in a society oppressed by
British misgovernment and by an economy with no industrial alternative to primitive, manorial agriculture. Relatively, Ireland has
donated more of her children to the United States than any other country. Smaller than most American states, this island on the western
fringe of Europe has sent about five million of her sons and daughters

to the United States since 1820, most of them young, single and Catholic.[7]

Rural Ireland has furnished the overwhelming majority of Irish emigrants. Between 1850 and 1865 over 84 percent of Irish Catholics entering the United States were peasants. Although Irish and Irish-American bishops joined many nationalist journalists in a plea to the emigrants to avoid wicked and worldly cities, about 90 percent of Irish Americans chose urban industrial America.[8] Motives more compelling than unfortunate rural experiences in Ireland, and money shortages binding them to ports of entry, persuaded Irish immigrants to avoid rural America.[9] Urbanization was compatible with their economic potential and their religious personalities.

Centuries of English colonialism had deprived the Irish Catholic majority of property, education, opportunity, expectations and basic civil rights. During the eighteenth century most of the Catholic aristocracy and gentry turned Protestant to preserve property, status and political influence. Those who kept the old faith practiced it quietly and deferentially. They sent many of their children abroad for education and careers. While penal laws prohibiting papists from acquiring property multiplied the urban Catholic middle class, the vast majority of Catholics were involved with agriculture. A few strong farmers rented farms of twenty-five acres or more, a larger number of tenants cultivated plots of fifteen acres or less, usually about five, and a majority of rural folk were agricultural laborers. Some laborers (cottiers) exchanged their toil for the use of a one-room cottage on a small plot of ground where they planted potatoes to feed large families; others worked for a small wage, barely enough to rent the land (conacre) on which to grow potatoes.[10]

During the eighteenth and early nineteenth centuries the standard of living for the Catholic rural masses steadily declined. Despite the miseries of famine, plague and infant mortality, a population explosion which raised the number of Irish from 3,042,000 to 8,175,000 between 1725 and 1841 overstrained the agrarian economy, raising rents, reducing farm sizes and driving many tenant farmers into the ranks of agricultural laborers.[11]

Ireland's static economy and inefficient landlord system maimed the people's skills, sapped their energy, and diminished their ambition to cultivate the land with intelligence or enthusiasm. As primitive spade, hoe and scythe subsistence farmers, they lacked the skill to work the vast, fertile fields of America properly.

Contrasts in rural life between Ireland and the United States also directed the Irish to American cities. Men working on small Irish farms chatted with neighbors on the opposite sides of ditches, hedges or stone walls, and in the evening took brief strolls to a neighbor's cottage for tea and conversation. A number of the Irish in rural America wrote home describing spaciousness and expressing loneliness. To counteract the loneliness, the immigrant Irish majority crowded into ugly, dreary urban ghettos where they had the comfort of being with their own kind.

Catholic bishops warned Irish immigrants that American cities contradicted their rural cultural values and threatened their religious loyalties, but Catholicism's corporate and communal emphases encouraged the Irish and other Catholics who would follow them to the United States to choose the urban scene. In general, Catholic ethnics tend to be more social and less individualistic and self-sufficient than Protestants, who seem religiously and psychologically better attuned to country life.[12]

Irish peasants were almost as useless in cities as they were in the country. When able to find employment they had to settle for casual, unskilled, difficult, dirty, unhealthy and low-paying labor.[13] Irishmen worked in stables, drove horses as draymen or cabbies, lifted freight on docks and swept out factories and saloons. With picks and shovels they dug building foundations or carried bricks and mortar over their shoulders on construction sites. They mined coal in Pennsylvania, gold in California, copper in Montana. In hotels Irishmen worked as doormen, janitors, bellhops and barmen.

The Irish in New Orleans, the second leading entry port, competed with blacks, free and slave, for employment as servants, cabbies or stevedores. They loaded Mississippi river boats and served on them as crew members, often sweating below deck "screwing" down the size of cotton bales or in engine rooms where they risked life and limb in frequent boiler explosions. Elsewhere in Louisiana many Irish perished draining malaria-infested swamps for road building or tillage. Promoters of such projects preferred the Irish to black slaves because the supply of cheap immigrant labor seemed inexhaustible, while slaves represented considerable capital investment.

When the transportation revolution began, "Paddies" dug canals and cut railroad trails through forest and mountain before laying track. Canals and railroads brought the Irish west to the urban frontier. Graveyards along the banks of the Erie and Illinois and Michigan canals and railroad tracks are full of Irish bones. Military service also moved the Irish around the United States. Bright red uniforms, prospects for adventure, a little money and an escape from the boredom of rural life enlisted many young Irishmen in the British army and navy. Military life in the United States had a similar allure for poor ethnics. The Irish contributed more than their fair share of servicemen in the

Mexican and Civil wars. In the latter they made considerable sacrifice to both sides. After Appomattox the Irish were a significant portion of the western frontier army, and many lost their lives in the Seventh Cavalry fighting with General George Armstrong Custer at the 1876 Battle of the Little Big Horn.

Women were more prominent in the Irish than in other European emigrations. As the nineteenth century progressed, more Irish women came to the United States than Irish men. As a group they became more successful than other immigrant women. Since they tended to emigrate as singles, and because of patterns of late or no marriage and gender segregation, as well as choices and customs emerging from the Great Famine in Ireland, Irish women were independent, aggressive and ambitious for economic independence. Unhappy relationships between Irish husbands and wives did not encourage them to marry. But once they did, and if not abandoned or widowed, they were less likely to be in the work force than women of other nationalities. Instead they concentrated on managing large families. Women were the dominant force in Irish homes, eventually leading Irish America to middle-class respectability.

Anglo-American women considered domestic service degrading. Fathers in ethnic groups that featured family emigration did not want daughters living in other peoples' homes. Unencumbered by this kind of family pressure, Irish women flocked to well-paid situations that provided food, housing, uniforms and a taste of cultivated living. They cleaned the houses, served and sometimes cooked meals, and minded the children of affluent Anglo-American Protestants. Widowed or deserted Irish women or those residing within a family unit drifted toward mill or factory or sewing in the garment industry. Irish men followed the women into the textile and shoe industries.[14]

Struggling to survive in urban America, early Irish-American Catholics played an unconscious historical role. Oscar Handlin said that they made Boston industrialism possible:

> Before their arrival the rigid labor supply had made industrialization impossible. It was the function of the Irish to thaw out the rigidity of the system. Their labor achieved the transition from the early commercial to the later industrialization of the city. Without it "the new and larger establishments could not have operated." Capitalists readily admitted that they could not "obtain good interest for their money, were they deprived of this constant influx of foreign labour."[15]

This Irish function was repeated in other American cities.

The Irish social problem offset their contribution to American industrialization. They were a "massive lump in the community, undigested, undigestable."[16] Their poverty cultures added to the psychological problems involved in their move to the United States, and made the Irish this country's first massive urban social problem. Life in damp cellars, steamy attics, overcrowded and unsanitary tenements and drafty tar paper shacks nurtured vice and disease. Well into the twentieth century tuberculosis afflicted the Irish on both sides of the Atlantic. Depressing ghettos and economic hardships encouraged the Irish tendency to drink excessively, and drink often resulted in violence and family poverty.

Present-day Irish Americans take pride in family, but through much of the nineteenth century working mothers, widowed or abandoned, and frequently unemployed or absent fathers, many working on canals or railroads, further eroded family organization weakened by emigration from a more socially structured rural Ireland. Wife battering and desertion were not uncommon Irish male responses to failure in the United States. Both men and women were defeated and degraded in urban America. A massive urban blight, they filled jails, sanitariums, hospitals, almshouses and insane asylums.

Convinced that Irish poverty, filth, alcoholism, crime, violence, improvidence and mental and physical disorders polluted the nation, Anglo-American Protestants resented their presence. They also objected to the financial burden imposed by police and institutional responses to the Irish social plague. But Irish poverty and misconduct offended Anglo-Protestant sensitivities far less than did their religion. Originating in the English historical experience, anti-Catholicism was the essence of Anglo-American Protestant nativism. But in the republic's early years the enemy was miniscule. In 1807 there was only one Catholic bishop, resident in Baltimore, with authority over eighty churches, seventy priests and about seventy thousand lay people. So no-popery was more paranoia than reaction to a significant Catholic presence. Commencing with the Irish, however, millions of Catholic immigrants moved into urban America in a way that seemed to confirm nativist anxieties concerning papists.[17]

In addition to its religious core, eighteenth-century liberal values— the United States was conceived and brought forth in the Enlightenment—shaped American nativism. The educated class considered Catholicism a superstitious, anti-intellectual and despotic alien tumor eating away at American culture and institutions. Jeffersonian democracy insisted that the nation's liberties could survive only in a fundamentally agrarian society, emphasizing citizen ownership of small farms as a symbol of and protection for individual dignity and freedom. Consequently, Irish poverty-culture Catholics expanding the "degenerate" urban dimension of the United States contradicted the

Protestant, rural and individualistically liberal definition that Anglo-Americans gave to their country. Protestant America's negative response to the Irish as an urban social plague and Catholic menace persuaded Irish Presbyterians to cultivate a separate identity as Scotch-Irish, guaranteeing that Irish America would have a Catholic image and personality.

In the Irish, Anglo-American nativism battled a tough foe. Protestant anti-Catholicism in the United States strengthened the links between the Irish and Catholic identities first forged by English colonialism in Ireland. Because of their numbers and religious commitment as faith and nationality, Irish Catholics took command of the American Catholic Church, incorporating it into an Irish spiritual empire functioning throughout the English-speaking world. Resisting the "Protestant Crusade," the Catholic hierarchy successfully appealed to the financial generosity and religious enthusiasm of the Irish and created an alternative Catholic institutional complex of schools, hospitals, asylums and orphanages. In reacting to real dangers and fulfilling real needs, the Catholic alternative institutional structure unfortunately fed the nativist appetite for evidence that Catholicism was indeed alien and divisive.

Working-class Protestants could be more anti-Irish than their more affluent coreligionists. They resented the Irish as unfair labor competition and as extrinsic to the United States. Unlike a number of English and German immigrants with urban experiences, the Irish came from a rural society with no appreciation for or experience with trade unionism. This and their willingness to toil long hours in less than human conditions for barely subsistence wages hindered the progress of the American labor movement and limited the potential of the strike as a weapon against harsh employers.[18] On the other hand, the availability of unskilled Irish labor not only made possible rapid American industrialization, but also promoted non-Irish workers to skilled and semi-managerial levels in mines, mills, factories and on railroads.

Antagonisms within the work force indicated that ethnic, religious and racial loyalties took precedence over class solidarity. Compensating for the psychological and physical wounds that they received from nativism and their low position in the working-class hierarchy, the Irish projected their anger and their inferiority complex on to blacks. Irish white racism indicated that they were assimilating the American value system. Protestant abolitionists also irritated the Irish. They were nativists who demanded emancipation and civil rights for blacks in the rural South, but who had no sympathy for the Irish urban outcasts of the North. Irish Americans also saw free blacks as their competition for unskilled jobs and as scab labor strikebreakers.[19]

In July 1863, Irish protests against the Draft Act melded with their racial prejudice to touch off one of the greatest urban riots in American history. Mobs of Irish, including many drunks, roamed about, murdering, burning and looting. They killed eleven blacks and an American Indian mistaken for a black, incinerated a black orphanage and, altogether, destroyed about three million dollars worth of property. Police power proved inadequate so the authorities summoned soldiers. During the five days of arson, pillage and violence, policemen and soldiers killed twelve hundred rioters. Mob members took the lives of three and injured a number of policemen. Most of the policemen and many of the servicemen were as Irish as the rioters. Irish-born John Hughes helped to disperse the mobs by telling the people to get off the street and into their homes.[20]

New York's infamous Draft Riot is not a true picture of the Irish response to the Civil War. From 1861 to 1865 they demonstrated their love of country on battlefields throughout the war zone. Their patriotism and courage diminished for a time some of the intensity of Anglo-American nativism. The rapid acceleration of postwar industrialism demanded a vast supply of unskilled labor, taking pressure off the Irish and other immigrants and helping inspire a melting pot rather than an exclusive concept of the United States. As ex-peasants from Southern and Eastern Europe joined urban industrial America, they pushed the Irish up the occupational ladder in the same way that the Irish had shoved Protestant workers earlier in the century.

In addition to new immigrants less skilled than they, American industrial needs, and a temporary retreat of nativism, Irish mobility owed much to the success of the Catholic institutional alternative in educating and civilizing them, and to the improved quality of the newly-arrived Irish. In radically reducing the Irish population, particularly among the economically and culturally-deprived agricultural laboring class, the famine brutally but effectively lifted the Irish standard of living by increasing the proportion of landholders and the size of their farms. Dollars from Irish America, as well as rising agricultural prices and stable rents, enabled the people to live in more comfortable cottages, wear better clothes and eat more nourishing food.[21]

Mass education also lifted the minds and spirits of the rural masses in Ireland. Introduced by the British government in 1831, the national school system raised literacy from 50 percent in 1850 to over 95 percent in 1900. Irish immigrants at the turn of the century could read and write better than most Americans.[22] While they might still have lacked technological skills, they had the intellectual equipment to acquire them.

If material comfort and mass education increased sophistication, a reformed Catholicism disciplined the Irish character. Previous to the famine, superstition competed with Catholic dogma. Clerical education and discipline were far from exemplary, and the hierarchy exhibited publicly quarreling factions.[23] By exterminating the most ignorant portion of the population, the famine aided religious instruction and practice. Nationalism's growing hold over the public mind awakened the people to the inseparability of their Catholic and Irish identities. Victorian English puritanical influences in Ireland also prepared the way for a "Devotional Revolution."[24]

From 1849 to 1875 Paul Cardinal Cullen directed the "Devotional Revolution." Under his guidance the Catholic Church built chapels, rectories, convents and schools; improved clerical education and discipline; and harmonized differences within the hierarchy which displayed a united front. The Irish became the most orthodox and pious Roman Catholics in Western Europe. They frequently attended Mass and received the sacraments, and participated in a variety of devotions—Benediction of the Blessed Sacrament, the Rosary, Stations of the Cross, Forty Hours—and parish missions.[25] This "Devotional Revolution" spread throughout the Irish spiritual empire, encouraging the Irish already in the United States and those about to come to be more sober, industrious and respectable.

Politics also speeded Irish-American mobility. In contrast with their technological ignorance, the Irish arrived in the United States relatively knowledgeable in democratic politics. Daniel O'Connell, Irish nationalism's founding father, had successfully mobilized a large portion of the Irish peasantry in the 1820s to pressure the British government into conceding Catholic emancipation. His massive 1843 agitation to cancel out the Act of Union with Britain failed, but O'Connell's Catholic and Repeal associations were masterpieces of political organization and models for Irish-American urban machines.

In its passage to the United States, Irish politics abandoned much of its nationalist associated idealism to concentrate on the acquisition and retention of power. Irish Americans comprehended power as a weapon against nativism and as an avenue to social mobility.[26] The Democratic Party's egalitarianism and welcoming attitude toward immigrants enlisted the Irish. By 1890 they controlled most of the large cities in the United States. During World War I, Cecil Spring Rice, the British ambassador to the United States, described them as the best politicians in the country with unsurpassed organizational ability.[27]

For bright Irish lads excluded from the Anglo-Protestant dominated financial world, politics offered fame and fortune. They feathered their own nests with graft, yet took care of their constituents. Irish politicians were always visible at christenings, first communions, confirmations, weddings and wakes, and they provided patronage jobs for employment seekers and coal, food and clothing for the poor. Since cities spent money for roads, bridges and public buildings, Irish politicians could award building contracts to their own people. Politics is a major reason for the large number of first-, second- and third-generation Irish Americans in the construction business. In 1870, 17 percent of American contractors were born in Ireland, three times the number that came from Germany or England.[28]

By the late nineteenth century a large number of Irish Americans had advanced from the ranks of unskilled labor to become foremen of work crews in mines, factories, mills, packing houses, foundries and on the docks. On railroads there were fewer and fewer of them among section gangs and more and more of them as engineers, switchmen, levermen, clerks and telegraphers. Irish bricklayers, carpenters, plasterers, plumbers and, after the turn of the century, electricians began to outnumber Irish hod carriers on construction sites. The middle-class status and security of the civil service appealed to the Irish. They also offered generation after generation of young men to police and fire departments. Many of the urban transport people on streetcars, elevated railroads and subway trains spoke with Irish brogues. Curiosity, skill with a story, a sense of adventure and a gift of words made the Irish natural journalists. Irish families gave their best talent to the Catholic Church, providing most of her bishops, priests, nuns and brothers. Affinities between law and politics harvested an abundance of Irish lawyers. Many also were attracted to the medical profession, where they earned reputations as dedicated general practitioners and specialists. The Irish at home and abroad have positive reputations as cardiologists and surgeons. Considering the associations between the Irish and alcohol, it is not surprising that many were saloon proprietors. Others owned more conventional small businesses.

Early twentieth-century Irishwomen entered business as routine office help or as trained typists or shorthand secretaries. When telephones became a standard form of communication, many Irishwomen worked as operators. Unlike most other ethnics, the Irish often educated their daughters to higher levels than their sons. While not opposed to the latter working with their hands and their backs at steady, well-paying jobs, they sought gentility for the former in professions like teaching and nursing. Since the late nineteenth century Irishwomen have been essential to American public education and community health.[29] Irish nuns taught in parochial schools, nursed in Catholic hospitals and staffed orphanages and sanitariums. Before women from other ethnic backgrounds, Irishwomen achieved leadership positions as school principals, college presidents and hospital directors.

Irish America's progress from unskilled to skilled worker, with some penetration of the middle class, was not nationally uniform. In the East, especially New England, they succumbed to nativist prejudice and low self-esteem. They isolated themselves psychologically as well as physically, building ghettos of the mind as well as of place. True, the New England Irish did acquire political office, but they did not balance it with economic success or social respectability.[30]

For a number of reasons the Irish on the "urban frontier," Buffalo and points west, were more successful. Common sense indicates that emigration is a selective process. The Irish who came to the United States probably were more ambitious and energetic than those who remained at home. Those who moved on to the West and Midwest were more likely motivated by success than those who settled in the bleak ghettos of the East. "Urban frontier" cities developed when Ireland began to export a new kind of immigrant—young people civilized by mass education and a higher standard of living, and disciplined by the "Devotional Revolution." A large percentage of them went west.[31]

Compared to the East, anti-Catholicism was muted and the economy more dynamic and multi-dimensional on the "urban frontier." Since production and profit took priority over prejudice, opportunity and hard work propelled the "urban frontier" Irish up the success ladder. Those who recently arrived in the United States surpassed the mobility of third- and fourth-generation New England Irish Americans.[32]

Eastern Catholicism wore the paranoid mask of the Irish ghetto. Suspicious of America's Protestant and secular features, quite a few eastern Irish Catholic bishops attempted to keep their people separate from the country's cultural mainstream. They cooperated with midwestern German prelates in an alliance to combat liberal trends in American Catholicism. Both partners agreed that ethnic and Catholic identities were mutually dependent.[33]

Interpreting social reform movements, including labor unions, as manifestations of socialism, eastern Irish bishops advised the laity to suffer poverty with Christian fortitude, relying on God's justice for happiness in the next world. They attributed social evils to Original Sin, prescribing Christian charity as a response to hunger, unemployment and poor housing. They said that prosperous Christians must be generous to the less fortunate, while the poor should accept this generosity with gratitude.[34]

Success and acceptance gave the "urban frontier" Irish a more optimistic vision of the United States. Their religious leaders tended to appreciate American pluralism, interpreting the healthy condition of the church as evidence that Catholicism flourished in a free and diverse society. Midwest Irish bishops urged the Americanization of the church in the United States. They took liberal positions on public education and a variety of social issues, defending labor unions, collective bargaining and the right to strike.[35] Because they became important in the labor movement, the attitude of the American Catholic hierarchy toward unions was significant for Irish Americans.

Post-Civil War competition for urban turf and jobs and their inferiority complex convinced the Irish that they had white and yellow as well as black enemies. During the 1880s Patrick Ford of the influential *Irish World* (New York) expounded an anti-capitalist populism stained with hostility toward Jews.[36] At the same time another Irish-American populist, Denis Kearney of California's Workingman's Party, threatened to burn the rich off of Nob Hill and campaigned against the Chinese, attempting to exclude the latter from the United States.[37]

Viewing them as labor competitors and strikebreaking scabs, the Irish often lacked empathy for other Catholic ethnics and ridiculed their non-English speaking cultures. American Catholicism's ethnic parish structure encouraged Irish prejudices. As Ellen Skerrett has explained, Irish-American parishes produced a paradox. By stressing American values, particularly patriotism, the work ethic and respectability, parochial schools speeded Irish assimilation. At the same time, the ethnic exclusiveness of church and school contradicted the cosmopolitanism that should have been a main feature of the multi-national Roman Catholic Church.[38]

Gradually Irish Americans developed a working-class consciousness beyond their own enclave. Some of their hostility to laissez-faire capitalism took violent forms. Named after a secret agrarian society in Ireland, the Molly Maguires in the late 1870s killed nine people in the Pennsylvania coal fields. Popular legend has portrayed the Mollies as gallant warriors against oppression. In fact, they acted out Irish hatred of English, Welsh and Scotch mine bosses as much as they did resentment against low wages, high prices in company stores and excessive rents for company houses.[39]

However, there were genuine Irish radicals such as the Cork-born Chicagoan, Mary Harris "Mother" Jones (1880-1930) of the syndicalist Industrial Workers of the World (Wobblies). She served several jail sentences for organizational activities, mainly among miners. In 1914 James Larkin (1876-1947), founder of Ireland's Transport and General Worker's Union, came to the United States, collaborated with the IWW and helped create the American Communist Party. Elizabeth

Gurley Flynn (1890-1964), William Z. Foster (1881-1961) and "Big Bill" Haywood (1869-1928) were other Irish Americans who were Wobbly and Communist leaders.[40]

Contrary to the fears of some Americans that the labor movement profiled the violence of the Irish personality, most Irish-American labor leaders were collective bargainers seeking higher wages, shorter work days and weeks, and an improved industrial environment for their followers. In 1879 Terence V. Powderly, prominent in Irish-American nationalism, became Grand Master Workman of the Knights of Labor, the first significant attempt to organize workers across the nation. When the American Federation of Labor came into existence in 1881, the Irish were conspicuous at the top levels. In the first decade of the twentieth century, fifty of the 110 American Federation of Labor presidents were Irish.[41]

Lyrics of the many folk songs presenting the history of organized labor insist on its liberalizing impact on the United States. They claim that the union movement's struggle with irresponsible, unbridled capitalism advanced equality of opportunity, promoted social and economic mobility, and narrowed the gap between rich and poor. But in another chapter of this volume, Herbert Hill explains that the concerns of the labor movement, particularly the American Federation of Labor, had racial limitations. Unions could be as restrictive as the Anglo-Saxon business world. Irish and Jewish labor leaders did advance the welfare of white ethnics, but attempted to exclude non-Caucasians from union membership and its benefits.

In the mid-1930s, during the Great Depression, Irish and other union bosses sharpened their social consciences. This was most evident when the Congress of Industrial Organizations came along to challenge the relatively conservative, craft-union dominated AFL. Many Irish Americans were active in the CIO campaign to organize workers in mass production industries. The most prominent, Philip Murray, the organization's second president (1940-1942), was a liberal Democrat and a social justice Catholic. Another Irishman, George Meany, became the first president of the merged AFL-CIO in 1955, and held that position almost until he died in 1979. A tough negotiator, Meany was a liberal Democrat and social justice Catholic, but an exuberant, anti-communist American patriot. While men like Murray and Meany denounced racism in their appeal for working-class solidarity, labor unionism has never done as much for blacks as it has for whites.

One of the frustrating mysteries of human nature is that seldom do those who experience the pain of persecution develop empathy for other victims of discrimination. At the same time that Irish labor leaders ignored the miseries of blacks and Asians, nativism continued to oppress their own people. Post-1880 recessions and depressions convinced many Americans that their country's opportunities and resources should be reserved for the native born, and that immigrants transported radical and class hatred ideologies from Europe to the United States. Social Darwinism added a racist dimension to American nativism. Jews from Eastern Europe and Catholics from Eastern and Southern Europe joined the Irish as targets for nativist organizations like the American Protective Association and the revived Ku Klux Klan.[42]

Racial nativism did not bypass the usually light-complexioned, often blue-eyed, fluent English-speaking, literate and increasingly respectable-in-conduct Irish. Anglo-Saxon racism on both sides of the Atlantic had a strong anti-Celtic Irish component,[43] and theories of racial superiority and inferiority did not supersede the fundamental anti-Catholicism of American nativism. Fears of Catholicism as mysterious, authoritarian and alien remained a powerful emotion, as strong in intellectual circles as in rural and small town America.[44] Anti-Catholicism continued to contain strong antipathy toward the Irish because they led the American Catholic community. No matter what their country of origin, Catholic immigrants entered a church attached to the Irish spiritual empire, joined labor unions with Irish leaders, and voted with and for Irish-controlled political machines. Every increase in the Catholic population meant a growth in Irish power, perpetuating nativist hatred of the Irish.

In 1914 a large number of Anglo Americans championed the British cause and resented the Irish- and German-American coalition that campaigned to keep the United States out of World War I. They agreed with the British that the 1916 Easter Week Rising in Dublin was a German-engineered Irish stab in Britain's back. Following World War I they complained about Irish-American pressure on Woodrow Wilson and Congress to support Irish republicanism during the Anglo-Irish War of 1919 to 1921. Like the president, Anglo-Americans rejected hyphenated Americanism and protested when many of the Irish objected to Wilson's anglophilia by opposing the League of Nations.[45]

Irish America was sure that Al Smith, a product of Tammany Hall and a quintessential Irish politician, lost his bid for the presidency in 1928 because he was a Catholic. This episode intensified Irish-American insecurity. Still the Irish in the United States continued their steady march toward middle-class respectability. With other Americans they suffered through the Great Depression, but their importance in the ruling Democratic Party, in the civil service and in urban government patronage systems, and their large numbers among the employees of railroads, which kept operating during hard times, meant that the Irish survived the 1930s in better shape than many other segments of the population.

Common misery during the depression and common cause in World War II united all Americans, banking the fires of nativism. Popular entertainment, particularly the movies, also diminished prejudice against Catholicism by giving it a favorable image. Such stars as Spencer Tracy, Bing Crosby, Gregory Peck and Pat O'Brien portrayed Catholic priests as social problem solvers in the American tradition, rather than preachers of Catholic dogma or ministers of Catholic liturgy.

At the beginning of the 1940s the Irish-American community had advanced to the borders of the middle class. In some cities over one-fourth of Irish secondary school graduates went on to college or university.[46] After 1945 the G.I. Bill of Rights radically increased that percentage. Many of the Irish receiving bachelor degrees entered graduate and professional schools. The G.I. Bill sparked an American social revolution; for the Irish it completed their long journey from unskilled workers to a middle-class community.[47]

Irish progress in urban America often has been marked by geographic as well as economic and social mobility. Writers Finley Peter Dunne and James T. Farrell described the movement of Chicago's South Side Irish from lower working-class Bridgeport and Canaryville in the 1890s to upper working-class/lower middle-class Washington Park in the first two decades of the twentieth century; then to the solidly middle-class South Shore in the 1920s. Farrell's Studs Lonigan and Danny O'Neill novels discuss how the Irish fled in panic from the advance of the black ghetto.[48]

Finally, in the 1950s quite a few Irish Americans packed up their university degrees and their middle-class respectability and headed toward the suburbs. This migration became a mass exodus when northern cities experienced in the 1960s a massive expansion in the number of black people fleeing discrimination and poverty in the South. As the most successful Catholic ethnics, the Irish were the first to abandon the cities.

Success transformed the politics as well as the geography of Irish America, encouraging a merger of power interests with more idealistic concerns.[49] This change occurred when Irish politics began to extend beyond the narrow focus of urban America. In Albany, New York, during the 1920s, Governor Al Smith previewed the New Deal. In the 1930s, President Franklin D. Roosevelt applied it on a national level and awarded Catholics, most of them Irish, for their long loyalty to the Democratic Party with a fair share of places in the federal government, where they helped reform the American social system.[50] In 1960 Irish Catholics arrived at last when one of their own, John Fitzgerald Kennedy, became president of the United States.

Kennedy was less culturally Irish Catholic than his name or public image suggested.[51] Still, his charm, self-deprecating wit and the energy of the New Frontier obscured the less-than-promised accomplishments of his administration. Most important, Kennedy made Americans feel good about themselves and to take pride in their country as a bastion of liberal democracy, feelings and convictions they have not experienced since that shattering late November 1963 day in Dallas. The president's popularity transferred to the Irish, increasing their self-confidence and their respectability. Kennedy also altered the public impression of the Irish-American politician from provincial, cynical, corrupt city boss to cosmopolitan, issue-minded statesman, still a power seeker and broker, but with pragmatism modified by idealism.[52] Even before Kennedy's presidency Irish Americans had achieved leadership roles in the House of Representatives and the Senate.[53] Since his death they have continued as prominent and articulate liberal voices within the Democratic Party.

Not all contemporary Irish Americans are well-educated, liberal, confident middle-class suburbanites. In the mid-1970s television viewers from all over the United States and many in Europe saw angry Irish faces confronting blacks and their police protectors, and heard hate-filled Irish voices shouting obscenities and racial insults at frightened black teenagers exiting from buses that transported them from Roxbury to South Boston. They also observed gangs of Irishmen assaulting blacks, and lines of Irishwomen marching with religious banners, praying the rosary and beseeching the Blessed Virgin to protect their neighborhood from black encroachment. The Irish response to school busing in Boston brought out the frustrations of people who continue to lag behind the achievements of their co-ethnics in the rest of the country.[54] Pockets of paranoia and self-pity also exist in Irish sections of the Bronx, Queens, Manhattan, Brooklyn and the Southwest side of Chicago.[55]

Some members of the working-class Irish have joined with other Catholic ethnics in resisting black efforts to leave depressing ghettos for more attractive neighborhoods with good schools. Catholic ethnics have also opposed, at times with violence, busing to create racially-mixed schools. Certainly racial prejudice is involved in these actions, but so are economic fears and cultural differences between evangelical black Protestants and white Catholics. Worried about the value of their homes, the safety of their streets and the education of their children, and protective of traditional family values, white Catholic ethnics, who have struggled so long in the United States for economic security and social respectability, do not want to integrate with the southern Protestant poverty culture which blacks represent to them. They interpret it as reverse mobility. And few of them can afford to escape to wealthy suburbs or fancy downtown high-rise apartments.

Boston Irish anti-busing protests and white Catholic ethnic reactions to blacks in other cities have confirmed long-held opinions by many Anglo-American Protestant and Jewish liberals, namely, that the Irish and other Catholic ethnics are a reactionary force in American life and the leading barrier to racial harmony in the urban North.[56] They believe that Irish resistance to racially integrated education and housing represents the same kind of un-Americanism manifested in Catholic ethnic support in the 1930s for the anti-Semitic fascism of Father Charles Coughlin, the radio priest from Royal Oak, Michigan, and the anti-communist witch-hunting of Senator Joseph McCarthy of Wisconsin in the early 1950s. This intellectual nativism distorts the present reality of Catholic ethnic America, particularly its Irish dimension.

Despite Boston, and there is improvement there, and enclaves of Irish frustration and slow mobility in other cities, Irish America is successfully middle class. According to the National Opinion Research Center (NORC), 71 percent of the Irish in Chicago and Minneapolis are white-collar workers. In the former city 39 percent are professionals or managers; the figure is 38 percent for the latter. Fifty percent of Irish Chicagoans earn more than $25,000 a year.[57] And it must be remembered that a large number of blue-collar Irish Americans in skilled trades earn substantial yearly incomes. NORC's 1977 and 1978 General Social Survey indicated that

> in terms of education, occupation and income, Irish Catholics are notably above the national average for other whites. In education and occupation they are also now even with the British Protestant group and substantially ahead of that group in income. Finally, while they lag somewhat behind Jews in occupational prestige and education, their average income in the years from 1975 to 1978 is slightly ahead of both the British Protestants and the Jews.[58]

Only a few hundred Irish immigrants now enter the United States each year. Some of them represent a "brain drain" of university and professional school graduates, but most resemble those who have come in the past: sons without a chance of inheriting the farm, daughters without bright marriage prospects, young people from farms, towns and cities seeking excitement and opportunity. New immigrants often feel uncomfortable with and resentful toward the generally well-educated, middle-class Irish-American community, yet they experience comparatively rapid occupational and social mobility. Since their numbers are small it is hard for them to remain isolated in ghetto situations. They are able to take advantage of Irish political power and thus are more fortunate in finding steady, well-paying jobs, particularly in construction, than are other European Catholic immigrants, blacks, Puerto Ricans or Chicanos. Recent Irish immigrants have invested a considerable portion of their incomes in higher education for their children. After attending college or university, sons and daughters of Irish-born parents join middle-class Irish America. Consequently, the contrasts between "greenhorns" and "narrowbacks" tend to fade within a generation.[59]

On sentimental occasions new immigrants, like the old, shed tears for and sing sad songs about "that dear land across the sea," but for Irish immigrants America always has been the country of opportunity and their journey to its shore a one-way trip. They have demonstrated their love for the United States in hard work, patriotism, military service, rapid citizenship and active political participation. Their lingering affection for Ireland pales in comparison with their love for America.

Prosperity and class mobility have altered the political allegiances of some Irish Americans. While a majority still cast Democratic ballots, a substantial minority vote Republican. Probably more would make a switch if the Republican Party did not cultivate such a rural, small town, Anglo-Protestant image. Despite some defections from the Democratic Party, evidence indicates that American Catholics are more compassionate than American Protestants on such issues as civil rights, social justice (including the race issue) and peace, and that the Irish tend to be more liberal than other Catholics.[60]

As a nation the United States could do much more in response to poverty, disease, prejudice, injustice and militarism, but compared to other Americans, except for Jews, the Irish have the most laudable record on these issues. The liberalism of so many Irish politicians reflects the community they came from and a Catholic education that has extended its Christian message beyond Catholic dogma. It combines love of neighbor with love of God.[61]

Contemporary Irish-America's Catholicism as well as its political and social opinions bespeak a confidence and a sense of belonging. Catholic patriotism no longer articulates a neurotic "my country right or wrong" perspective. Formerly, American Catholic bishops tended to give unreserved support to United States Cold War foreign and military policies. Lately, many members of the hierarchy, including a number of Irish Americans, have criticized their country's support for despotism in Latin America, and they have taken a strong line, with little dissent, against the nuclear weapons buildup, insisting that these instruments of death and destruction cannot be used by civilized peoples. The moral courage of the bishops and the general Catholic concern for peace and social justice signify that the Irish and other Catholics are ready to function as a positive force in the restructuring of American society and more as a national conscience than as a jingoistic battalion.

NOTES

[1] L. M. Cullen, *The Emergence of Modern Ireland, 1600-1900* (New York: Holmes and Meier Publishers, Inc., 1981) discusses Ireland as the leading recipient of immigrants among the countries bordered by the Atlantic.

[2] Carl Wittke, *The Irish in America* (New York: Russell and Russell Publishers, 1970); W. F. Adams, *Ireland and Irish Immigration to the New World from 1815 to the Famine* (New York: Russell and Russell Publishers, 1967); and Audrey Lockhart, *Some Aspects of Emigration from Ireland to the North American Colonies Between 1660-1775* (New York: Arno Press, 1976) discuss pre-1815 Irish entry into America.

[3] Lockhart's *Some Aspects of Emigration,* op. cit., is the first examination of the indentured servant/transported convict dimensions of Irish immigration. Since eighteenth-century punishment for crime was excessive, transportees were not necessarily hardened or brutal criminals.

[4] For discussions of the Irish in Britain see John Archer Jackson, *The Irish in Britain* (Cleveland, Ohio: The Press of Western Reserve University, 1963); Kevin O'Connor, *The Irish in Britain* (London: Sidgwick & Jackson Ltd., 1972); John Hickey, *Urban Catholics* (London: Geoffrey Chapman Ltd., 1967); and Lynn Hollen Lees, *Exiles of Ireland: Irish Migrants in Victorian London* (Ithaca, N.Y.: Cornell University Press, 1979).

[5] Patrick Blessing, "The Irish," in Stephan Thernstrom, ed., *Harvard Encyclopedia of American Ethnic Groups* (Cambridge, Mass.: Belknap Press, 1980), pp. 525-528, and Adams, *Ireland and Irish Immigration,* op. cit., provide information on pre-famine Irish immigrants.

[6] Oliver MacDonagh, "Irish Emigration to the United States of America and the British Colonies During the Famine," in R. Dudley Edwards and T. Desmond Williams, eds., *The Great Famine* (New York: New York University Press, 1957) and Cecil Woodham Smith, *The Great Hunger, Ireland, 1845-1849* (New York: Harper and Row Publishers, Inc., 1962). Joel Mokyr, *Why Ireland Starved: A Quantitative and Analytical History of the Irish Economy, 1800-1850* (Boston: Allen & Unwin, 1983) discusses the poverty and deficiencies of the pre-famine Irish economy and the significance of the absence of an industrial alternative. He also updates the famine's casualty figures.

[7] Blessing, "The Irish," op. cit., and Marjorie R. Fallows, *Irish-Americans: Identity and Assimilation* (Englewood Cliffs, N. J.: Prentice-Hall, Inc., 1979), pp. 22-26, discuss post-famine emigration from Ireland to the United States.

Terry Coleman's *Going to America* (New York: Doubleday & Co. Inc., Anchor, 1973) and Philip Taylor's *The Distant Magnet* (New York: Harper & Row Publishers, 1971) detail the emigration process. Taylor includes the Irish in his examination of the entire scope of European emigration, including the journey to the New World and the problems encountered there. Coleman concentrates on the voyage and tribulations of ship passengers, mostly Irish, sailing from Liverpool to America.

[8]Dennis Clark, *The Irish in Philadelphia* (Philadelphia: Temple University Press, 1973), p. 62, presents a figure of 84.5 percent for rural emigration. Blessing, "The Irish," op. cit., p. 530, estimates that in 1920, 90 percent of Irish Americans were urban. James P. Shannon, *Catholic Colonization on the Western Frontier* (New York: Arno Press, 1976) describes Catholic clerical efforts to keep the Irish away from American cities.

[9]Oscar Handlin, *Boston's Immigrants* (New York: Atheneum, 1968) argues that poverty limited the Irish presence in the United States to port cities.

[10]For discussions of the agricultural situation see James S. Donnelly, Jr., *Landlord and Tenant in Nineteenth Century Ireland* (Dublin: Gill and MacMillan, 1973) and *The Land and People of Nineteenth Century Cork* (London: Routledge & Kegan Paul, 1975); L. M. Cullen, *The Emergence of Modern Ireland*, op. cit.; Joel Mokyr, *Why Ireland Starved*, op. cit.; and Gearoid O'Tuathaigh, *Ireland Before the Famine* (Dublin: Gill and MacMillan, 1972).

[11]Kenneth Connell, *The Population of Ireland, 1750-1845* (London: Oxford University Press, 1950) explained the population explosion as the result of early marriages with consequent high fertility. He said that the easy availability of the potato encouraged early marriage. Cullen's book established a historical consensus that survived until the 1970s. O'Tuathaigh's *Ireland Before the Famine* presents the population problem in more complicated terms. So does Mokyr's *Why Ireland Starved*, which admits that Irish parents had large families but denies that they married younger than other Europeans.

[12]Lawrence J. McCaffrey, *The Irish Diaspora in America* (Washington, D.C.: The Catholic University Press of America, 1984) emphasizes the differences between rural life in Ireland and America and the Catholic personality as factors in Irish-American urbanization.

[13]Clark, *The Irish in Philadelphia*, op. cit.; Handlin, *Boston's Immigrants*, op. cit.; Blessing, "The Irish," op. cit.; Earl F. Niehaus, *The Irish in New Orleans* (New York: Arno Press, 1976); Stephan Thernstrom, *Poverty and Progress* (Cambridge, Mass.: Harvard University Press, 1964); Brian C. Mitchell, *Immigrants in Utopia: The Early Irish Community of Lowell, Massachusetts, 1821-1861* (Ph.D. Dissertation, University of Rochester, 1981. Ann Arbor: University Microfilms-International); and William V. Millett, *The Irish and Mobility Patterns in Northampton, Massachusetts, 1846-1883* (Ph.D. Dissertation, University of Iowa, 1980. Ann Arbor: University Microfilms International) provide valuable information for the following comments on early Irish-Catholic contributions to the American work force.

[14]For a brilliant description and analysis of the world of nineteenth-century Irish-American women see Hasia Diner, *Erin's Daughters in America: Irish Immigrant Women in the Nineteenth Century* (Baltimore: The John Hopkins University Press, 1983).

[15]Handlin, *Boston's Immigrants*, op. cit., p. 82.

[16]Ibid., p. 55. Handlin's fourth chapter, "The Physical Adjustment," is an excellent portrait of a bleak Irish ghetto.

[17]The two most important volumes on anti-Catholic American nativism are Ray Allen Billington, *The Protestant Crusade, 1800-1860*, paperback ed. (Chicago: Quadrangle Books, Inc., 1964); and John Higham, *Strangers in the Land: Patterns of American Nativism, 1860-1925*, paperback ed. (New York: Atheneum Publishers, 1965).

[18]George Taylor, *The Transportation Revolution* (New York: Holt, Rinehart and Winston, 1964), p. 287. Taylor's generalization has to be modified. David Doyle, *Irish-Americans, Native Rights, and National Empires: The Structure, Divisions, and Attitudes of the Catholic Minority in the Decade of Expansion, 1890-1901* (New York: Arno Press, 1976) does point out that some Irish immigrants came from towns and cities where unionism did exist. This was particularly true for Dublin. And T. Desmond Williams, ed., *Secret Societies in Ireland* (New York: Barnes and Noble Books, 1973) and James S. Donnelly, Jr. and Samuel Clark, eds., *Irish Peasants: Violence and Political Unrest* (Madison, Wis.: University of Wisconsin Press, 1983) make clear that in rural Ireland, agricultural laborers and tenant farmers often organized into secret societies or into open agitations to achieve decent wages and/or fair rents and security of tenure, and employed violent as well as legal forms of coercion.

[19]In William V. Shannon, *The American Irish* (New York: Collier Books, 1974), p. 55, the author lists "obsessive preoccupation with their own problems" as the basic reason for Irish opposition to abolition. They complained that the northern middle class was insincere when it pitied the black slaves in the South and ignored the tribulations of poor whites in the urban North. Shannon quotes Congressman Mike Walsh of New York who said in the 1854 House of Representatives that: "The only difference between the negro slave of the South and the white wage slave of the North is that one has a master without asking for him, and the other has to beg for the privilege of becoming a slave . . . The one is the slave of an individual; the other is the slave of an inexorable class."

[20]The Irish role in the New York riot is discussed in chapters ten through twenty-one of Joel Tyler Headley, *The Great Riots of New York: 1712-1873*, introduced by Thomas Rose and James Rodgers (Indianapolis, Ind.: Bobbs-Merrill, 1970). In Richard Shaw, *Dagger John: The Unquiet Life and Times of Archbishop John Hughes of New York* (New York: Paulist Press, 1977), pp. 362-369, the author describes Hughes' response to Irish participation in the riot.

[21]For examinations of the rising rural standard of living in Ireland see Barbara Lewis Solow, *The Land Question and the Irish Economy, 1870-1903* (Cambridge, Mass.: Harvard University Press, 1971); Joseph Lee, *The Modernization of Irish Society, 1848-1918* (Dublin: Gill and MacMillan, 1973); James S. Donnelly, Jr., *The Land and People of Nineteenth Century Cork*, op. cit.; Samuel Clark, *Social Origins of the Irish Land War* (Princeton, N. J.: Princeton University Press, 1979); and L. M. Cullen, *The Emergence of Modern Ireland*, op. cit.

[22]According to Patrick Blessing, "From the earliest years of the 19th century unskilled rural peasants were common to the movement to the New World, and from 1850 to 1920 they accounted for about 80 percent of all departures. Nevertheless, at mid-century about 75 percent and by 1910, 97 percent of all the Irish admitted to the United States could read and write English." "The Irish," op. cit., p. 529. Of course the 1845-1849 famine conditions took the biggest toll on the illiterate portion of the population. People who emigrated probably were better able to read and write than those who remained in Ireland.

[23]David W. Miller, "Irish Catholicism and the Great Famine," *The Journal of Social Studies*, 9:1 (September 1975): 81-98; and S. J. Connolly, *Priests and People in Pre-Famine Ireland, 1780-1845* (New York: St. Martin's Press, 1982) describe pre-famine Irish Catholicism.

[24]Eugene Hynes, "The Great Hunger and Irish Catholicism," *Societas*, VIII:2 (Spring, 1978): 137-156, argues that post-famine Irish peasants became more devout to avoid future calamities and to achieve or maintain economic security because the discipline and rigid sexual standards of their religion helped control population, preventing a slide back into desperate poverty. In *Ireland From Colony to Nation State* (Englewood Cliffs, N. J.: Prentice Hall, Inc., 1979), p. 80, Lawrence J. McCaffrey emphasizes the ties between Catholicism and Irish nationalism to explain the new vitality of the former.

[25]In "The Devotional Revolution in Ireland, 1850-1875," in *The Historical Dimensions of Irish Catholicism* (Washington, D.C.: The Catholic University Press of America, 1984) and *The Making of the Roman Catholic Church in Ireland, 1850-1860* (Chapel Hill, N. C.: University of North Carolina Press, 1980), Emmet Larkin defines and describes Cullen's "Devotional Revolution."

[26]For a perceptive interpretation of Irish-American politics see Thomas N. Brown, "The Political Irish: Politicians and Rebels," in David Noel Doyle and Owen Dudley Edwards, eds., *America and Ireland, 1776-1976* (Westport, Conn.: Greenwood Press, 1980), pp. 133-150. James P. Walsh, ed., *The Irish: America's Political Class* (New York: Arno Press, 1976) offers numerous, often interesting essays on Irish-American politics.

[27]Alan J. Ward, *Ireland and Anglo-American Relations, 1899-1921* (London: Weidenfeld and Nicolson, 1969), p. 94.

[28]David Montgomery, "The Irish and the American Labor Movement," in Doyle and Edwards, eds., *America and Ireland, 1776-1976*, op. cit., p. 211.

[29]Hasia Diner's *Erin's Daughters*, op. cit., offers an excellent discussion of Irish-American women teachers, religious and lay. Male Catholic bishops and priests ignored women's problems, but nuns, overwhelmingly Irish in numbers, sheltered the poor and afflicted and educated young women for economic independence rather than marriage. Diner emphasizes that nuns were primarily concerned with women, with the result that Irishwomen were much better educated than Irishmen in the United States, thus enhancing their role as a civilizing force. Since Irishwomen had more reservations about marriage than others of their sex, many of them entered a profession like teaching which often excluded those who were married. According to Patrick Blessing in "The Irish," op. cit., p. 532, "In 1900 daughters of Irish born parents composed 10 percent of all female teachers of foreign born parentage in the United States, exceeding the combined total of female teachers with English and German parents." During the early 1920s, Chicago's George Cardinal Mundelein estimated that about 70 percent of the city's public school teachers graduated from Catholic secondary schools. (*The New World* (January 25, 1920).) Chicago Normal School's yearbook, *The Emblem*, indicated that over 50 percent of its graduates were Catholics, most with Irish names.

[30]The best study of almost frozen New England Irish economic mobility is Stephan Thernstrom's *Poverty and Progress*, op. cit., a discussion of the Irish working class of Newburysport, Massachusetts.

[31]Irish success on the urban frontier is a major subject in JoEllen McNergney Vinyard, *The Irish on the Urban Frontier: Detroit, 1850-1880* (New York: Arno Press, 1976). See also R. A. Burchell, *The San Francisco Irish, 1848-1880* (Berkeley, Cal.: University of California Press, 1980); and Charles

Fanning, Ellen Skerrett and John Corrigan, *Nineteenth Century Chicago Irish* (Chicago: Center for Urban Policy, Loyola University of Chicago, 1980).

[32]David Noel Doyle's *Irish-Americans, Native Rights, and National Empires*, op. cit., pp. 59-66, sustains the "urban frontier" thesis.

[33]John Cogley, *Catholic America* (New York: Dial Press, 1973); Andrew Greeley, *The Catholic Experience* (New York: Doubleday Image Books, 1969); and John Tracy Ellis, *American Catholicism* (Chicago: University of Chicago Press, 1955) are intelligent, well-written and brief interpretations of American Catholic history.

[34]James Edmund Roohan, *American Catholics and the Social Question, 1865-1900* (New York: Arno Press, 1976); and Arthur Mann, "Irish Catholic Liberalism: The Spirit of 1848," in *Yankee Reformers in the Urban Age: Social Reform in Boston, 1880-1900* (New York: Harper and Row Publishers, Harper Torchbooks, 1954), pp. 25-51.

[35]Robert D. Cross, *The Emergence of Catholic Liberalism in America* (Chicago: Quadrangle Books, Inc., 1967); James H. Moynihan, *The Life of Archbishop John Ireland* (New York: Arno Press, 1976); and Harry J. Brown, *The Catholic Church and the Knights of Labor* (New York: Arno Press, 1976).

[36]James Paul Rodechko, *Patrick Ford and His Search for America: A Case Study of Irish-American Journalism, 1870-1913* (New York: Arno Press, 1976).

[37]Burchell, *The San Francisco Irish*, op. cit., pp. 153-154.

[38]Ellen Skerrett, "The Catholic Dimension," in Lawrence J. McCaffrey, ed., *Chicago's Irish* (Champaign-Urbana, Ill.: University of Illinois Press, in press).

[39]William A. Gudelunas, Jr. and William J. Shade, *Before the Molly Maguires: The Emergence of the Ethno-Religious Factor in the Politics of the Lower Anthracite Region, 1844-1872* (New York: Arno Press, 1976).

[40]Shannon, *The American Irish*, op. cit., pp. 389-390; Emmet Larkin, *James Larkin* (Cambridge, Mass.: MIT Press, 1965); and McCaffrey, *The Irish Diaspora in America*, op. cit., pp. 101-102.

[41]Montgomery, "The Irish and the American Labor Movement," op. cit., p. 206.

[42]Higham, *Strangers in the Land*, op. cit., is the best comprehensive study of post-Civil War American nativism. Also consult Donald L. Kinzer, *An Episode in Anti-Catholicism: The American Protective Association* (Seattle, Wash.: University of Washington Press, 1964). The original Ku Klux Klan, a Reconstruction white terrorist organization, concentrated on blacks. Jim Crow laws passed by southern states and approved by the United States Supreme Court spelled victory for the KKK. The new Klan, founded in 1915, was more concerned with blocking the progress of Catholics and Jews in American society.

[43]L. P. Curtis, Jr., *Anglo-Saxons and Celts: A Study in Anti-Irish Prejudice in Victorian England* (Bridgeport, Conn.: Conference on British Studies, 1968), and *Apes and Angels: The Irishman in Victorian Caricature* (Newton Abbot, England: David and Charles, 1971); Richard Ned Lebow, *White Britain and Black Ireland* (Philadelphia: Institute for the Study of Human Issues, 1976); John J. and Selma Appel, *The Distorted Image* (New York: Anti-Defamation League of B'nai B'rith, 1974)—a slide collection containing examples of anti-Irish cartoons in American newspapers and periodicals; Stephan Gar-

rett Bolger, *The Irish Character in American Fiction, 1830-1960* (New York: Arno Press, 1976).

[44]"More than one person has noted that anti-Catholicism is—or perhaps was—the anti-semitism of the intellectual." Michael Novak, *The Rise of the Unmeltable Ethnics,* paperback ed. (New York: MacMillan Co., Inc., 1973), p. 163. D. W. Brogan discussed American intellectual anti-Catholicism in *American Aspects* (New York: Harper & Row, 1964), p. 164; so too does Andrew M. Greeley in *The Irish Americans: The Rise to Money and Power* (New York: Harper & Row, 1981), pp. 107 ff.

[45]Francis M. Carroll, *American Opinion and the Irish Question, 1910-1923* (New York: St. Martin's Press, 1978); Joseph Edward Cuddy, *Irish-America and National Isolationism, 1914-1920* (New York: Arno Press, 1976), and "The Irish Question and the Revival of Anti-Catholicism in the 1920s," *The Catholic Historical Review,* LXVII:2 (April 1981): 236-255.

[46]Andrew M. Greeley claims that already in the World War I era one out of four Irish-American secondary school graduates went on to higher education. See Greeley, *The Irish Americans: The Rise to Money and Power,* op. cit., p. 112. Many of them must have been women in teaching or nursing training.

[47]McCaffrey, *The Irish Diaspora in America,* op. cit., p. 158.

[48]Charles Fanning has discussed Dunne and Farrell as social historians of the Chicago Irish in a number of places including Charles Fanning, *Finley Peter Dunne and Mr. Dooley: The Chicago Years* (Lexington, Ky.: The University of Kentucky Press, 1978); Charles Fanning, ed., *Mr. Dooley and the Chicago Irish* (New York: Arno Press, 1976); "James T. Farrell: A Reappraisal," *Irish Literary Supplement,* 2:2 (Fall 1983): 30; and Charles Fanning, "The Literary Dimension," in McCaffrey, ed., *Chicago's Irish,* op. cit. Also consult Skerrett's "Catholic Dimension" in *Chicago's Irish,* op. cit.

[49]Thomas N. Brown, "The Political Irish: Politicians and Rebels," in Doyle and Edwards, eds., *America and Ireland, 1776-1976,* op. cit., pp. 144-147.

[50]George Q. Flynn, *American Catholics and the Roosevelt Presidency* (Lexington, Ky.: University of Kentucky Press, 1968).

[51]Gary Wills in *The Kennedy Imprisonment* (Boston: Little Brown, 1982) claims that Joseph Kennedy and sons were more impressed with upper-class British values than Irish ethnicity. For more favorable estimates of Kennedy's Irishness see Arthur Schlesinger, Jr., *A Thousand Days: John F. Kennedy in the White House* (New York: Fawcett World Library Premier Book, 1971); Kenneth P. O'Donnell and David F. Powers with Joe McCarthy, *Johnny We Hardly Knew Ye* (Boston: Little Brown, 1972); Benjamin Bradlee, *Conversations With Kennedy* (New York: W. W. Norton & Co., Inc., 1975); William V. Shannon, *The American Irish,* op. cit., pp. 292-438; William Manchester, *One Brief Shining Moment: Remembering Kennedy* (Boston: Little Brown, 1983); and Ralph G. Martin, *A Hero for Our Time* (New York: MacMillan, 1983). Herbert S. Parmet's two volumes, *Jack: The Struggles of John F. Kennedy* and *JFK: The Presidency of John F. Kennedy* (New York: Dial Press, 1980 and 1983) add up to the most scholarly portrait of the late president.

[52]The old image of the Irish politician exaggerated their faults as much as the new magnifies their virtues. In his well-written, beautifully illustrated, generally perceptive *A Portrait of the Irish in America* (New York: Charles Scribners & Sons, 1981), pp. 114-136, William D. Griffin repeats Daniel P. Moynihan's charge in "The Irish" in Daniel P. Moynihan and Nathan Glazer,

Beyond the Melting Pot (Cambridge, Mass.: MIT Press, 1963), pp. 137-180, that the Irish functioned as a static, peasant conservative force in American urban politics. In "Urban Liberalism and the Age of Reform," *The Mississippi Valley Historical Review*, 49 (September 1962): 231-241, J. Joseph Huthmacher said that the Catholic ethnic poverty experience, religious values, and welfare-orientated political machines created the main attack on laissez-faire liberalism. John B. Buenker, *Urban Liberalism and Progressive Reform* (New York: Charles Scribner's Sons, 1973) applies Huthmacher's thesis to politics in such cities as Providence, Cleveland, Chicago, Pittsburgh and New York. When Kennedy was glossing up the Irish-American political image and giving it a national dimension, Richard J. Daley controlled the most effective urban machine in American history. For discussions of Daley's Irishness see William F. Gleason, *Daley of Chicago* (New York: Simon and Shuster, 1970); Milton Rakove, *Don't Make No Waves—Don't Back No Losers* (Bloomington, Ind.: University of Indiana Press, 1975); and Eugene Kennedy, *Himself: The Life and Times of Mayor Richard J. Daley* (New York: The Viking Press, 1978). Edward M. Levine, *The Irish and Irish Politicians* (South Bend, Ind.: University of Notre Dame Press, 1966) is an interesting analysis of the Chicago Irish political style in the Daley era.

[53] During Kennedy's presidency, Mike Mansfield of Montana was Senate Majority Leader, John W. McCormack of Massachusetts was Speaker of the House of Representatives, and John Bailey of Connecticut was chairman of the Democratic National Committee. They were not members of the president's "Irish Mafia." Their power preceded and survived him. Since Kennedy's death his brothers Robert and Edward, Senator Eugene McCarthy of Minnesota, Governor Jerry Brown of California and Speaker of the House of Representatives Thomas P. O'Neill of Massachusetts, are among Irish politicians who have been important in the United States.

[54] Stephan Thernstrom's *The Other Bostonians: Poverty and Progress in the American Metropolis, 1860-1970* (Cambridge, Mass.: Harvard University Press, 1970) reveals how the Irish lagged behind all whites, except Italians, in terms of economic and social mobility in Boston. Andrew Greeley, *The Irish-Americans: The Rise to Money and Power*, op. cit., p. 116 ff., reinforces Thernstrom's thesis.

[55] In "Race and Housing: Violence and Communal Protest in Chicago, 1940" in Melvin G. Holli and Peter d'A. Jones, eds., *The Ethnic Frontier* (Grand Rapids, Mich.: William B. Eerdmans Publishing Co., 1977), Arnold Hirsh's description of Chicago Irish resistance to black expansion into South Side white neighborhoods indicates that they could be as insecure as the Boston Irish. Jimmy Breslin's *World Without End, Amen* (New York: Viking Press, 1973) indicts Irish racism in Queens.

[56] A best-selling novel which was turned into a successful film, Judith Rossner's *Looking for Mr. Goodbar* (New York: Simon and Shuster, 1975) identifies Catholics as bigots. The novel's half-Irish, half-Italian main character, Theresa Dunn, describes her mother and father to her English professor as "very prejudiced you know, typical lower-middle class Roman Catholics . . . I grew up with all that stuff you know, the niggers are coming. They don't even like Martin Luther King." (p. 39.) Irish-American writers have done more to perpetuate an image of their own people as anti-intellectual, conservative prudes, hypocrites and bigots than Anglo-American Protestant or American Jewish writers and intellectuals. From James T. Farrell through Harry Sylvester to Jimmy Breslin, Pete Hamill, Joe Flaherty and John Gregory Dunne, Irish-American writers have complained of the Jansenism, narrow-mindedness and prejudices of their co-ethnics. In doing so they have created some excellent

literature and provided insight into some Irish character flaws. But in exercising their role of the writer as rebel and exile, these Irish-American writers often attribute the vices of a minority to a total community, have failed to judge the Irish in relationship to other segments of America, and have ignored the considerable changes in Irish-American values and attitudes since James T. Farrell's time.

[57]Andrew M. Greeley, *The Irish Americans: The Rise to Money and Power*, op. cit., p. 118. The National Opinion Research Center's alcohol study showed 54 percent of the Boston Irish as white collar and 26 percent as managers or professionals. Twenty-seven percent of the Irish in Boston, 32 percent in New York and 33 percent in Minneapolis-St. Paul earned more than $25,000 a year.

[58]Greeley, *The Irish Americans*, op. cit., p. 111. Greeley's comparison of the Irish to others is based upon the following statistics that he records on the same page:

> 26 [sic] percent of families in America reported an annual income in excess of $20,000; of those who describe themselves as British Protestant, 30 percent reported more than $20,000 in income; and 47 percent of the Irish-Catholic families reported more than $20,000 in income, a little higher than the 46 percent of Jewish families and 43 percent of Italian families. Irish occupational prestige, on a scale of 100, was 42.0 as compared to 39.8 for all American white families, 38.6 for Italian families, and 42.1 for British Protestant families. The mean number of years of schooling of Irish Catholics is 12.6 as compared to the national average of 11.8, 12.7 for British Protestants, and 11.4 for Italian Catholics and 13.7 for Jews. Of the Irish Catholics, 32 percent were professionals or managers, as compared to a national average of 25 percent, an Italian figure of 22 percent, a British Protestant figure of 33 percent, and a Jewish figure of 40 percent.

Greeley (p. 113) also points out that Irish Catholics are more "likely to attend graduate school and choose academic careers" than white Protestants.

[59]Lawrence J. McCaffrey, "The Recent Irish Diaspora in America," in Dennis L. Cuddy, ed., *Contemporary American Immigration* (Boston: Twayne Publishers, 1982), pp. 37-58. Greenhorns are Irish immigrants; narrowbacks are their American-born offspring.

[60]Andrew M. Greeley has discussed the social conscience liberalism of Irish-American Catholics in a number of books besides *The Irish Americans: The Rise to Money and Power*, op. cit., including *The Catholic Experience* (New York: Doubleday, 1967); *Why Can't They Be Like Us* (New York: E. P. Dutton, 1971); and *Ethnicity in the United States: A Preliminary Reconnaissance* (New York: John Wiley & Sons, 1974).

[61]Evidently, Catholics who attend Catholic schools are more liberal in a social conscience way than Catholics who attend secular educational institutions. This point is made in a number of Greeley's books and articles, particularly Andrew M. Greeley and Peter H. Rossi, *The Education of Catholic Americans* (Chicago: Aldine, 1966).

THE ECONOMIC ACTIVITIES OF ITALIAN AMERICANS

Humbert S. Nelli

University of Kentucky

Italian emigration to the United States has been accurately divided at about 1880 to differentiate between two movements. The smaller movement, composed largely of Northern Italians, arrived before 1880; the large-scale migration from the South began around 1880 and continued until World War I. Although the groups generally arrived in different eras, both Northern and Southern Italians typically started with few financial resources and at or near the bottom of the socioeconomic ladder. Both settled in the highly urbanized and industrialized states of the East and Midwest. There were, however, two notable exceptions to this generalization. In contrast to other American cities, New Orleans attracted Southern Italians from the beginning of the colony in the 1850s, while San Francisco remained Northern Italian long after other cities were inundated by immigrants from the South. Furthermore, in both cities the Italian communities were wealthier than those in other urban centers.

Immigrants from Northern Italy typically did not work as common laborers. Instead, they generally held semi-skilled or skilled jobs, or found employment in service and trade occupations. Although some Northern Italian immigrants possessed considerable wealth, most, like the later-arriving Southerners, had very limited financial resources when they arrived in the United States. Both groups increased family incomes by withdrawing children from school, either putting them to work or assigning them household chores in order to free mothers for outside jobs.

In San Francisco, generally regarded to be the "model colony," Northern Italians enjoyed success in banking and small industry; they prospered as fishermen, fish brokers and commission merchants, truck gardeners, viticulturists, horticulturists and food processors. The two most important industries they established in the Bay Area were truck farming and commercial fishing. The San Francisco colony also produced a number of business entrepreneurs. The most famous and successful was Amadeo Giannini, founder of the Transamerica Corporation and the Bank of Italy, later renamed the Bank of America.[1]

In New York, Chicago and other eastern and midwestern cities, Northern Italians became prosperous merchants, importers, manufacturers, building contractors, bankers and other businessmen, as well as physicians and lawyers. Still others realized more modest but substantial success as peddlers, vendors, artisans, bakers, restaurateurs, store owners, saloon-keepers and barbers.[2]

The post-1880 Southern Italian immigrants generally were able to find employment only as common laborers. They appeared to make little economic progress, at least in part because of a steady stream of new arrivals who settled in Italian districts and started at the bottom of the economic ladder. Many immigrants remained unskilled laborers throughout their working lives and contributed to the nation's economic growth through construction, maintenance or factory work. Others became affluent merchants, small manufacturers, professionals or businessmen, or qualified for jobs as skilled workmen.

In contrast to the experience elsewhere, Southern Italians composed the majority of the early as well as post-1880 arrivals in New Orleans. The city offered numerous economic opportunities to newcomers, particularly through its importance as a seaport. Although the Irish and blacks monopolized waterfront jobs, numbers of Sicilians and other Southern Italians found jobs as fishermen, stevedores and longshoremen. Others became importers, exporters and retail merchants; still others, fruit and vegetable peddlers and dealers.[3]

During the decades of large-scale immigration, Southern Italian newcomers were generally regarded by the native American population as an aggregation of unskilled construction workers. Thus one popular writer observed in 1906 that "they are to be found wherever a shovel of earth needs to be turned or a bed of rock is blasted."[4] This belief stemmed at least in part from the justly deserved notoriety surrounding the padrone, or labor boss, system. The extensive, and perhaps excessive, attention devoted to the boss system had the unfortunate result of obscuring the fact that during the peak of padrone activity, as well as in the period after its decline, Italians were employed in a wide variety of economic activities.

Southern Italian immigrants who flooded into the United States after 1880 generally understood little of the English language. They also lacked contacts with potential employers in America, and knew nothing about local labor practices. To compensate for these deficiencies they looked for an intermediary—someone who spoke both languages, understood Old World traditions, and had contacts with American employers needing unskilled workers. This intermediary was the labor boss, the padrone.

Some form of boss system seemed to be typical of non-English-speaking immigrant groups newly arrived in industrial America, including Italians, Greeks, Austrians, Bulgarians, Macedonians and Mexicans. It was the method by which these groups overcame three immediate problems: language difficulties, financial exigencies and differences in labor practices. It was, in fact, part of the price that the newcomer had to pay for his newness.[5]

The Italian padrone system functioned in the United States from the 1860s to the beginning of the twentieth century. Prior to the passage of the Foran Act in 1885, which forbade the importation of immigrant labor under contract, the padrone recruited men in Italy, paid their transportation and arranged work for them in the United States, generally in construction. Usually the padrone brought only adult males into the country, but some preferred to recruit entire families, employing the men in manual labor, often forcing the women into prostitution and sending the children into the streets to shine shoes, play the mouth organ or steal. After the Foran Act the padrone functioned merely as a private, unlicensed labor agent—in fact, most probably functioned in this capacity before 1885.

Bosses hired men in New York, Chicago and other cities, and sent them out to their places of work. The padrone system was best suited to particular lines of work, especially those demanding a large supply of unskilled labor on short notice and in relatively isolated areas. Bosses on rare occasions supplied skilled workers, including masons, carpenters, stonecutters and machinists.

Because of its role as the principal port of arrival for Italian immigrants, New York City became the center of the padrone system in the United States. It appears that the methods used by bosses in other large cities, except San Francisco, were similar to those practiced in New York. Although San Francisco contained a large Italian colony, the padrone system did not become an important factor in the city's labor picture. According to an 1897 United States Department of Labor study of the boss system, the reason for this difference stemmed from the high cost of transportation across the country. Economics therefore served as an effective barrier to a large direct importation, and precluded the arrival of the impoverished and least fortunate immigrants. The presence of a large and long-settled contingent of Northern Italians was probably also an important contributing factor to the different labor patterns in San Francisco.

Bosses directed Italian immigrant laborers to most parts of the United States and even into Canada to build railroads and to work at other construction jobs. Chicago became an important padrone stronghold, partly because of the city's position as a railroad center, and partly because of its geographical location. Railroad and other construction jobs tended to be seasonal, and Chicago served as a clearinghouse for seasonal workers from the entire country.

The padrone (usually of Italian birth or extraction, although some were Irish or American) met arriving immigrants at the docks in port cities and at railroad stations in other urban centers, and promised steady work at high wages. Some immigrants did not succumb to padrone promises at once. In Italian sections of any large city, however, stubborn newcomers met with padrone-promoted pressures and enticements intended to recruit their services for the boss. It should be noted that not all immigrants needed to be forced into service for the boss. Many turned toward the padrone because he offered opportunities to make ready money.

Generally the labor agent negotiated directly with the contractor and received from him or from representatives of a corporation a definite order for a specified number of men. In order to obtain employment through the padrone, immigrants paid a commission (bossatura) ranging from one to fifteen dollars per man, the size of the fee depending on such factors as length of employment, amount of wages and whether the men were to use padrone facilities.

Not all bosses deliberately made illegal profits, and not all set out to cheat the laborer, but enough did so as to give notoriety to the entire group. Many labor agents made use of every available opportunity to overcharge, shortchange or otherwise take advantage of the men from the moment of hiring to the time of sending them back to the city where they had been hired.[6]

Despite obviously undesirable characteristics, the labor boss performed a valuable function: he brought together American capital and Italian immigrant labor. Most immigrants lacked education and money, but they had strong arms, a willingness to work and an ambition to earn as much money as possible. What they lacked was the ability to communicate with prospective employers who needed manual laborers. The padrone provided this service for them as well as for employers who as a rule did not have the means to locate and hire large numbers of dependable immigrant workers.

In addition to locating jobs, the boss provided workers other needed services. He collected wages, wrote letters, acted as banker, supplied room and board and handled dealings between laborers and employers. Often he abused his trust.

The decade of the 1890s formed a "golden era" for the Italian padrone. Of central importance, however, is the fact that Italian immigration reached its peak in the fourteen years following the turn of the century. It would seem that fortuitous opportunities for unscrupulous labor agents would best present themselves at this time, yet in 1911 the United States Immigration Commission (the Dillingham Commission) found that the boss system could be found "only in a few isolated cases among Italians."[7] The rapid decline of bossism was due in part to the efforts of social workers and others in the larger outside community concerned about the welfare of immigrants, who pressured state governments to pass legislation greatly restricting the power of labor agents.

Along with the activities of interested agencies and groups in the American community (which dated from the years after 1900), factors of a long-range nature operated within the immigrant colony. The increasingly stable nature of immigration after the turn of the century helped to reduce the need for the boss. As early as 1897, a report published in the *United States Department of Labor Bulletin* pointed out that Italian immigrants had become more settled, a condition indicated by the large numbers who came to the United States to join their immediate families or relations, and were "thus probably to a large extent put out of the reach of the padroni."[8]

The more stable nature of the immigration, increased familiarity with American labor practices and the English language, and the resultant rise in economic status all helped to end the boss system among Italians. By the turn of the century, as the United States Industrial Commission found in its investigations, Italians worked not only as common laborers on railroads and other construction and excavation jobs, but also in a variety of trades and professions, and many had become successful merchants, manufacturers and businessmen. Among these were many whose lives were rags-to-riches success stories. One example, among others, is New Orleans hotel owner Antonio Monteleone.

A native of the town of Contessa Entellina in the province of Palermo, Monteleone arrived in New Orleans in 1870, an impoverished immigrant boy. He began working as apprentice to a shoemaker, later opened his own store, and then started the first shoe factory in the city. By 1890 Monteleone was a shoe manufacturer with $37,000 in taxable property; he had become one of the Italian colony's success stories. In the early 1890s he built the Commercial Hotel on Royal and Customhouse (now Iberville) streets; later he expanded and renamed the building. The Monteleone Hotel still stands, one of the famous hostelries in the French Quarter. Monteleone became a director of two banks (the Whitney-Central Bank of New Orleans and The Bank of Hammond,

Louisiana, where he owned extensive property) and the owner of a brewery.

Early in the immigration process, Southern Italians recognized the benefits that accrued in their new homeland from involvement in politics. Political machines in New York, Chicago, New Orleans and other cities granted patronage jobs to Italians (and to members of other immigrant groups as well) in exchange for support on election days.

In Italian wards, political bosses generally came from Irish backgrounds and found that they needed a contact man or intermediary between themselves and the ethnic masses. The machine found it expedient to employ as go-betweens men who spoke the language of the community and who knew its customs, prejudices and the best means of molding opinion and winning votes.

Despite diligent efforts, Italians enjoyed only limited political success in the decades prior to World War I, although they did benefit from patronage. Robert F. Foerster noted this fact in 1919, when he observed that the level of achievement to that date was on the ward and, occasionally, the city level and, even more rarely, to elected or appointed state office. "In national affairs," he correctly judged, "the Italians have so far been all but negligible."[9]

Italians began to move into public employment by at least the early 1890s. Such employment generally offered to unskilled laborers relatively steady income and job security, while to ethnic groups it gave convincing proof of the benefits to be gained from participation in local politics. With the turn of the century Italians moved into this employment sector in ever-increasing numbers, even though in the last years of the nineteenth century such work came increasingly under the control of civil service commissions. This shift was important because it suggested the element of education at a time when tenement dwellers generally did not have much schooling. To Italians and other immigrants, civil service meant the loss of a job to a middle-class resident of a neighborhood on the periphery of the city.

Although Italians benefited from opportunities both in public and private employment, which made it possible for some to realize great financial success, most Italian immigrant males remained laborers throughout their lives. For these men success was achieved if they were able to rise to semi-skilled or skilled status. They and their compatriots who remained unskilled laborers contributed substantially but undramatically to the economic growth of the country, performing construction, mining, factory or maintenance work. As S. Merlino wrote in 1893, the Italian immigrant laborer "tills the soil, builds railroads, bores mountains, drains swamps, opens here and there to the industry of American workmen new fields which would not perhaps be opened but for his cheap labor."[10]

For the typical immigrant the work day was long and the pay low. The United States Commissioner of Labor surveyed living and working conditions in Italian neighborhoods of Baltimore, Chicago, New York and Philadelphia for the years 1893 and 1894, and found that common laborers put in a sixty-hour work week for an average weekly wage between six and nine dollars. In order to pay for food, housing, clothes and other necessities (which were often priced exorbitantly high), many found it necessary to put as many members of the family as possible to work.

Two problems facing the immigrant generation were child labor and the employment of women. By the age of fourteen and often earlier, children were removed from school and sent into the job market to supplement the family income. In a break from European habits, women went out to work or brought piecework home.

In New York, Chicago and other manufacturing centers, Italian women were heavily represented in the garment industry and in the manufacture of lace, artificial flowers, candy, paper and tobacco products. As early as 1902 Mable Hurd Willett, who studied the employment of women in the clothing trades in New York City, found that Italians had gained "a complete monopoly of part of the work, the felling and finishing of ready-made clothing."[11] By 1910 Italian women comprised the largest proportion (36.2 percent) of the female work force in the garment industry in New York City. They dominated the artificial flower industry, totaling 72 percent of the entire work force in that line of activity. Italian women (along with women of other immigrant groups) went into this kind of work because the peculiar nature of such industries often permitted them to work at home. Production processes were decentralized and the factory work, if the job could not be done at home, required little or no machinery. Such conditions suited women with small children, and also made it possible to put girls under sixteen years of age to work.

Whether at home or in a factory, Italian women worked long hours for low pay under sweatshop conditions. In 1895 reformer Jacob Riis described the experience of a New York school teacher who decided to visit the home of one of her students because the "little Italian girl, hardly yet out of her teens, stayed away from her class in the Mott Street Industrial School so long" the teacher was worried. The teacher went to the girl's apartment and "found the child in a high fever, in bed, sewing on coats with swollen eyes, though barely able to sit up." Sickness, Riis concluded, "unless it be mortal, is no excuse from the drudgery of the tenement."[12]

In 1919 Louise Odencrantz observed that in the pre-war era of large-scale immigration, "the assertion was frequently heard that the Italian girl underbids her fellow-workers in every occupation she enters, that the most poorly paid home work is largely in her hands, and that Italian standards of living are a menace to American industry."[13] Yet Italian women did not always accept these conditions without complaint. By the eve of World War I they had begun to join labor unions. Although they were less active than Eastern European Jews, they did seem to be more amenable to organization than Slavic women, or even native Americans.

School teaching was the most popular line of employment for middle-class Italian women, particularly those of the second-, or American-born, generation. The numbers involved were, however, quite small. Thus of twenty-eight Italians teaching in Chicago in 1914, twenty-four were female. Of the 407 Italians teaching in the New York City school system in 1915, 334 were women. Relatively few Italians worked in any of the professions; most were concentrated in manufacturing. In New York, for example, only some 150 women, or 1.2 percent of all Italian women employed in the city in 1900, were in professional services, compared with 9,391, or 77.1 percent, of the Italian working women who in the same year were employed in manufacturing.

Italian men moved into organized labor somewhat earlier than did women. During the first years of the immigration before Italians learned American labor practices, they were often used as strikebreakers. As early as 1874, Southern Italian immigrants were transported into the Pennsylvania coal fields to break a strike. In subsequent years and continuing into the twentieth century, new arrivals from the Italian South continued to serve as strikebreakers. To cite but two examples: in 1882 Italians helped to break up a strike by freight handlers on the New York docks and railroads, while in 1912 they served as strikebreakers for the trunk and valise makers in Chicago. Through such activities, Italians gained an unsavory but not fully deserved reputation as scabs. During the same years, Italians joined existing unions or organized new ones in the stone, garment and building industries in the eastern areas of the United States. In following years they continued their union interests and activities there and in other parts of the nation.

When they had resided for a time in America, Italians from the South as well as those from the North joined fellow workers (foreign-born and American) in supporting the rights of labor. In 1903, Italians in America made an early, although not fully successful, effort at union activity when excavation workers on New York's subways went on strike. Under the leadership of Tito Pacelli, an articulate and intelligent young labor organizer, Irish, Polish, Southern Italian and other workers concluded that their job situation was unbearable. They organized the Rockmen's and Excavators' Union and struck for higher wages, shorter hours and better job conditions. After more than five weeks of sacrifice, the laborers settled for a pay raise of about twenty-five cents a day instead of the seventy-five cents to one dollar a day they had demanded. What was more important however, according to historian Edwin Fenton, was that "they had also gained a union." During the course of the strike, the American Federation of Labor "chartered them as Excavators' Union No. 10,630 and Rockmen's Union No. 10,631, both of which won seats on the Central Federated Union. This formal recognition from the AFL enabled the Italians to win some successes in the following years."[14] The 1903 strike was just one of the organizational efforts among Italian workers.

Discussing the labor situation in the New York area, historian George Pozzetta observed that "virtually all trades having large Italian representation experienced labor turmoil during the years after 1900."[15] This unrest included the longshoremen, garment workers, laborers, shoemakers, masons and bricklayers, among others.

In addition to supplying rank-and-file support, Italians served as leaders of union locals and even of national organizations. One such organization was the International Hod Carriers' and Building Laborers' Union of America (now the Laborers International Union of America), formed in 1903 as a member union of the American Federation of Labor. Domenico D'Allessandro of Boston became its general president in 1908 and directed the organization during its early, difficult years until his death in 1926, when Chicagoan Joseph V. Moreschi (like D'Allessandro, an Italian immigrant) was elected president.

In the garment trades, Anzuino D. Marimpietri of Chicago, one of the founders of the Amalgamated Clothing Workers of America, served as a vice-president of that union. Under the militant leadership of Luigi Antonini, Salvatore Ninfo, who became a vice-president of the International, and A. Baffa, Italians also entered the International Ladies Garment Workers' Union and formed powerful ethnic locals in New York City.

Italians produced some of America's foremost radical leaders, among them Arturo Giovannitti and Giuseppe Ettor of the Industrial Workers of the World (the IWW), who led Southern Italian workers in the famous 1912 textile strike in Lawrence, Massachusetts. A cut in wages at the city's textile mills precipitated the Lawrence strike in January 1912. Consisting largely of unskilled immigrants (Italians, Poles, Germans, French, Belgians, French-Canadians, Jews, Lithuanians,

English, Portuguese and Syrians), the work force quickly came under the control of the Industrial Workers of the World. Led by Giovannitti, a prominent radical union organizer and editor of the syndicalist-controlled newspaper *Il Proletario*, and Ettor, then a member of the IWW executive board, Italians formed the backbone of the strike. During a fight between police and strikers on January 29, Anna Lo Pezzi, a young Italian woman striker, was shot and killed. Giovannitti and Ettor were arrested and in September stood trial on the charge of being accessories to murder. After nearly two months of testimony, the anarchist leaders were found innocent, but in the process the strike was broken.

Italians moved a long distance from the early years of the immigration when, as Fenton has shown, "provincialism, fatalism, and self-reliance made it difficult for unions to control them." As Southern Italians moved into organized labor, economic concerns and grievances influenced them rather than philosophical tenets of radicalism and socialism. The key factor in the successful organization of immigrants was "bargaining power"—that is, some assurance that a union might achieve its stated objectives, an assurance that socialists and anarchists often could not offer. Where such prospects existed, Italian immigrants organized rapidly and effectively. They became, in Fenton's words, "faithful members of conservative AFL locals."[16]

One form of economic enterprise that attracted some immigrants as well as members of the second generation, and which brought money (if not favorable publicity) to the Italian community, was crime. This included gambling, prostitution, labor racketeering and the activities of Black Hand extortion gangs.

During the pre-World War I immigrant era, the groundwork was laid for the creation of the powerful criminal syndicates which emerged and expanded during the Prohibition Era that followed the end of the war. The number of Italians involved in gambling, Black Hand and other illegal activities before the Prohibition period—or since then, for that matter—was small. Nevertheless, the influence they exerted and the power they wielded was out of all proportion to their numbers. This impact was in part the result of the vast amounts of money they were able to amass. Of even greater importance were the connections they formed with machine politicians and the role they played as power brokers in immigrant colony and city politics.

The general prosperity that began during World War I and continued until late 1929 (except for the recession of 1920-1921) facilitated the upward social and economic movement of Italians and members of other "new" immigrant groups. Their improved economic status brought greater self-esteem to the Italian community. During the twenties the increased affluence of many immigrants made possible, even speeded, the dispersion of Italians throughout all parts of urban and suburban America.

For most Italians, economic gains enjoyed during the twenties were modest; but to the individuals concerned, advances were significant. A comparison of occupations in New York City in 1916 and 1931 shows Italians moving away from employment as unskilled laborers. Although 50 percent worked as laborers in 1916, only 31 percent were still in this occupational category just fifteen years later. By 1931 Italians could be found in increasing numbers as chauffeurs, clerks, mechanics, carpenters, salesmen, painters and plasterers. Upwardly mobile Italians in the city generally took advantage of opportunities in the construction and consumer trades or as small proprietors. One source noted in the late thirties that "every trade, business, and profession in the New York area has its representatives among the Italians."[17] Most professional men still came either from the small Northern Italian element or from the small portion of the Southern Italian group who came from non-peasant backgrounds. The largely Northern Italian, San Francisco group enjoyed outstanding success in business during the inter-war decades, especially in banking. During this period, the level of achievement experienced by Italians in the northern California metropolis was not typical of the Italian population in other American cities.

For their part, Italian women dominated the garment industry in these years. During the 1920s Italian women became the largest single group in the needle trades, displacing the Jews. By 1937, according to David Dubinsky, president of the International Ladies Garment Workers' Union, immigrant and second-generation Italians numbered about 100,000 out of a total membership of 250,000 in the New York area.

Political patronage continued to provide economic benefits for Italian colony residents in all large American cities. Organized crime was an even more lucrative source of income. On January 16, 1920, the Eighteenth Amendment and the Prohibition Enforcement Act (Volstead Act) went into effect, forbidding the manufacture, sale or transportation of intoxicating liquors. Supporters of the Eighteenth Amendment predicted that it would usher in a new era of "clean thinking and clean living." The results of prohibition were far different from the lofty objectives envisioned by reformers. For young, upwardly mobile Italians and other urban ethnics, the "Noble Experiment" was a godsend, an opportunity to amass amounts of money and power undreamed of in earlier days. The Capones, O'Banions and Lanskys were willing to take the risks necessary to build their businesses into successful enterprises. Unlike many of their native American contemporaries, the "businesses" they went into involved the illegal manufacture, importation, transportation and sale of alcoholic beverages.

Prohibition provided the means by which young Italians, Jews and other ethnics entered the mainstream of American entrepreneurial crime, but repeal of the Eighteenth Amendment did not bring about a decline in their fortunes. After repeal—and, in fact, during the Prohibition Era—criminal entrepreneurs engaged in other types of illegal but highly lucrative activities, including gambling, narcotics, prostitution and business and labor racketeering. In the process of developing their businesses, syndicate leaders created organizations loosely and imperfectly patterned on those in existence in the legitimate business world. These organizations effectively provided for the needs for which they were created.

Entrepreneurial crime offered an important avenue of upward economic mobility for members of the American generation. Although group unity and cooperative effort figured prominently in Italian successes within the highly competitive world of American syndicate crime during the 1920s and 1930s, certain individuals played roles of key importance. These men had a profound impact on the high level of criminal achievement Italians enjoyed during that era. The situation in entrepreneurial crime from the enactment of the Eighteenth Amendment until American entry into World War II exhibited considerable fluidity; during this period syndicate leaders were highly receptive to ideas that promised to maximize profits and reduce risks and uncertainty. The institutions and procedures created in cities throughout the country during the late twenties and the thirties provided the framework within which criminal syndicates have functioned ever since.

During the decades since the end of World War II, more than 500,000 Italian immigrants have entered the United States. Nearly one-half (228,000) came in the decade following the passage of the 1965 immigration law. That law gave all nations the same access to an overall quota, but assigned priority status to immediate relatives of American citizens and resident aliens as well as to professional and skilled workers in short supply among the native population. The 1980 United States Census counted over twelve million Italian Americans and found them in every state in the Union, although almost 70 percent still resided in the heavily industrialized and urban Northeast.

Italian Americans have shared fully in the general prosperity the nation enjoyed between World War II and the 1970s. Movement out of the ethnic districts slowed during the 1930s because of the depression, and during the 1940s because of wartime housing shortages, but by the

1950s the process had accelerated and the formerly heavy concentrations of Italians in immigrant neighborhoods thinned out. By the 1960s and 1970s Italian Americans had entered the mainstream of American life.

Many veterans of World War II, as well as of the Korean and Vietnam wars, used the G.I. Bill to finance college educations and take professional training; they obtained jobs in industry or started businesses of their own. A 1963-64 study of occupational patterns among Italian Americans found that 48 percent of the respondents were employed in white-collar jobs and 52 percent in blue-collar jobs. In contrast, 26 percent of the fathers of the respondents held white-collar positions, 71 percent were in blue-collar jobs and 3 percent were employed as farmers. Furthermore, Italians in working-class occupations had shifted from unskilled to semi-skilled and skilled jobs.

Based on research conducted by the National Opinion Research Center (NORC), Andrew Greeley in 1974 stated that "Italians have reached the national average in the percentage of those who have become managers or owners or professional or technical workers." Referring to studies conducted by NORC over the previous several years, Greeley concluded that the evidence "leaves little doubt" that Italians "have moved rapidly into the upper-middle class of American society during the last two decades."[18]

Syndicated columnist George Will noted in an August 12, 1983 article that Italian Americans "are increasingly important, from coast-to-coast. One runs Yale and, even more impressive, one manages the Los Angeles Dodgers. (The Dodgers are doing better than Yale but not as well as Chrysler, which is run by . . .)" another Italian American, of course.[19] In fact, a *New York Times Magazine* feature article identified a wide range and variety of successful Italian Americans. As a group, "in recent years they have attained a kind of critical mass in terms of affluence, education, aspiration and self-acceptance—so much so that the political analyst Theodore H. White, in his 1982 book *America in Search of Itself*, identifies Italian Americans as 'the most important among the rising ethnic groups.'"[20]

In their move up the economic ladder Italians have followed, on a smaller scale and a generation later, a pattern noted among Jews, whereby "the children of storekeepers and small businessmen went to college and became professionals." Italians are attending college in ever-increasing numbers. By 1970 they accounted for approximately one-third of the students in the City University of New York system and half of the student body at Fordham University. As a result of their stronger qualifications and better educational background, the grandchildren of Italian immigrants "are moving into the professions

and the higher white collar fields."[21] They are filling the great bureau-
cracies of government and business and moving into such glamourous
fields as advertising, sports and entertainment.[22]

According to Alfred J. Tella, special advisor to the director of the
Census Bureau, the 1980 Census and other recent studies document the
fact that Italian Americans have realized dramatic economic success.
One telling sign of this is that the income of Italian Americans is $2,000
a year more than the average for all American families.[23]

Historians Thomas Kessner and Betty Boyd Caroli suggest that
Italian Americans have attained their high level of achievement
through individual or family efforts rather than by group action. Kessner and Caroli suggest that Italian-American strength resides "in individual achievement, eked out in years of hard work and within a framework of family solidarity." Ethnic unity is seldom seriously considered
as "a way to shorten the route" to success. "It is not so much that the
rules of loyalty to one's townsmen have endured but rather that the
advantages of cooperation beyond narrow lines have never become apparent. Most attempts to unify in large power blocks founder." Italian
Americans are simply too new to the nuances of group action and not
yet fully aware of the vast potential available from such activity to
make effective use of it.[24]

If the Italian-American experience holds a lesson for other, more recent ethnic groups, perhaps this is it: Employ any means at your
disposal. As long as the goals are clearly perceived and are held firmly
in view, it really does not matter whether individual effort, family co-
hesion or group solidarity is the way success is achieved.

NOTES

[1]Raymond Stevenson Dondero, "The Italian Settlement of San Francisco"
(Unpublished Masters Thesis, University of California, Berkeley, 1953), pp.
76-79.

[2]Frederick H. Wright, *The Italians in America* (New York: Missionary Education Movement, 1913); Federal Writers' Project, *The Italians of New York*
(New York: Random House, 1938); Robert F. Foerster, *The Italian Emigration of Our Times* (Cambridge, Mass.: Harvard University Press, 1919), Chap.
XXI.

[3]*Soards' New Orleans City Directory for 1890* (New Orleans: 1890); *Bio-
graphical and Historical Memoirs of Louisiana* (Chicago: Goodspeed Publishing Co., 1892).

[4]Edward Steiner, *On the Trail of the Immigrant* (New York: Revell, 1906),
p. 262.

[5]United States Congress, Senate, *Reports of the Industrial Commission*
(Washington, D. C.: 1901), xv, 432.

[6]A number of descriptions of padrone camps exist. One is by Domenick Ciolli, "The Wop in the Track Gang," *The Immigrants in America Review*, II:2 (July 1916): 61-66.

[7]United States Congress, Senate, *Reports of the Immigration Commission*, Vol. 2 (Washington, D. C.: 1911), p. 392.

[8]John Koren, "The Padrone System and Padrone Banks," *United States Department of Labor Bulletin*, II:ix (March 1897): 115-116.

[9]Foerster, op. cit., p. 400.

[10]S. Merlino, "Italian Immigrants and Their Enslavement," *Forum*, XV (April 1893): 184.

[11]Mabel Hurd Willett, *The Employment of Women in the Clothing Trade* (New York: Macmillan, 1902), p. 99.

[12]Jacob A. Riis, Robert A. Wood, et al., *The Poor in Great Cities* (New York: Charles Scribner's Sons, 1895), pp. 92-95.

[13]Louise C. Odencrantz, *Italian Women in Industry: A Study of Conditions in New York City* (New York: Russell Sage Foundation, 1919), p. 4.

[14]Edwin Fenton, *Immigrants and Unions: Italians and American Labor, 1870-1920* (New York: Arno Press, 1975), p. 214.

[15]George E. Pozzetta, "The Italians of New York City, 1890-1914" (Unpublished Ph.D. Dissertation, University of North Carolina at Chapel Hill, 1971), p. 359.

[16]Edwin Fenton, "Italian Immigrants in the Stoneworkers' Union," *Labor History*, III:2 (Spring 1962): 206-207.

[17]Federal Writers' Project, op. cit., p. 171.

[18]Andrew M. Greeley, *Ethnicity in the United States: A Preliminary Reconnaissance* (New York: Wiley, 1974), p. 51.

[19]*Washington Post*, (August 12, 1983).

[20]Stephen S. Hall, "Italian-Americans Coming Into Their Own," *New York Times Magazine* (May 15, 1983), p. 31.

[21]Nathan Glazer and Daniel Patrick Moynihan, *Beyond the Melting Pot: The Negroes, Puerto Ricans, Jews, Italians, and Irish of New York City*, 2nd ed. (Cambridge, Mass.: MIT Press, 1970), p. 206.

[22]Thus four of the most successful moving picture directors during recent years have been Italian Americans: Francis Ford Coppola *(Godfather I* and *II* and *Apocalypse Now)*, Martin Scorsese *(Taxi Driver* and *Raging Bull)*, Brian De Palma *(Carrie* and *Dressed to Kill)* and Michael Cimino *(The Deer Hunter)*, while numerous Italian Americans have won wide acclaim as actors and singers.

[23]*New York Times* (October 15, 1983).

[24]Thomas Kessner and Betty Boyd Caroli, *Today's Immigrants: Their Stories* (New York: Oxford University Press, 1982), pp. 217-218.

IS RACE SURMOUNTABLE?
THOMAS SOWELL'S CELEBRATION OF
JAPANESE-AMERICAN "SUCCESS"

Ronald Takaki

University of California, Berkeley

This volume entitled *Ethnicity and the Work Force* provides a valuable forum for a critical comparative analysis of a question of profound social significance: Is there a difference between the experiences of racial minorities (Japanese Americans, blacks, Mexican Americans and Native Americans) and the experiences of white ethnic groups (Irish Americans, Jewish Americans, Italian Americans and Polish Americans)? Fortunately, or perhaps unfortunately, this question has already been answered by Thomas Sowell in his book, *Ethnic America: A History*.[1] Why, one may ask, give Sowell's book such attention? After all, it is not a serious work of scholarship. True, but I think it would be unwise to ignore it. Sowell is a senior fellow at the Hoover Institute, an adviser to President Ronald Reagan; his book has been widely read and discussed, especially in public policymaking circles; and he has raised a question of vital intellectual and social importance: Is race surmountable?

Sowell's response is cheerfully affirmative. "There are wide variations in the rates of progress among Americans," he states sanguinely, "but progress itself is pervasive."[2] According to Sowell, examples to support such a contention not only abound; they are also dramatic. Descendants of slaves today sit in Congress and on the Supreme Court, and O. J. Simpson is hailed as an "American phenomenon." Everywhere, "ethnic" groups have made it, or are rapidly making it into middle-class and affluent America. Many of them, notably Jews and Asian Americans, have family incomes above the national average. And even Mexican Americans and blacks are on the road to progress.[3]

This assessment has led Sowell to dismiss or de-emphasize the importance of prejudice or group discrimination: "If bigotry alone was a sufficient causal explanation [for inequality], Jews and Japanese would not be among the most prosperous American ethnic groups."[4] "Color," to be sure, did play "a major role" in determining the fate of many Americans, Sowell acknowledges. But it was not an all-powerful determinant, he counters, and it has been and can be surmounted.[5]

Sowell's study, subtitled "a history," is no mere inquiry into the past: it is mainly a prescription for the present. *Ethnic America* is a public policy manual designed to describe the "progress" of "ethnic" groups, particularly Jews and Asian Americans, in order to delineate what has "worked," and to instruct "ethnic" groups which are still striving toward success how they should behave and what values they must internalize in order to be assimilated into middle-class America. Sowell's study has public policy significance, for if race has indeed diminished as a force in American society, then we no longer need and should not have affirmative action. In other words, Sowell's book can be viewed as a sequel to Nathan Glazer's *Affirmative Discrimination: Ethnic Inequality and Public Policy.*[6]

This chapter focuses on the case of the Japanese Americans—a group Sowell celebrates as a model of "ethnic" success and progress, as *prima facie* evidence that racism can indeed be overcome. What makes the Japanese-American case so crucial to the construction of Sowell's general argument is the undeniable fact that Japanese Americans were victims of racial oppression. As Sowell points out, "few [groups] met such repeated rebuffs and barriers—including barriers of mass internment camps."[7]

Indeed, Japanese immigrants encountered formidable barriers both in Hawaii and on the mainland. Emigrating from the southern prefectures of Japan, they came by the tens of thousands. Between 1880 and 1920 (four years before the Immigration Law of 1924, which prohibited immigration from Japan), the Japanese population in Hawaii increased from a little more than one hundred to 109,274, and on the mainland from less than one hundred to 111,010. Japanese immigrants found themselves denied citizenship and access to the political process in both places. Hawaii reserved citizenship to natives and whites; then, as a territory of the United States in 1900, Hawaii was subject to federal law, including the 1790 Naturalization Act which restricted eligibility for naturalized citizenship to "whites."[8]

While the Japanese were racially excluded from the body politic, they were incorporated as laborers into the process of production. In fact, sugar planters in Hawaii systematically recruited and transported Japanese immigrants to cultivate cane. The number of Japanese plantation workers increased dramatically from fifteen laborers or 0.1 percent of the work force in 1882, to 31,029 or 73.4 percent in 1902. Japanese workers were also heavily involved in agricultural production on the mainland. In 1909 Japanese farm laborers constituted 40 percent of the Japanese population, with thirty thousand in California alone. Large numbers of Japanese were located in other sectors of the economy: ten thousand in railroad construction and operations, fifteen thousand in domestic services, 3,300 in canneries in Alaska and Washington, 2,240 in the lumber mills and logging camps in Washington and two thousand in the mines of states like Wyoming and New Mexico.

Employed in a wide range of economic sectors, the Japanese experienced racial discrimination in the form of occupational stratification. They often found themselves excluded from skilled and supervisory positions. In 1909, for example, only three of the two thousand Japanese employed in the western coal mining and metalliferous industries were foremen. A similar pattern existed in Hawaii where a stratified racial/ occupational structure on the plantation was based on a formal policy of the Hawaiian Sugar Planters' Association. In 1904 the association instructed plantation managers to reserve all skilled positions for "American citizens, or those eligible for citizenship."[9] While this policy did not specify or even mention race or a racial group, it did have a racial function, for it excluded from skilled occupations Japanese or immigrants regarded by federal law as not "white." Little wonder the Japanese were mostly field hands and mill laborers. A racial line of demarcation was particularly evident in supervisory positions. In 1915, of the 377 foremen, only two were Chinese and seventeen Japanese; 313 of all foremen or 83 percent were white. Yet the Japanese constituted over 60 percent of the entire plantation work force. Thus field and mill laborers, predominantly Japanese, took orders from foremen, usually white men.[10]

Japanese workers were very aware of the plantation hierarchy and the limits on the possibility of occupational advancement for them. "Lunas [foremen] were all Portuguese," observed Minoru Hayashida of the Puunene Plantation on Maui. "Above that was the Caucasian field boss called 'o luna,' the big foreman."[11] Another Japanese worker, knowing he would never be able to get ahead on the plantation, expressed his frustration. Told by an interviewer that he would be promoted and become a "big shot" if he had "the stuff," the laborer retorted: "Don't kid me. You know yourself I haven't got a chance. You can't go very high up and get big money unless your skin is white. You can work here all your life and yet a haole [white man] who doesn't know a thing about the work can be ahead of you in no time."[12]

But even where Japanese workers were employed in the same occupational categories as whites, they found themselves paid different and lower wage rates. In the lumber industry in Washington, according to the Immigration Commission in 1909, the Japanese had been "without exception, paid lower wages than men of other races engaged in the same occupations. . . . While the Japanese were employed as trimmers, edgermen, planing-mill feeders, lumber graders, lathe mill men, and carpenters at wages varying from $1.65 to $2 per day, at other mills white men engaged in these occupations were paid from $2.75 to $3.50 per day."[13] Also in 1909 in California, white employers paid $1.80 per day to white workers and only $1.54 per day to Japanese workers. Meanwhile, in plantation Hawaii, "American" or white carpenters earned $4.36 in average wages per day, while Japanese carpenters made only $1.28. The wage differential between "American" foremen and Japanese foremen was enormous—they were paid $3.01 and $1.25 per day respectively.[14]

The dual wage system in Hawaii set apart Japanese male and female laborers. Japanese women represented an important part of the plantation work force. In 1920, for example, 14 percent of all Oahu plantation laborers were women, and the preponderance of them—over 80 percent—were Japanese. Japanese women were concentrated in field operations such as hoeing, leaf-stripping, cane cutting and even cane loading, a strenuous and backbreaking activity. Though women were given many of the same work assignments as men, they were paid less than their male counterparts. Japanese female field hands, for example, received only an average wage of 55¢ per day in 1915, compared to 78¢ for Japanese male field hands.[15]

The dual wage system also involved wage differentials between different groups of Asian workers. For example, Filipino cane cutters in 1910 were paid only 69¢ per day, compared to 99¢ for Japanese cane cutters. This use of differential wages was part of a general management strategy to create ethnic divisions within the work force. George H. Fairfield, manager of the Makee Sugar Company, frankly stated, "Keep a variety of laborers, that is different nationalities, and thus prevent any concerted action, in case of strikes, for there are few, if any, cases of Japs, Chinese, and Portuguese entering into a strike as a unit." In their business and private correspondence, planters wrote that they needed Korean laborers in order to "pit" them against the Japanese and defuse Japanese attempts to form "a combination to put up wages."[16] The manager of the Hawaiian Agricultural Company complained to C. Brewer and Company about the high wages which the "Japs" on his plantation were demanding. On August 7, 1913, he wrote to the company, "If possible for you to arrange it I should very much like to get say 25 new Filipinos to put into our day gang. . . . In this way perhaps we can stir up the Japs a bit."[17]

Housing arrangements on the plantation reinforced the ethnic divisions within the work force. Camps for the laborers and their families were usually segregated on the basis of nationality or ethnicity.

Describing the racial divisions and "pyramid" structure of plantation housing, the son of a plantation laborer wrote:

> At the tip was Mr. Nelson [the manager], then the Portuguese, Spanish and *nisei lunas* in their nicer-looking homes, then the identical wooden frame houses of Japanese Camp, then the more run-down Filipino Camp. . . . The [company town] was planned and built around its sewage system. The half dozen rows of underground concrete ditches, two feet wide and three feet deep, ran from the higher slope of camp into the concrete irrigation ditch on the lower perimeter of camp. An outhouse built over the sewage ditch had two pairs of back-to-back toilets and serviced four houses. Shit too was organized according to the plantation pyramid. Mr. Nelson was top shit on the highest slope, then there were the Portuguese, Spanish, and *nisei lunas* with their indoor toilets which flushed into the same ditches, then Japanese Camp, and Filipino Camp.[18]

As they experienced interethnic divisions within the work force, Japanese laborers in Hawaii found themselves restricted to plantation employment and even confined to the islands. In 1903, for example, the legislature of Hawaii passed a law stating that Asiatic laborers should not be employed on public works in the territory because the workers were needed on the plantations. Four years later, President Theodore Roosevelt issued an executive order which prohibited Japanese in Hawaii from moving to the mainland.

On the mainland, as the Japanese left the farm labor class to become tenant farmers and small farmers, they faced legislation designed to deny them the right to land ownership. In 1913 California enacted the Alien Land Law which made it illegal for aliens ineligible for naturalized citizenship to own land. One of the authors of the law, State Attorney U. S. Webb, declared that the purpose was to "limit their [Japanese] presence by curtailing their privileges which they may enjoy here; for they will not come in large numbers and long abide with us if they may not acquire land."[19] Commenting on the Alien Land Law in 1926, a magazine writer observed, "If he [Japanese] could have been kept as a laborer, it would have been a great benefit to California."[20] The California law was not an isolated development. Similar alien land laws were also enacted in Washington, Arizona, Oregon, Idaho, Nebraska, Texas, Kansas, Louisiana, Montana, New Mexico, Minnesota and Missouri.

Japanese workers of the second generation or *nisei* also found themselves excluded from participation in certain levels and sectors of employment. In Los Angeles, for example, no *nisei* was a public school teacher, fireman, policeman or mailman in 1940. Even college-educated *nisei* experienced bleak employment prospects in professional fields. A

Stanford University official bluntly stated, "It is almost impossible to place a . . . Japanese of either the first or second generation in any kind of position, engineering, manufacturing, or business. Many firms have general regulations against employing them; others object to them on the ground that the other men employed by the firms do not care to to work with them."[21]

In 1942 this history of racial exclusionism—discrimination in employment, alien land laws, immigration restriction—culminated in the World War II internment of over 110,000 Japanese Americans, a majority of whom were United States citizens by birth. In the early 1980s the Commission on Wartime Relocation and Internment of Civilians concluded that the massive evacuation of Japanese Americans from the West Coast was not justified by military necessity, and that the broad historical causes behind it were a failure of political leadership, war hysteria and race prejudice.

Thirty-seven years later, reviewing this unhappy and tragic past, Sowell hails the remarkable "triumph" of Japanese Americans. He proudly reports that they have median family incomes 32 percent above the national average, and that they earn "more than whites in general." They have more education than whites; indeed, "88 percent of the *Sansei* [third generation] have attended college, and 92 percent intend to become professionals."[22] But is the Japanese-American "success" as "remarkable" as Sowell makes it out to be?[23]

Here we may have a situation where the means of measurement may be the message. In other words, *how* we measure success may determine our conclusions. Sowell knows that certain "ethnic" groups are located in particular regions of the United States; yet he insists on comparing their incomes to national averages. What this allows Sowell to do is highlight the "high" incomes of Japanese families compared to families nationally, and to downplay two crucial characteristics of this group.

First, more Japanese-American families have two or more income earners than American families generally. In 1970 both husband and wife worked in over half of all Japanese-American families, compared to 39 percent of all families in the country. Hence the fact that Japanese-American families are earning more than the average family indicates that there are more members of each Japanese-American family working. Second, Japanese Americans are concentrated in urban areas and also in Hawaii and California, states which have considerably higher average incomes and higher costs of living than the nation as a whole.

Moreover, when we compare Japanese-American incomes in terms of education, we find that single-income, Japanese-American male-headed families earned only 84 percent of the national average for families in the same category where the male family head had four years of college, and only 83 percent where he had two or more years of post-graduate study. When we make comparisons within a region, we find that in the San Francisco-Oakland area in 1970 the median income of Japanese-American men was only 81 percent of that of white men.

Further, we need to analyze not only incomes but also the number of weeks worked per year. Here we find that Japanese-American men in 1969 worked 3.5 percent more weeks than white men annually. Thus their earnings, compared to that of white men, would be even less if they worked the same number of weeks as white men. Clearly, we need to be careful in making statistical comparisons; otherwise, they might only yield conclusions we are looking for rather than ones we need in order to understand reality.[24]

But what about Sowell's observation concerning the high numbers of Japanese Americans in the professions? If we take four western states (California, Washington, Oregon and Arizona), we will find that 28.3 percent of Japanese males (25-44 years of age) were professionals in 1960, compared to 20.5 percent of white males in the same age co-hort, while for females the percentages were 13.5 percent for Japanese and 15.8 percent for whites. In 1970, for the San Francisco-Oakland SMSA, 24 percent of Japanese males were in the professional/techni-cian occupations, compared to 20 percent of white males. We can see from these data the entry of Japanese Americans into professional em-ployment, but we must be careful to remember that the figures for whites included Spanish-surnamed Americans and hence were biased downward. We must also place all of this kind of information within the context of a pattern of Japanese-American overconcentration in specific fields such as engineering and the sciences, and under-representation in the social sciences and human services fields. Thus, Japanese Americans are not participating in the full range of profes-sional activities. Furthermore, we should not overlook the other areas of employment—the craft occupations where only 11 percent of Japa-nese-American males in the San Francisco-Oakland SMSA were em-ployed in 1970 compared to 20 percent of white males, and the clerical occupations where Japanese-American females tend to be low-echelon workers such as file clerks and typists rather than receptionists and secretaries.[25]

But Sowell's main purpose is not to prove empirically Japanese-American "success" but to explain it. How did they do it, he asks.

Politics could not have been an important factor, Sowell contends, noting how "the Japanese . . . studiously avoided political agitation for their rights. . . ."[26] They shunned the "confrontationist" meth-ods of "militant" blacks; "quiet" and "persistent," they did not rely on government intervention and welfare.[27] Neither was education the key to Japanese-American mobility. "The educational panacea is undermined by the history of groups like . . . the Japanese, who first rose by their labor and their business sense and only later on could afford to send their children to college."[28]

Thus, the most important factor, Sowell argues, was their business sense—their "middle class" orientation and values of discipline, obedience, politeness, hard work, thrift, industry, diligence and self-reliance.[29] Sowell sings praises to the Japanese gardener: "What made these humble occupations avenues to affluence was the effort, thrift, dependability, and foresight that built businesses out of 'menial' tasks and turned sweat into capital."[30]

As paragons of middle-class virtues, Japanese Americans practiced restraint in the home as well as in the marketplace, argues Sowell. The most important area of restraint, for him, involves sexual activity or family size. The average Japanese-American woman in the thirty-five to forty-four-year-old bracket, Sowell reports, has only 2.2 children compared to three children for the average American woman in the same age category.[31] On the other hand, women of less successful groups, blacks and Mexican Americans, have the highest fertility rates.[32]

Sowell correctly cautions us that "history is what happened, not what we wished had happened." To read Sowell's "history"—his "explanation" of how and why the Japanese succeeded—is to be given the impression that the Japanese were gardeners and to be told that the "successful" ethnic groups made it through enterprise. But to write this kind of history is to minimize or ignore much of "what happened."[33]

Take, for example, Sowell's observation that "all Japanese" neighborhoods became virtually non-existent or "unusual" in the postwar continental United States, indicating the success of Japanese-American assimilation. But such a residential pattern should be viewed differently by one familiar with history. After all, the forced mass evacuation of Japanese Americans from the West Coast during World War II had destroyed their *nihonmachis* or communities. And Sowell is familiar with this history. But what he does in his discussion on internment is to transform it into an event which had a "positive effect," emancipating the *nisei* from the "old bonds of a narrow ethnic world."

In the camps, *nisei* were allowed to work in a wider range of employment than in civilian life, and their resettlement in eastern and midwestern areas gave them "opportunities" to pursue new fields. "In this regard," Sowell remarks, "many Japanese Americans themselves—including Senator S. I. Hayakawa—have credited the internment experience with improving their long-run mobility."[34] But to highlight Hayakawa is to hide the current campaign for redress and reparation led by angry Japanese Americans who remember the "years of infamy" in camp, and to shroud the fact that Hayakawa himself was never interned. Born in Canada and living in Chicago in 1942, Hayakawa did not suffer the humiliation and loss of civil and human rights experienced by Japanese Americans of the West Coast. Little wonder he has frivolously called the years behind barbed wire a "vacation." Hayakawa is hardly a reliable source, yet Sowell puffs him up to support his point.

Sowell's insensitivity and carelessness are also illustrated in his discussion on fertility rates. According to Sowell, statistically, black and Mexican-American women have more children than Japanese-American women. What does this finding mean? Here Sowell tritely quips: "The rich get richer, and the poor have children." He views the high fertility rate of black and Mexican-American women as the cause of their poverty: it "directly lowers the standard of living of a group by spreading a given income more thinly among family members."[35] But a case can be made that the high fertility rate is actually an effect of poverty. And historically a high fertility rate for Japanese Americans actually contributed to the economic advancement of many of them. The *issei* or first generation had large families; the birth rate of the early immigrant Japanese population was four times greater than the rate of white Americans. Many Japanese-American families relied on the labor of their children to work on the plantations, help cultivate farms and operate small businesses.

Moreover, to argue that Japanese Americans "made it" through "diligence," "obedience" and "enterprise" is to simplify and distort history.   Most Japanese Americans were laborers, not petty capitalists, and their responses to racial oppression were more varied and complex than Sowell describes them. "The Japanese," he writes, "accepted low pay, long hours, and difficult working conditions without complaint."[36] To make such a statement is to betray a limited knowledge of Japanese-American history. It is simply not true that Japanese laborers "accepted" low pay and did not complain. Actually, many of their responses were hardly "polite," certainly not accommodationist. Japanese workers founded in 1900 the Japanese Labor League, an organization which sprang from the Japanese Socialist Revolutionary Party and which had a membership of two thousand laborers. Hundreds of Japanese farm laborers joined Mexican farm workers in the Oxnard strike of 1903, and Japanese produce workers in Los Angeles organized unions in the 1930s.

Meanwhile, in Hawaii, Japanese laborers viewed the plantation as a "contested terrain"—a place where they had to struggle to acquire greater control over their work and a greater share of plantation earnings, and where they sometimes violently confronted their bosses. The records show that Japanese laborers physically fought "haole" or white foremen and committed acts of arson, including burning cane fields and plantation buildings, to protest mistreatment and exploitation.[37] In the fields and mills, many of them engaged in work slowdowns and were intentionally lazy and inefficient. The Japanese Consul in Hawaii reported to his government that Japanese plantation workers took "breaks during working hours to have a leisurely smoke" and "indulged in gossip with their co-workers."[38] A white foreman found the supervision of Japanese women workers to be a frustrating task:

> Hoeing was more pleasant and would have been all right except for the fact that the gangs on this work were largely composed of Japanese *wahines* [women], and it always seemed impossible to keep them together, especially if the fields were not level. The consequence was that these damsels were usually scattered all over the place and as many as possible were out of sight in the gulches or dips in the field where they could not be seen, where they would calmly sit and smoke their little metal pipes until the luna [foreman] appeared on the skyline, when they would be busy as bees.[39]

In their work songs, Japanese plantation laborers described the changing weather and their absence from the fields:

> When it rains I sleep;
> When it's sunny I stay away from work;
> And, when cloudy, I spend the day
> in drinking wine.[40]

Japanese plantation workers also feigned illness in order to secure a medical excuse from work; in fact, one of the main responsibilities of the plantation doctor was to ferret out malingerers. To deceive the plantation doctor, some Japanese laborers even resorted to drinking soy sauce to raise their body temperatures. Thousands of Japanese workers also sought a more permanent form of escape from work: they broke their labor contracts (which required them to labor for three years on their assigned plantation) and ran away. Between 1890 and 1892, reported Marshall Charles B. Wilson, 5,706 laborers were arrested for desertion. In their diaries, plantation managers filled many pages with references to runaway contract laborers. On one such page, Anton Cropp of the Koloa Plantation listed the "Deserters Japanese":

> #5 — Nakajin recaught & redeserted
> #8 — Kaneki

#12 — Murohisa recaught & redeserted
#16 — Kako
#17 — Toshida recaught
#19 — Iwamoto
#21 — Iamamoto Furokishi
#24 — Murakami
#323 — Asahare recaught
#326 — Hayashi
#400 — Imatzu
#418 — Saito recaught
#409 — Uyeda
#416 — Murakami recaught
#655 — Nakane
#619 — Seto
#621 — Kuba recaught Honolulu[41]

More important, Japanese plantation laborers also engaged in collective acts of resistance—strikes. In 1900 alone, Japanese workers, over eight thousand of them, participated in over twenty strikes. Nine years later, seven thousand Japanese laborers organized a protracted four-month-long strike on the island of Oahu and shut down all of the island's major plantations. In 1920, five thousand Japanese workers united with three thousand Filipino workers in another massive strike. Strike leaders told workers of both nationalities that they should work together on the strike "shoulder to shoulder," and that there were no "barriers of color" between the two groups. In 1946, Japanese laborers, along with workers of other nationalities, again went out on strike—this time under the leadership of the International Longshoremen's and Warehousemen's Union, and successfully extracted from management higher wages and the right of collective bargaining.[42]

"History," writes Sowell, "can sometimes help to assess our beliefs about the past or about the present or future."[43] To do this in a responsible way, however, we must be sure history or our study of the past is precise and comprehensive. We should not sloppily state, as does Sowell, that "more than 300,000 Japanese Americans fought in World War II,"[44] when in fact the total Japanese population in the United States in 1940 was only 284,853! We should also not hastily and recklessly urge blacks to learn lessons for "ethnic" success from the history of Japanese Americans. For one thing, the Japanese represent only a fraction of a percent (.3 percent in 1980) of the U.S. population, while blacks constitute a significantly larger racial minority (nearly 12 percent in 1980). The difference in size alone between the two groups demands the exercise of caution in proposing solutions for blacks based on an analysis of Japanese Americans.

In the use of statistics to study the incomes of Japanese Americans, we must be certain we do not compare "apples and oranges," or the average Japanese family income and the average national family income, regardless of the number of income earners within the family, or the average income of a regional group and the national average income. In our examination of the ways Japanese Americans responded to racial oppression, we must note not only their efforts as enterprisers but also the fact that much of their "progress" was due to their ability to organize as workers and to raise their wages. To accept Sowell's prescription for ethnic progress in the 1980s—his advice to blacks and Mexican Americans—is not only to deny much of Japanese-American history, but also to ask racial minorities to strive for entry into a world which no longer exists, a shopkeeper economy of individual enterprise and opportunity where "sweat" and even "cleanliness" could be turned into "capital."[45]

But, finally, what does Sowell's analysis of Japanese Americans in particular and "ethnic America" in general mean in terms of public policy—the focus of concern in this volume? While Sowell does not explicitly relate his historical thesis to public policy, he does present data and an argument which question the need for, and political wisdom of, affirmative action. If Japanese Americans can succeed through their own efforts and without government intervention, then so can blacks and other racial minorities. "Controversial" affirmative action programs, Sowell contends, have had "little or no effect beyond what had already been achieved under 'equal opportunity' policies in the 1960s." Moreover, the "public perception" of affirmative action has engendered "strong resentment" among whites generally.[46] Thus what we have in Sowell's celebration of the "progress" of "ethnic America," especially Japanese America, is a criticism of affirmative action.

Curiously, Sowell seems to have found some support or tacit agreement in radical or left circles—as from Christopher Jencks in the *New York Review of Books*. In the conclusion of his two-part review of Sowell, Jencks remarked, "In today's political environment the only argument that will persuade minorities not to seek protection from competition is prudential: certain short-term benefits, especially those that derive from reverse discrimination, may cost blacks more than the benefits are worth."[47] This statement is an extraordinarily provocative one, for Jencks considers himself a "radical" as opposed to a "conservative." Jencks identifies Sowell as the latter and explains what it means to be a conservative in terms of the affirmative action issue: essentially it involves an assessment of affirmative action as "reverse discrimination" and as "harmful" governmental efforts to eliminate discrimination.[48]

But what does it mean to be a "radical" on the issue of affirmative action? Here Jencks reveals something about his own "radical" thinking which needs to be explored critically. In his evaluation of Sowell, Jencks assumes the validity of the theory of "reverse discrimination." He states, for example, that it is a "fact" that Title VII has sometimes led to discrimination against whites. But he neither questions whether this fact is really a fact, nor provides a definition of racial discrimination which would enable us to determine if the term can be applied to anyone regardless of whether or not the person belongs to a group which has historically been oppressed or discriminated against because of race. Such an attempt at a definition might have clarified the difference between the *racial* experience and the *white ethnic* experience in America (a difference which Sowell overlooks or downplays), and offered a way to assess the prospects or lack of them for racial minorities to overcome inequality without the government acting affirmatively to eliminate it.[49]

What Jencks does instead is to give scholarly legitimacy to the theory and claims of "reverse discrimination" (as does Sowell), and to contribute, albeit inadvertently, to the very "political environment" which is warning racial minorities that affirmative action is not "prudential." Thus, in the end, Jencks, like Sowell, pushes upward the cost of benefits derived from affirmative action as he asks racial minorities whether the price might not be too high.

NOTES

[1] Thomas Sowell, *Ethnic America: A History* (New York: Basic Books, 1981).

[2] Ibid., p. 275.

[3] Ibid., p. 14.

[4] Ibid., p. 274.

[5] Ibid., p. 4.

[6] Ibid., pp. 5, 6, 14.

[7] Ibid., p. 155.

[8] *Debates and Proceedings in the Congress of the United States, 1789-1791*. 2 vols. (Washington, D.C.: 1834), Vol. 1, pp. 998, 1284; Vol. II, pp. 1148-1156, 1162, 2264.

[9] Hawaii Sugar Planters' Association, "Resolution," Grove Farm Plantation Records (Grove Farm Plantation, Kauai, Hawaii: November 18, 1904).

[10]U.S. Department of Labor, Bureau of Labor Statistics, *Report of the Commissioner of Labor on Hawaii* (Washington, D.C.: 1916), pp. 120-153.

[11]Ethnic Studies Oral History Project, *Stores and Storekeepers of Paia and Puunene, Maui* (Honolulu: University of Hawaii, 1980), p. 401.

[12]Machiyo Mitamura, "Life on a Hawaiian Plantation, An Interview," *Social Process in Hawaii*, Vol. 6 (Honolulu: University of Honolulu Sociology Club, 1940), p. 51.

[13]Yamato Ichihashi, *Japanese in the United States* (New York: Arno Press, 1969, originally published 1932), pp. 151-152.

[14]U.S. Department of Labor, Bureau of Labor Statistics, *Report of the Commissioner of Labor on Hawaii* (Washington, D.C.: 1910), p. 20.

[15]U.S. Department of Labor, *Report* (1910), op. cit., p. 20; Republic of Hawaii, *Report of the Labor Commission on Strikes and Arbitration* (Honolulu: 1895), p. 36.

[16]Wayne K. Patterson, "The Korean Frontier in America: Immigration to Hawaii, 1896-1910" (Ph.D. Dissertation, University of Pennsylvania, 1977), pp. 100, 129, 134, 146, 169-171.

[17]Letter, manager of Hawaiian Agricultural Company to C. Brewer and Company, August 7, 1913, in Hawaiian Agricultural Company Records, University of Hawaii Library (Honolulu, Hawaii).

[18]Milton Murayama, *All I Asking For Is My Body* (San Francisco: Supa Press, 1975), pp. 28, 96.

[19]Robert Higgs, "Landless by Law: Japanese Immigrants in California Agriculture to 1941," *Journal of Economic History*, 38:1(March 1978): 215.

[20]From the May 1926 issue of *Survey*, quoted in Carey McWilliams, *Factories in the Fields* (Santa Barbara, Cal.: Peregrine Publ., 1971), p. 112.

[21]Quoted in Ichihashi, op. cit., p. 357.

[22]Sowell, op. cit., pp. 5, 176, 177.

[23]Ibid., p. 177.

[24]For statistical studies of Japanese-American incomes, see Amado Y. Cabezas and Harold T. Yee, *Discriminatory Employment of Asian Americans: Private Industry in the San Francisco-Oakland SMSA* (San Francisco: Asian American Service Institute for Assistance to Neighborhoods, 1977); Harold H. Wong, "The Relative Economic Status of Chinese, Japanese, Black, and White Men in California" (Ph.D. Dissertation, University of California at Berkeley, 1974); U.S. Commission on Civil Rights, *Social Indicators of Equality for Minorities and Women* (Washington, D.C.: Government Printing Office, 1978); Barry Chiswick, "An Analysis of Earnings and Employment of Asian-American Men," *Journal of Labor Economics*, 1:2(April 1983): 197-214; Barbara Varon, "The Japanese Americans: Comparative Occupational Status, 1960 and 1950," *Demography*, 4:2(1967): 809-819; Calvin F. Schmid and Charles E. Nobbe, "Socioeconomic Differentials among Nonwhite Races," *American Sociological Review*, 30:6(December 1965): 909-922; Robert M. Jiobu, "Earnings Differentials Between Whites and Ethnic Minorities: The Cases of Asian Americans, Blacks, and Chicanos," *Sociology and Social Research*, 61:1(October 1976): 24-38; Emma Gee, ed., *Counterpoint: Perspectives on Asian America* (Los Angeles: Asian American Studies Center, UCLA, 1977), pp. 554-585; Ki-Taek Chun, "The Myth of Asian American Success and

Its Educational Ramifications" (New York: Columbia University Institute for Urban and Minority Education, 1980).

[25]Varon, op. cit., p. 813; Cabezas and Yee, op. cit., p. 135; Chun, op. cit., p. 7.

[26]Sowell, op. cit., p. 168.

[27]Ibid., p. 294.

[28]Ibid., p. 274.

[29]Ibid., pp. 162, 168.

[30]Ibid., p. 283.

[31]Ibid., p. 178.

[32]Ibid., pp. 7, 8.

[33]Ibid., p. 273.

[34]Ibid., p. 176.

[35]Ibid., p. 7.

[36]Ibid., p. 162.

[37]Richard Edwards, *Contested Terrain: The Transformation of the Workplace in the Twentieth Century* (New York: Basic Books, 1977).

[38]James Okahata, ed., *A History of Japanese in Hawaii* (Honolulu: United Japanese Society of Hawaii, 1971), p. 122.

[39]Jack Hall, *A Luna's Log*, a reprint of articles appearing in the *Honolulu Advertiser* in June 1927 (Kohala, Hawaii: 1927), p. 6.

[40]Yukuo Uyehara, "The Horehore Bushi," *Social Process in Hawaii*, Vol. 28 (Honolulu: University of Honolulu Sociology Club, 1980-1981), p. 116.

[41]Anton Cropp, "Diary—1892," Grove Farm Plantation Records (Grove Farm Plantation, Kauai, Hawaii), pp. 4, 12, 13.

[42]Takashi Tsutsumi, *History of Hawaii Laborers' Movement*, translated from the Japanese (Honolulu: Hawaiian Sugar Planters' Association Library, 1922), pp. 175, 242-243.

[43]Sowell, op. cit., p. 273.

[44]Ibid., p. 174.

[45]Ibid., pp. 7, 283.

[46]Ibid., p. 223.

[47]Christopher Jencks, "Special Treatment for Blacks?" in *New York Review of Books* (March 17, 1983), p. 19.

[48]Christopher Jencks, "Discrimination and Thomas Sowell," *New York Review of Books* (March 3, 1983), p. 36; Jencks, "Special Treatment," op. cit., p. 14.

[49]Ibid.